Matthew

New International Biblical Commentary

Matthew

Robert H. Mounce

New Testament Editor,
W. Ward Gasque

HENDRICKSON
PUBLISHERS
PEABODY, MASSACHUSETTS 01961-3473

Library of Congress Cataloging-in-Publication Data

Mounce, Robert H.
    Matthew / Robert H. Mounce.
        p. cm. — (New International biblical commentary; 1)
    Includes bibliographical references and indexes.
    ISBN 0-943575-18-4
    1. Bible. N.T. Matthew—Commentaries.   I. Bible. N.T.
Matthew. English. New International. 1991. II. Title.
III. Series.
BS2575.3.M68   1991
226.6'2077—dc20   90-29866
                                                            CIP

Table of Contents

Foreword
New International Biblical Commentary

Although it does not appear on the standard best-seller lists, the Bible continues to outsell all other books. And in spite of growing secularism in the West, there are no signs that interest in its message is abating. Quite to the contrary, more and more men and women are turning to its pages for insight and guidance in the midst of the ever-increasing complexity of modern life.

This renewed interest in Scripture is found both outside and inside the church. It is found among people in Asia and Africa as well as in Europe and North America; indeed, as one moves outside of the traditionally Christian countries, interest in the Bible seems to quicken. Believers associated with the traditional Catholic and Protestant churches manifest the same eagerness for the Word that is found in the newer evangelical churches and fellowships.

We wish to encourage and, indeed, strengthen this worldwide movement of lay Bible study by offering this new commentary series. Although we hope that pastors and teachers will find these volumes helpful in both understanding and communicating the Word of God, we do not write primarily for them. Our aim is to provide for the benefit of every Bible reader reliable guides to the books of the Bible—representing the best of contemporary scholarship presented in a form that does not require formal theological education to understand.

The conviction of editor and authors alike is that the Bible belongs to the people and not merely to the academy. The message of the Bible is too important to be locked up in erudite and esoteric essays and monographs written only for the eyes of theological specialists. Although exact scholarship has its place in the service of Christ, those who share in the teaching office of the church have a responsibility to make the results of their research accessible to the Christian community at large. Thus, the Bible scholars who join in the presentation of this series write with these broader concerns in view.

A wide range of modern translations is available to the contemporary Bible student. Most of them are very good and much to be preferred—for understanding, if not always for beauty—to the older King James Version (the so-called Authorized Version of the Bible). The Revised Standard Version has become the standard English translation in many seminaries and colleges and represents the best of modern Protestant scholarship. It is also available in a slightly altered "common Bible" edition with the Catholic imprimatur, and a third revised edition is due out shortly. In addition, the New American Bible is a fresh translation that represents the best of post-Vatican II Roman Catholic biblical scholarship and is in a more contemporary idiom than that of the RSV.

The New Jerusalem Bible, based on the work of French Catholic scholars but vividly rendered into English by a team of British translators, is perhaps the most literary of the recent translations, while the New English Bible is a monument to modern British Protestant research. The Good News Bible is probably the most accessible translation for the person who has little exposure to the Christian tradition or who speaks and reads English as a second language. Each of these is, in its own way, excellent and will be consulted with profit by the serious student of Scripture. Perhaps most will wish to have several versions to read, both for variety and for clarity of understanding—though it should be pointed out that no one of them is by any means flawless or to be received as the last word on any given point. Otherwise, there would be no need for a commentary series like this one!

We have chosen to use the New International Version as the basis for this series, not because it is necessarily the best translation available but because it is becoming increasingly used by lay Bible students and pastors. It is the product of an international team of "evangelical" Bible scholars who have sought to translate the Hebrew and Greek documents of the original into "clear and natural English . . . idiomatic [and] . . . contemporary but not dated," suitable for "young and old, highly educated and less well educated, ministers and laymen [*sic*]." As the translators themselves confess in their preface, this version is not perfect. However, it is as good as any of the others mentioned above and more popular than most of them.

Each volume will contain an introductory chapter detailing the background of the book and its author, important themes, and other helpful information. Then, each section of the book will be expounded as a whole, accompanied by a series of notes on items in the text that need further clarification or more detailed explanation. Appended to the end of each volume will be a bibliographical guide for further study.

Our new series is offered with the prayer that it may be an instrument of authentic renewal and advancement in the worldwide Christian community and a means of commending the faith of the people who lived in biblical times and of those who seek to live by the Bible today.

W. WARD GASQUE
Provost
Eastern College
St. Davids, Pennsylvania

Abbreviations

Abbott-Smith	*A Manual Greek (Lexicon of the New Testament)*
Amplified	Amplified New Testament
Ann.	Tacitus, *Annals*
Ant.	Josephus, *Antiquities*
ASV	American Standard Version (1901)
AV	Authorized Version (King James Version)
b.	Babylonian Talmud
BA	*Biblical Archaeologist*
BAGD	Bauer, Arndt, Gingrich, Danker, *A Greek-English Lexicon of the New Testament and Other Early Christian Literature* (2d ed., 1979)
Beck	*The New Testament in the Language of Today*
Berkeley	Gerrit Verkuyl, *The Berkeley Version of the New Testament*
cf.	compare
chap. (chaps.)	chapter(s)
Dead Sea Scrolls	
CD	Cairo Damascus Document
1QH	Thanksgiving Hymns
1QM	War Scroll
1QS	Rule of the Community
1QSa	Messianic Rule
disc.	discussion
ExpT	*Expository Times*
f. (ff.)	and following verse or page (verses or pages)
Gk.	Greek
GNB	Good News Bible
Goodspeed	*The New Testament: An American Translation*
HDB rev.	Grant and Rowley, *Dictionary of the Bible* (edited by James Hastings)
Eccl. Hist.	Eusebius, *Ecclesiastical History*
IBD	*The Illustrated Bible Dictionary*

IDB	*The Interpreter's Dictionary of the Bible*
ISBE rev.	*The International Standard Bible Encyclopedia rev.* (1979–1988)
JBL	*Journal of Biblical Literature*
JTS	*Journal of Theological Studies*
Knox	The New Testament in the Translation of Monsignor Ronald Knox
Lamsa	The New Testament According to the Eastern Texts
LT	Edersheim, *The Life and Times of Jesus the Messiah*
LXX	Septuagint (the pre-Christian Greek translation of the OT)
m.	Mishnah
MM	Moulton and Milligan, *The Vocabulary of the Greek Testament* (1930)
Moffatt	The New Testament: A New Translation
Montgomery	The Centenary Translation: The New Testament in Modern English
MT	Masoretic Text
NEB	New English Bible
NIDNTT	*New International Dictionary of New Testament Theology*
NIV	New International Version
Norlie	The New Testament: A New Translation
NT	New Testament
NTS	*New Testament Studies*
OT	Old Testament
Phillips	*The New Testament in Modern English*
Pss. Sol.	Psalms of Solomon
Rieu	The Four Gospels
Rotherham	*The Emphasized New Testament: A New Translation*
RSV	Revised Standard Version
RV	Revised Version
sg.	singular
Sifra	Tannaitic Midrash
Str.-B.	Strack, H. L. and Billerbeck, P. *Kommentar zum Neuen Testament aus Talmud und Midrasch* (1922–38)

TCGNT	Metzger, *A Textual Commentary on the Greek New Testament*
TCNT	*The Twentieth Century New Testament*
TDNT	Kittel, *Theological Dictionary of the New Testament*
UBS	United Bible Societies
v. (vv.)	verse(s)
Weymouth	*The New Testament in Modern Speech*
Williams	*The New Testament: A Translation in the Language of the People*
WPNT	Robertson, *Word Pictures in the New Testament*
WSNT	Vincent, *Word Studies in the New Testament*

Introduction

When the four Gospels were arranged (in the order we now have them in the New Testament) it was natural that the Gospel of Matthew should be placed first. Its distinctive structure and specific purpose made it an ideal Gospel for the growing church, with its need to instruct its converts in the life and teachings of Jesus. This early recognition has not diminished in the years that have followed. Though Mark continues to attract readers on the basis of vivid narrative, and Luke appeals to those of broad and benevolent concerns, Matthew is the Gospel that over the years has shaped the life and thought of the church. Renan, the nineteenth-century historian, called it the most important book ever written.[1]

Authorship

The Gospel has traditionally been assigned to Matthew the apostle, although nowhere is there any clear indication of authorship. Some note that in the listing of the apostles, only in the first Gospel is Matthew identified as "the tax collector" (Matt. 10:3; cf. Mark 3:18, Luke 6:15, Acts 1:13). Supposedly this occupation would qualify him to be the official recorder of what Jesus said and did.

The view that Matthew was the earliest Gospel rests primarily on a statement of Papias (a church father who lived until about A.D. 130) as recorded by Eusebius (the "father of church history," who became Bishop of Caesarea in the early fourth century). The statement reads, "Matthew composed [or collected] *ta logia* in the Hebrew dialect, and each one interpreted [or translated] them as best he could" (*Eccl. Hist.* 3.39.16). Ralph Martin, in his book *New Testament Foundations*, surveys the possible meanings of the key term (*logia*) and places them in one of three categories. The term may refer to an earlier Aramaic edition of the Gospel that was written by the apostle and later translated into our Greek canonical Gospel. If the term refers only to part of Matthew's Gospel, then the reference could be either to Old Testament prophetic "oracles" used by the church to prove that Jesus

came in fulfillment of prophecy or to a collection of "sayings" of
Jesus (scholars use the designation "Q") that the writers of Matthew and Luke used when they compiled their Gospels. Martin
favors a third possibility, that *ta logia* refers to an undefined collection of material that was used later in the composition of the
entire Gospel.[2]

Scholars who hold that the apostle Matthew did not write
the Gospel feel that it would be highly unlikely for one of the
Twelve (Matthew) to rely so heavily on the writing of someone
who was not an apostle (i.e., Mark; New Testament scholarship
is almost completely committed to the priority of Mark). However, according to the same Papias who identifies Matthew as the
author or compiler of *ta logia*, Mark was the "interpreter of Peter"
(*Eccl. Hist.* 3.39.15), and it is possible that Matthew would find
little problem deferring to the early leader of the Christian church.
It is also objected that an eyewitness of the events would include
more vivid and lifelike details in his writing. This objection is less
weighty when we remember that Matthew abbreviated much of
Mark's (Peter's?) material and wrote not so much to tell the story
of Jesus as to supply an organized compendium of Jesus' life and
teachings for the instruction of new converts to the Christian faith.

In favor of the apostolic authorship of the Gospel is the
strong witness of the early church fathers. In the early third century Origen wrote, "The first Gospel was written by Matthew,
who was once a tax collector, but who was afterward an apostle
of Jesus Christ."[3] Irenaeus, Eusebius, and Jerome gave similar
evidence. It can also be argued that if the apostle did not write
the Gospel, how did his name become attached to it, and what
became of the person who did write it? Though it is difficult to
answer with any certainty the question of authorship of a Gospel that makes no claims for itself, the most reasonable answer
is that Matthew the apostle was responsible for the Gospel in its
earliest form and that behind the canonical Gospel lies the authority of Matthew the tax collector, one of the Twelve.

Setting and Date

Though earlier writers tended to favor Judea as the place
of origin for the Gospel of Matthew, modern scholarship favors
some place in Syria, probably Antioch. Early in the second cen-

tury Ignatius of Antioch reveals in his writings a knowledge of the Gospel. The date of composition is difficult to determine. The references in 27:8 and 28:15 to events that are remembered "to this [very] day" suggest that a considerable period of time had elapsed between the events and the time when the Gospel was written down. Certain observations, such as the existence of a trinitarian formula for baptism (28:19) and the general impression that the church had settled into a rather fixed ethical code and pattern of organization and worship, suggest a rather late date for composition. On the other hand, if the Gospel were written after the fall of Jerusalem (A.D. 70), it seems strange that the author did not refer to such a dramatic event as a fulfillment of Jesus' predictions in chapter 24. Sometime between A.D. 70 and 80 seems to fit the evidence best.

Structure

It is widely recognized that Matthew is a literary masterpiece. F. C. Grant writes that "the Gospel is clearly the work of a first-rate literary artist and teacher, who has reflected long and deeply upon the substance of the Christian Gospel."[4] While following the order of Mark and preserving almost all its material, Matthew organizes his Gospel into five blocks of teachings separated by narrative sections. The clue lies in the formula "when Jesus had finished saying these things," which is repeated with only minor variations at the close of each section (7:28; 11:1; 13:53; 19:1; 26:1). This fivefold structure is common in ancient Jewish literature (cf. the five books of Moses, the five divisions of the Psalms, the five Megilloth, etc.). Barker, Lane, and Michaels point out that Matthew's five "books" deal with the ethics of the Kingdom (5:1–7:27), mission (10:1–42), redemptive history (13:1–52), church discipline (18:1–35), and eschatology (23:1–25:46).[5] These would be major concerns of an early church desirous of instructing new converts.

Leading Characteristics

Several characteristics set Matthew off from the other Gospels. Perhaps most prominent is his extensive use of Old Testament quotations. In addition to the more than fifty clear quotations, the Gospel contains innumerable single words, phrases, and echoes of the Old Testament. For this reason alone, the Gospel of Matthew served as a natural link between God's people of the old covenant and the new Israel, the church. Gundry's *The Use of the Old Testament in St. Matthew's Gospel* is especially helpful at this point.

Attention is often drawn to the "Jewishness" of the Gospel: for example, the genealogy in chapter 1, interest in fulfilled prophecy (a variation of "that it might be fulfilled" occurs repeatedly) and interest in the law and the traditions of Judaism. At the same time, Matthew expresses a great deal of concern for the Gentiles. It was wise men "from the east" who first came to search out the birthplace of the Messiah (2:1–12). A missionary motif runs throughout the entire Gospel. The Great Commission in 28:19–20 sends the eleven out to "make disciples of all nations." Though it is not true that the basic message of the Gospel is that "the Gentiles have displaced the Jews,"[6] there is no doubt that Matthew is universalistic in outlook.

Matthew evidences a great deal of interest in the organized church. Only in Matthew, among the Gospels, does the word *ekklēsia* ("church") occur. His entire Gospel is organized around the catechetical needs of the growing community. The abridgment of Marcan material is intended to make it more easily learned and remembered by new believers. The emphasis on the teaching ministry of Jesus is prominent. The Sermon on the Mount (chaps. 5–7) is the largest single block of Jesus' teaching to be found in any of the four Gospels. Other emphases that should be mentioned are Matthew's stress on the inevitability and serious nature of divine judgment, his concern with apocalyptic eschatology, and his insistence that Jesus the Messiah is the Lord of the worshiping church.

Interpretive Approach

One final word needs to be said about the view that certain portions of Matthew (basically, the infancy narratives and various amplifications of the passion and resurrection narratives) are examples of a Jewish-Christian midrash (imaginative elaborations that bring out the deeper meaning of the text). Grant says that such things as the flight into Egypt (2:13–18), Peter's walking on the water (14:28–31), and the resurrection appearance in Galilee (28:16–20) "must be viewed as fancies—pious fancies, no doubt, but still only the poetic or imaginative embellishment of the central narrative and message of the NT."[7]

There is, of course, no way to prove or disprove in any final sense the validity of one's hermeneutical methodology. What may seem obvious to one scholar may not be nearly so convincing to another. The basic assumptions one brings to Scripture determine to a great extent what the text will turn out to mean; we are all affected by the mind-set with which we approach a text. If, for example, we are of the general opinion that miracles do not (and never did) happen, then the miracles of Jesus will have to be interpreted to fit. On the other hand, if we believe that God is able to act from time to time in ways that seem to defy "natural law," then Peter's walking on the water (to say nothing of the resurrection) will be taken at face value.

The approach followed in this commentary is to let the Gospel speak for itself. Since there is no indication that the early church discussed at length the historicity of Jesus' life and work vis-à-vis the possible deeper and allegorical significance of each event, to take up the task some nineteen centuries later has little promise of success. To deny the historical nature of the central events in the redemptive activity of God is to treat narrative as though it were poetry and in the process sacrifice the heart of the Christian gospel.

Notes

1. F. V. Filson, *A Commentary on the Gospel According to St. Matthew,* Harper's New Testament Commentaries (New York: Harper & Brothers, 1960), p. 1.

2. R. Martin, *New Testament Foundations,* 2 vols. (Grand Rapids: Eerdmans, 1975–78), vol. 1, pp. 238–40.

3. Origen, *Ecclesiastica Historia* 6.14.5

4. F. C. Grant, "Matthew, Gospel of," *IDB,* vol. 3, p. 304.

5. G. W. Barker, W. L. Lane, and J. R. Michaels, *The New Testament Speaks* (New York: Harper & Row, 1969), p. 265.

6. K. W. Clark, "Gentile Bias in Matthew," *JBL* 66 (1947), p. 172.

7. Grant, "Matthew," 307.

Note: A list of the abbreviations used in the commentary is found at the beginning of the book (see pp. xi–xii). See also, "For Further Reading" (pp. 271–74); full bibliographical references for works referred to in short-form notes within the commentary are supplied there.

§1 The Birth of Jesus (Matt. 1:1–25)

Genealogical records were important to the Jewish people of Jesus' day. They were maintained by the Sanhedrin and used to ensure purity of descent. Josephus, the famous Jewish historian who served in the court of Rome, began his autobiography by listing his ancestral pedigree. Similarly, Matthew opens his Gospel by tracing the lineage of Jesus. It has often been noted that, from David forward, the Lucan genealogy has forty-one generations traced through Nathan rather than twenty-six generations traced through Solomon. Possibly Luke records the actual descent of Joseph whereas Matthew follows the royal lineage.

1:1 / At the very beginning Matthew establishes the two most significant points about Jesus' family history: he was **the son of David** (therefore of royal lineage) and also a descendant **of Abraham** (he belonged to the people of God who had their origin with the great patriarch who moved out of ancient Ur and by faith followed the leading of God to a new land.) The title **son of David** occurs frequently in Matthew and stems from God's promise to King David in 2 Samuel 7:12: "I will raise up your offspring to succeed you, . . . and I will establish his kingdom." In Jewish usage the title was messianic; that is, it pointed ahead to the coming of the long-awaited Messiah.

1:2–17 / The family record of Jesus (listed in vv. 2–16) is arranged in three divisions, which mark out three stages in Jewish history. Furthermore, according to verse 17, there are **fourteen generations** in each division. Several irregularities call for explanation. First, there appear to be only thirteen generations in the third division (vv. 12–16). A number of answers have been suggested: a name has been lost; Mary should be included; Jesus is the thirteenth, and Messiah (Jesus at his second coming) is the fourteenth. Schweizer is probably correct in his observation that, since ancient reckoning always included the first and last elements of a series, the sequence should be (1) Abraham to David,

(2) David to Josiah (the last free king), (3) Jeconiah (the first king of the captivity) to Jesus (p. 23). This would place fourteen generations in each division.

Another irregularity is the omission of three kings before Jotham (Joash, Amaziah, Azariah) and one after Josiah (Jehoahaz). The most reasonable answer is that Matthew is less concerned with supplying us with an exact family record than with arranging the names in groups of fourteen to coincide with the three important stages of Jewish history: the account of God's people leading up to Israel's greatest king; the decline of the nation, ending in Babylonian exile; the restoration of God's people with the advent of the Messiah. Some have noted that fourteen is the numerical value of the Hebrew letters in the name David (the three consonants have the numerical values D = 4, W = 6, D = 4, for a total of 14). In any case, the somewhat rough genealogical table serves Matthew's purpose of setting forth the royal and messianic ancestry of Jesus of Nazareth.

A third irregularity sets this family record apart from all others: it makes reference to five women. Since women had no legal rights in Jesus' day, this is indeed extraordinary. And note who the four (apart from Mary) were: **Tamar** was a Canaanite who seduced her father-in-law, Judah (Gen. 38). **Rahab** was a prostitute in Jericho (Josh. 2:1–21). **Ruth** was a Moabitess (Ruth 1:4; and Deut. 23:3 rules that "no . . . Moabite or any of his descendants may enter the assembly of the Lord"). Bathsheba (**Uriah's wife**) was the wife of a Hittite, and as a result of his lust for her, David committed both adultery and murder. If one searched the Old Testament for a more unlikely group of candidates for a messianic lineage, it is doubtful one could come up with a more questionable group.

Why did Matthew include women in his genealogical listing? They are not in the lineage in the same sense that all the men are. Since their names did not have to be included (he could have mentioned the mothers of all the other kings as well), Matthew must have had some specific reason for doing so. Of the many solutions offered, the most persuasive is that by including the women Matthew is calling attention to the strange ways in which God has brought about his purpose in times past and is thereby preparing the way for a truly unique event, the virgin birth of Jesus. Whether or not he is getting ready to argue that

God's activity embraces both Jew and Gentile (all four women were foreigners) is not quite clear. In any case, the family record reminds us of the fallen state of human nature and the redeeming activity of God in bringing back to himself the sinner as well as the saint.

1:18-21 / Matthew now turns to the events surrounding the birth of Jesus. It will be noticed at once that the account differs from what we find in Luke. In fact, neither Gospel writer includes anything dealt with by the other except the role of the Holy Spirit in Mary's pregnancy and the fact that Joseph and Mary were the parents of Jesus. This has led some scholars to conclude that the two accounts are historically irreconcilable.

There is no inherent necessity, however, for such a radical conclusion. For example, the angelic appearance to Mary (in Luke) and to Joseph (in Matthew) are not the same event. To Mary, the angel announces that, having found favor with God, she is to bear a son. In response to Mary's query as to how that could be, since she has no husband, the angel explains that the Holy Spirit will overshadow her, and the child will be the Son of God (Luke 1:30-35). To Joseph, the angel counseled that he **not be afraid to take Mary home as** his **wife,** since the child she will conceive is **from the Holy Spirit** (Matt. 1:20-23). There is no reason to question a twofold appearance of the angel. In fact, the situation calls for it. Other variations between the accounts are no more than what one would expect given the slightly differing purposes and perspectives of the writers.

Jewish weddings involved three separate steps. First, there was the engagement. This was often arranged by the parents or by a professional matchmaker while the couple were still children. At a later stage came the betrothal, a legally binding relationship lasting for one year. During this period the couple lived apart and had no sexual relations. Should either party not wish to go ahead with the marriage, a divorce was required. The penalty for sleeping with a virgin betrothed to another man was stoning for both (in Deut. 22:24, she is called "another man's wife"). The third step was the marriage itself.

It was during the second stage (the betrothal) that Mary was found to be pregnant. What bewilderment and dismay this must have brought to the virgin Mary. And what thoughts must have passed through the mind of Joseph. Matthew tells us that Joseph was **a righteous man** (v. 19), yet he did not want to expose Mary openly. Mosaic law called upon a man to divorce his wife if he "finds something indecent about her" (Deut. 24:1). Such was Joseph's duty, and he realized it. Yet compassion for his bride led him to make plans to break off the engagement privately, that is, before the minimum number of witnesses (two) and without pressing charges (cf. m. *Sotah* 1.5).

While he was considering this, an angel appeared to Joseph telling him to follow through with the marriage plans. The child Mary would bear would be by the Holy Spirit. He was to call him **Jesus**, for his mission would be to **save his people from their sins** (v. 21). With his Davidic bloodline, Joseph was to become the legal father of Jesus the Messiah. It has been noted that in certain respects Joseph is a reflection of his Old Testament namesake, who also was a righteous man, influenced by dreams, and forced to journey into Egypt.

1:22–25 / Five times in the first two chapters (and six more scattered through the Gospel) Matthew uses what are called "formula quotations" to point out that in the details of Jesus' life are being fulfilled many of the promises of the Old Testament. On this first occasion Matthew says that **all this** (the supernatural conception of Jesus in the womb of the virgin Mary) **took place to fulfill what the Lord had said through the prophet**. He then quotes Isaiah 7:14 from the LXX, which translates the Hebrew *'almâ* ("a young woman of marriageable age") with the Greek *parthenos* ("virgin"; note, however, that though *parthenos* normally assumes virginity, it is used in Gen. 34:3 for a girl who has been raped.) He sees beyond the promise made to King Ahaz (that by the time a child soon to be born reaches early childhood the international situation will change in favor of Israel) to a greater fulfillment in the birth of Christ. The child will be called **Immanuel**, explained by Matthew as meaning **God with us** (v. 23). In the Old Testament setting, God is with his people in the noble son of Ahaz (Hezekiah), who gave his undivided loyalty and allegiance to the God of Israel. Green notes that **God with us** in the Old Testament is "a semi-technical expression of God's helping presence with individuals" (p. 56). In the New Testament, Jesus is the very presence of God the Father who comes to live among his people (cf. John 1:14). It is fitting that the Gospel ends with an "Immanuel" promise—"I am with you always, to the very end of the age" (Matt. 28:20).

When Joseph awoke from his dream he carried out the instructions he had received from the angel. Mary and Joseph were married but had **no union** ("sexual relations," GNB) until after the child was born. One branch of the church, desiring to protect the "perpetual virginity" of Mary, holds that the couple never did have sexual relations. The mention of Jesus' brothers and sisters in Matthew 13:55–56 points to a different conclusion.

Additional Notes §1

1:16 / Of the three principal variant readings, the UBS follows the one that translates, "Joseph the husband of Mary, of whom Jesus was born, who is called Christ." Other readings avoid the expression "husband of Mary" as inappropriate in view of vv. 18ff.

1:19 / **Public**: Gk. *deigmatizō* means "to expose or humiliate in public." A *deigma* is a "specimen" or an "example."

1:20 / **In a dream**: In biblical times dreams were often used as vehicles of revelation. They seem to appear in clusters: in the patriarchal period, during the ministry of Daniel, and in the nativity narratives in Matthew.

1:21 / **Jesus**: The name is the Greek form of the Hebrew "*ye-(hô)šu'a*" (English "Joshua") which means "Yahweh is salvation." Jesus' mission is revealed in the name he is given. His mission is redemptive and spiritual rather than nationalistic. He is to save his people from their sins.

2:1-2 / Luke recounts Joseph and Mary's journey from Nazareth to Bethlehem in order to comply with census regulations (Joseph was a descendant of David, who was a son of "Jesse of Bethlehem," 1 Sam. 16:1); Matthew simply states that Jesus was born in the town of **Bethlehem in Judea** (there was another Bethlehem within the territory assigned to Zebulun, Josh. 19:15). The name Bethlehem means "house of bread." It was nestled in a fertile countryside some six miles south of Jerusalem, and its history was long and illustrious. It was there that Rachel died (Gen. 48:7) and there that Ruth lived after her marriage to Boaz (Ruth 1:22). Bethlehem was most important, however, as the city of David. Thus it was from Bethlehem that Israel expected David's greater son, the Messiah, to come (Mic. 5:2). So, in fulfillment of prophetic anticipation, Jesus was born in Bethlehem.

The birth of Jesus took place during the reign of **Herod** the Great. This crafty and cruel monarch secured his position as ruler over Palestine by successfully manipulating Marcus Antonius. Although he erected many ornate buildings (the temple in Jerusalem was one) and was on occasion exceptionally generous, he steadily lost favor with the Jewish people. His mixed lineage (half Idumean and half Jewish) would make him suspect to begin with. His Edomite blood (cf. Mal. 1:4) made him unacceptable.

Toward the end of his reign (which lasted from 40 until 4 B.C.) he became increasingly cruel. Suspicious that his own family was plotting his overthrow, he murdered his favorite wife (Mariamne), her mother, two of her sons, and his own eldest son. Augustus, the Roman emperor, who for years had retained confidence in Herod, finally acknowledged that it was safer to be Herod's pig (*hys* in Greek) than his son (*hyios*). He was, as it were, a second Pharaoh, that symbol of unbelief and coldheartedness in the Old Testament.

The first to visit the newborn child were astrologers from the East. The AV calls them "wise men" (NIV **Magi**, translating *magoi*) indicating that they were thought to possess secret wisdom concerning the movement of the stars and the influence that this would have on the course of human history. Beare notes that although astrology was a dominant influence at that time ("the real religion of many of the most elevated and clearminded spirits"), it was a pseudoscience, for it depended upon the theory that the earth is the center of the universe and that the planets are living powers (p. 74). The astrologers probably came from Babylonia, where they would have had contact with the Jewish exiles and the opportunity to develop an interest in the coming Messiah (cf. *TDNT,* vol. 6, pp. 356–59). The same word (*magos,* sg.) occurs in Acts 13:6, 8, of the magician Elymas (Bar-Jesus), but in the negative sense of one who practices magical arts (Paul calls him a "child of the devil . . . full of all kinds of deceit and trickery," Acts 13:10). The wise men who came to worship the Christ were not crafty magicians but highly respected members of the community (note, however, that Ignatius of Antioch took them in the bad sense, *Ign. Eph.* 19).

Tradition has expanded on the visitors from the East. Because they brought three kinds of gifts (v. 11), it is commonly held that they were three in number. The idea that they were kings was probably derived from such passages as Psalms 72:10, 15, and Isaiah 49:7. Some seven hundred years later they were given the names Caspar, Balthasar, and Melchior. There is no basis in the text for these conjectures.

The journey from the East was prompted by a remarkable phenomenon that they had seen in the heavens. It may have been the conjunction of Jupiter and Venus in the spring of 7 B.C. We know that ancient astronomers were able to calculate the orbits of planets years in advance. Stauffer holds that the Magi noted only the beginning of the conjunction (the appearance of Jupiter in the east; v. 2) and set out for Palestine. Upon arriving, they witnessed the extremely rare (once every 794 years) conjunction of Jupiter and Saturn in the Sign of the Fishes. Note that when they left Jerusalem for Bethlehem they saw "the star they had seen in the east" (v. 9) and were filled with joy. Stauffer goes on to say that since Jupiter was regarded as the star of the universe, Saturn the planet of Palestine, and the constellation of the Fishes the sign of the last days, this rare conjunction "could only mean that the ruler of the last days would appear in Palestine" (*Jesus and His Story,* p. 33).

2:3–6 / Upon arriving in Jerusalem the Magi asked where they could find the baby born to be king of the Jews. They had come with gifts and wanted to worship him. It is no surprise that the sudden arrival of these foreign visitors with their bold query caused considerable consternation among the ruling elite. Upon hearing the report, King Herod was "greatly agitated" (Weymouth). And well he should be. His hold upon the country was shaky at best. Should a bona fide Jewish king appear on the horizon, his own hegemony could be quickly overthrown. Herod was thrown into confusion and called together the chief priests and teachers of the law in order to inquire of them where the Messiah was to be born. At that time there was a widespread expectation that a universal king would appear and bring about a golden age of peace and prosperity.

The Jewish council answered Herod, telling him that the Messiah was to be born in **Bethlehem in Judea**. Matthew adds that this is in fulfillment of the prophecy of Micah, who said that from Bethlehem would come a **ruler** who would **shepherd** his **people Israel**. It is instructive to compare Matthew's quotation with the original in Micah 5:2. "Ephrathah" (probably the district in which Bethlehem lay) becomes the **land of Judah**; "clans of Judah" becomes **rulers of Judah**; and "though you are small" becomes **you . . . are by no means least**. What we have is a form of midrashic interpretation that combines scriptural interpretation with reflection of contemporary events. The Dead Sea Scrolls show that the Essenes (a Jewish ascetic order) of Jesus' day practiced this kind of messianic adaptation of Old Testament passages. For Matthew, it was a way of bringing out the deeper intention of prophetic passages by making the words of the prophet more specific. It is the fulfillment of ancient prophecy that allows for messianic clarification.

2:7–11 / Having discovered the town in which the Messiah was to be born, Herod summoned the Magi **secretly** in order to find out **the exact time the star had appeared**. Apparently he had already decided that if he were unable to find the child and destroy him he would go ahead and slaughter all the children up to a certain age (see v. 16). Note the parallels with the account of the birth of Moses. Pharaoh had instructed the Hebrew midwives to destroy every baby boy, but the mother of Moses, when she could hide him no longer, placed the infant in a papyrus basket and hid him in the reeds along the Nile (Exod. 2:1–4): Jesus is taken to Egypt to escape the wrath of Herod (Matt. 2:13–15). In a late Jewish midrash there is a somewhat parallel legend of the birth of Abraham involving a star, predictions of greatness that threaten his life, and the hiding of the child in a cave for three years (Vermes, *Scripture and Tradition in Judaism*, pp. 68ff.).

Herod sends the astrologers on to Bethlehem with instructions to search for the child and, upon finding him, to report back. The alleged purpose was so that Herod could also go and worship him. The cruel hypocrisy of Herod is obvious. It is what we would expect from a tyrant who shortly before he died ordered that a large group of prominent citizens be imprisoned and put to death at the moment of his own decease. In this way he guaranteed there would be sorrow and tears at the time of his death.

It is interesting that the Jewish religious leaders made no attempt to follow through on the possibility that the baby to be born might be the long-awaited Messiah. The first to understand and take action were dignitaries from a foreign land. Already at this early stage in the Gospel we have an indication of the universal implications of the incarnation. In Christ all people, not Jews only, may be brought into God's favor.

So the wise men left Jerusalem and journeyed toward Bethlehem. When they caught sight of the star, they were overwhelmed with joy. The way Matthew narrates the story supports the interpretation that an earlier conjunction started them on their way, and now a major and subsequent conjunction (see disc. on v. 2) proves that their reading of the stars was correct. The star is said to go **ahead of them until it stopped over the place where the child was** (v. 9). This has been taken either as a miraculous movement of the star leading them to the very house where the baby Jesus was (no problem for the ancients; a star is said to have led Aeneas to the spot where Rome was founded; Virgil, *Aeneid* 2.694ff.) or as no more than a way of saying that what they had seen in the heavens "led" them to find the newborn Messiah (cf. Plummer, p. 12).

Some time has passed since the earlier visit by the shepherds on the night Jesus was born. Luke 2:16 tells us that they found the babe (*to brephos*) lying in a manger (*phatnē*). By now (Matt. 2:11) the family has moved into a **house** (*oikia*), and Jesus is referred to as a **child** (*paidion*). Upon seeing the child with Mary his mother, the Magi fall on their knees and worship him. They open their treasure chests and lay before the child **gifts of gold and of incense and of myrrh**. Gold is the metal of kings. [Frank]incense is a sweet-smelling gum imported from Arabia (cf. Jer. 6:20). Myrrh is a fragrant gum used both medicinally (Mark 15:23) and as a perfume (Ps. 45:8; Prov. 7:17). Because gold was a royal metal, frankincense was used by priests in temple worship (Lev. 2:1, 2, 15–16), and myrrh was used to embalm the bodies of the dead (John 19:39), some writers have seen a special symbolism in the three gifts. Barclay writes, "Even at the cradle of Christ [the gifts] foretold that he was to be the true King, the perfect High Priest, and in the end the supreme Saviour" (vol. 1, p. 33).

2:12 / After presenting their gifts to the Christ child, the wise men returned to their homeland. They did not report back to Herod as he had ordered, but having been **warned** by God **in a dream** they returned home by another way. By secular observation these gentile astrologers had discerned the coming of the Jewish Messiah, sought him out in order to worship him, and now in obedience to a divine visitation return home without making contact with the religious authorities. All this time the religious leaders of Jerusalem know from their own Scriptures where the Messiah is to be born. But not even the visit of foreign dignitaries piques their curiosity enough to travel six miles to Bethlehem to find out if there is any truth in the report. As Jesus later said, "I have come into this world, so that the blind will see and those who see will become blind" (John 9:39).

2:13–15 / As soon as the Magi left, **an angel of the Lord appeared to Joseph in a dream**. This is the third time thus far in the Gospel that God communicates by means of a dream (in 1:20, to encourage Joseph to go ahead and take Mary as his wife; in 2:12, to warn the Magi to return to their country by a different route). On two subsequent occasions in chapter 2 Joseph will be instructed by means of a dream (vv. 19, 22). In the ancient world people attached great importance to dreams. The dream was viewed as a form of communication with the unseen world, and every primitive culture had its professionals who would interpret dreams (cf. Dan. 2:2). In Hebrew tradition the ability to interpret dreams comes from God (Gen. 40:8).

The angel who appears to Joseph in a dream warns him that Herod will **search for the child to kill him**. Joseph is to **take**

the child and his mother (note the order; even in infancy, the priority is given to Jesus) **and escape to Egypt**. It has often been noted that Egypt was a natural refuge for the Jews. Every city in Egypt of any size had a colony of Jews (in Alexandria, over 2 million). Certain later traditions attempt to convey the idea that it was in Egypt that Jesus learned magical tricks that he used later in connection with his miracles (cf. *Abodah Zarah* 16b–17a).

Joseph is to remain with his family in Egypt until the angel of the Lord returns and tells him to leave. In verse 8 Herod claimed he wanted to know where Jesus was so he could go and worship him. Now we see that his real intent was to murder the Christ child. So Joseph gathers his family and leaves for Egypt, where they remained **until the death of Herod**. This took place in 4 B.C. How Jesus could have been born B.C. (before Christ) is troublesome, until one realizes that the universal method of dating was not changed to take as its fixed point the birth of Christ until several centuries later and involved a miscalculation. If Kepler's astronomical calculations are correct, Jesus may have been born as early as 7 B.C. In any case, it was prior to 4 B.C. That Herod ordered the death of all boy babies two years old and younger (v. 16) supports a date between 7 and 5 B.C.

Once again Matthew points out that an event in the life of Jesus took place in order to make some prophetic utterance come true (cf. 1:22; 2:5, 17, 23). As spoken by the prophet, the statement "out of Egypt I called my son" (Hos. 11:1) referred to God's deliverance of Israel from the bondage of Egypt. Matthew interprets the Christ child as the embodiment or representation of the true Israel. Consequently, a number of parallels exists between the life of Jesus and the history of the nation. For example, Jesus is a second and greater Moses, who will lead his people out from spiritual bondage as his predecessor led the Israelites out from physical bondage. This "Moses typology" allows Matthew to find in Hosea's words a prediction that the Christ child will be called **out of Egypt**.

Revelation 12:1–6 tells of a great dragon who waited for the radiant woman to give birth to a son in order to devour him. The son, who is to rule the nations, is born but immediately snatched away to God's throne. The woman flees to the protection of the desert. Though the theme of a miraculous rescue of a young sovereign is not unusual in ancient literature (cf. Heracles, Romulus and Remus), there is no reason to doubt the historicity of the biblical account of the flight of Joseph and his family to Egypt.

2:16–18 / Herod was furious when he realized that the wise men had not returned to him with information about the newborn king. Immediately he ordered the death of all male children in Bethlehem and the surrounding area who were **two years old and under**. His decision regarding age rested upon what he had learned from the Magi about the time the star had first appeared. It suggests that a number of months had intervened between the "rising" of the star in the east (2:2; cf. NIV text note) and the return of the wise men to their own country. Undoubtedly Herod left a considerable margin for error. That Herod would carry out such a savage plan is not surprising. We already know that he murdered members of his own family, and, after all, Bethlehem was a tiny little village with not more than twenty or thirty children of that age. That Josephus the historian (or any other early writer) neglects to mention the slaughter tells us more about the cruelty of that day than it does about any lack of historicity of the event. Such purges were simply not noteworthy.

Once again Matthew finds prophetic background for the event. Jeremiah speaks of the weeping that took place in Ramah when Rachel mourned for her dead children (Jer. 31:15), giving a picture of the Israelites (Rachel's children) filing by her grave at Ramah as they are led into captivity. Since the route to Babylon would lead the exiles north from Jerusalem, this has led to some confusion regarding the location of Ramah. If it is to be identified with Er-Ram, it would be located about six miles north of Jerusalem; if with Ramat Rahel, it would be on the road south from Jerusalem toward Bethlehem. Tradition has placed the burial place of Rachel near Bethlehem (cf. Gen. 35:19; 48:7). How then would the captives pass by on their way into exile? But is such geographical precision necessary? All we are intended to understand is that as Rachel mourned for her children, so also do the mothers of Bethlehem mourn for theirs.

Some have noted that the larger context of the Jeremiah passages is one of hope. The prophet goes on to say that the exiles will return (31:16) and "there is hope for your future" (31:17). God will bring his people back from captivity (31:23), refreshing the weary and satisfying the faint (31:25). Since a particular passage may intend the entire context (cf. C. H. Dodd, *According to the*

Scriptures, p. 126), Matthew may be pointing beyond the immediate sorrow to the final result of the Messiah's entrance into the
world. Beyond pain and death there is certain victory.

2:19–23 / The angel of the Lord had told Joseph to remain in Egypt until he was told to leave (2:13). Now the angel
appears once again and instructs him to take his family and
go to the land of Israel. When Herod died in 4 B.C. his kingdom
was divided into three parts. Archelaus, the eldest son, was
placed over Judea, Samaria, and Idumea, but confirmation was
withheld by Augustus until the newly appointed ethnarch could
prove himself. This never happened. This ruthless leader opened
his reign by slaughtering three thousand prominent citizens.
Two years later, he was removed by the emperor, who then
placed the territory under a prefect responsible to the legate of
Syria.

It was during this two-year period that Joseph made preparations to return to Israel. Upon hearing that **Archelaus was reign-
ing in Judea in place of his father Herod** (though not as **king**
as in GNB), he was afraid to go there (presumably, to Bethlehem).
Once again Joseph receives instructions in a dream. He is to go
to the province of Galilee and make his home in a **town called
Nazareth.** Although Nazareth is not mentioned apart from the
Gospels, it was by no means an isolated and insignificant village
(in spite of the derogatory tone in John 1:46, "Nazareth! Can anything good come from there?"). Nestled in the hills in the south
of Galilee, it looked down on two of the most important caravan
routes in the ancient world: one leading from Damascus to Egypt
and the other from the seacoast to the lands to the east.

Matthew interprets the fact that Jesus makes his home in
Nazareth as a fulfillment of the prophetic statement, **He will be
called a Nazarene.** Since no such prophecy is to be found in the
Old Testament, we are faced with an interesting puzzle. The best
approach is that since Matthew speaks of prophets (plural) he
is providing a summary in indirect speech rather than quoting
a specific utterance. No totally satisfying solution to the Old
Testament background for the title Nazarene is forthcoming. Many
have noted the wordplay between *nēṣer* ("branch"; cf. Isa. 11:1) or
nāzîr ("Nazirite"; cf. Judg. 13:5, 7) and *Nazōraios* ("Nazarene"). In
spite of the linguistic difficulties in relating *Nazōraios* and Nazareth,
that is obviously the connection Matthew intends to establish.

Many writers have noticed Matthew's use of the Moses motif, especially in the nativity narratives (cf. W. D. Davies, *The Setting of the Sermon on the Mount*, pp. 78ff.). In Exodus 4:19 God tells Moses to leave Midian and "go back to Egypt, for all the men who wanted to kill you are dead." Matthew's use of "those who were trying to take the child's life" (2:20), referring to Herod and those he sent to carry out his nefarious scheme, may reflect the Old Testament parallel as well. Joseph is to go back from Egypt to Israel. In both cases, release from bondage is the ultimate purpose: physical in Moses' case, spiritual in Jesus'.

Additional Notes §2

2:1 / **King Herod**: For a full account of his reign, see S. Perowne, *The Life and Times of Herod the Great*.
The visit of the wise men is commemorated in the Christian celebration called Epiphany (January 6), also referred to as Twelfth Day or Little Christmas.

2:5 / The Gk. *gegraptai* may be taken in the sense of "the inspired text runs" (Albright-Mann, p. 13).

2:9 / **The place**: Justin Martyr said Jesus was born in a cave that served as a stall for cattle and donkeys. It would have been beneath the inn on the side of a hill.

2:11 / **Gifts**: The giving of gifts in the ancient East was an act of submission and allegiance (cf. Ps. 72:10–11, 15; Isa. 60:6).

2:14 / The Gk. *anachōreō* means "to withdraw from danger" (cf. 2:22; 12:15). Later it became a technical term in monasticism (an "anchorite" is one who has withdrawn from society).

2:15 / According to a Jewish tradition retained in the Talmud (b. *Shab.* 104b), Jesus "brought with him magic arts out of Egypt in an incision on his body."

2:23 / **Nazarene**: For a full discussion, see R. H. Gundry, *The Use of the Old Testament in St. Matthew's Gospel*, pp. 97ff.

At the close of chapter 2, Joseph, Mary, and the child Jesus returned from Egypt and took up residence in the Galilean town of Nazareth. The time would have been shortly after the death of Herod in 4 B.C. Chapter 3 begins with the prophetic ministry of John the Baptist some twenty-five to thirty years later. What had been going on in the life of Jesus during this time? Except for one incident, the Gospels remain silent. They were never intended to be taken as biographies. The only thing we know for sure is that at age twelve Jesus was taken to Jerusalem for the Passover. There he talked with the religious leaders about the things of God (Luke 2:41–50). Luke then notes that Jesus returned with his parents to Nazareth and "was obedient to them" and "grew in wisdom and stature, and in favor with God and men" (Luke 2:51–52).

Such meager information did not satisfy the curiosity of later writers. They felt moved to invent all sorts of miraculous tales and assign them to the early years of Jesus' life. For example, the *Infancy Gospel of Thomas* tells of Zeno (one of Jesus' young friends), who fell from the upper story of a house and died. Zeno's parents accused Jesus of causing him to fall, whereupon Jesus jumped down from the roof and brought Zeno back to life so he could tell them it wasn't so (9:1–3). Fortunately, the canonical Gospels include no such sensational vignettes. Jesus undoubtedly grew up in much the same way as any other Jewish boy.

Since Joseph does not appear in later accounts (e.g., no mention is made of him at the wedding at Cana, John 2:1–12), and since it appears that he was quite a bit older than Mary, most writers conclude that Jesus, as the eldest son, took responsibility for the family when Joseph died and provided for them until he entered into his public ministry (about thirty years of age, Luke 3:23).

3:1–6 / Matthew introduces the ministry of John the Baptist, saying that **in those days John the Baptist came, preaching in the Desert of Judea**. The temporal reference emphasizes that this was a critical period in history (cf. Gen. 38:1; Dan. 10:2). For four hundred years Israel had been without a prophetic voice. Now there appears on the scene the promised "Elijah," who is to usher in the great and dreadful day of the Lord (Mal. 4:5; Sir. 48:10; cf. Matt. 17:10–13). Like the Elijah of old, his clothes were made of **camel's hair,** and he wore a **leather belt around his waist** (v. 4; cf. 2 Kings 1:8; Zech. 13:4 speaks of a "prophet's garment of hair"). His food consisted of locusts and wild honey. The ceremonial instructions in Leviticus 11 allow the eating of "any kind of locust, katydid, cricket or grasshopper" (Lev. 11:22). Even today, the locust is eaten in many parts of the Eastern world. Wild honey was honey that came from nectar taken from uncultivated shrubbery.

John's ministry took place in the Judean desert, that rather barren wasteland to the west of the Dead Sea. Since John's execution was at the decree of Herod Antipas, who ruled over Galilee and Perea (Matt. 14:1–12), it is likely that the Baptist's travels took him into a wider area as well. Whether or not he came under the direct influence of an Essene group (the sectarians at Qumran?) has been widely discussed. It should be noted that though baptism was an important rite at Qumran, it differed in several respects from the baptism practiced by John (e.g., it was repeated frequently, had to do with ceremonial uncleanness, and involved entry into an exclusive sect that demanded unswerving obedience to the law).

John's basic message was a call to repentance. **Repent, for the kingdom of heaven is near.** To **repent** (*metanoeō*) does not mean simply to be sorry but to change one's way of life completely. The corresponding Hebrew verb means "to turn," that is, "to reverse completely the direction of one's life." The Jewish society of John's day would know full well the radical change of lifestyle indicated by genuine repentance. As recorded by Matthew, Jesus' initial message is exactly the same as John's (cf. Matt. 4:17). Repentance is both urgent and appropriate, because the long-awaited kingdom is about to appear. Matthew uses the term **kingdom of heaven** (rather than kingdom of God) out of Semitic reluctance to speak the divine name. God's kingdom is his reign or rule over his people.

Again Matthew finds the fulfillment of prophecy in the events of his day. It was John the Baptist that Isaiah was talking about when he spoke of **one calling in the desert, "Prepare the**

way for the Lord." That the Hebrew text punctuates the passage differently and joins **in the desert** with what follows makes little difference. In Isaiah 40 a highway for God is to be prepared along which the exiles will return home from Babylon. Ancient roads were notably poor. Efforts to make a road level and smooth were restricted to times when royalty was on its way. John calls for repentance so that God will have **straight paths** to travel into the hearts and lives of his people. Response to John's preaching was remarkable. People came from everywhere—Jerusalem, all of Judea, and the entire country around the Jordan River. **Confessing** openly **their sins, they were baptized by him in the Jordan River.**

3:7–12 / Among those who came were a number of **Pharisees and Sadducees.** Although apparently they came to be baptized, John immediately saw through their hypocrisy. The **Pharisees** were lay reformers who stressed obedience not only to the law but also to the oral tradition that had grown up around it. They were students of the law and centered their activity in the synagogue. The **Sadducees** were the priestly aristocracy, for whom the temple was the focal point for all religious life. Since the two groups were normally at odds with one another (cf. Acts 23:6–10), it is instructive to note that their differences did not prevent them from coming together at this point.

John's response is sharp: **You brood of vipers! Who warned you to flee from** God's punishment! The picture is one of serpents slithering quickly to escape a fire racing through a field of dry grass or weeds. It is unnecessary to find in John's words a reference to the serpent in the Garden of Eden (Gen. 3:1). Yet Jesus calls his antagonists children of the devil, who "was a murderer from the beginning" (John 8:44). Note that Jesus uses the expression "offspring of vipers" (ASV) on two occasions (Matt. 12:34; 23:33). John has no corner on vivid language! Barclay quotes Diogenes as saying, "He who never offended anyone, never did anyone any good" (vol. 1, p. 44).

Genuine repentance produces a changed life. The religious leaders of Israel must show by their conduct that they have turned from their sins. They are not to presume that having **Abraham** as their ancestor will keep them from punishment. The rabbis taught that Abraham was such an exceptionally good man that he had built up a treasury of merit that covered all the needs of his descendants (cf. *Mekilta Exod.* 14:15). They had forgotten that "fidelity, not race or class, is the only bond that binds us to God" (Senior, p. 43). The truth is that God can take stones and make of them children for Abraham. The comparison between "stones" and "children" is strengthened by the fact that in Aramaic the two words sound quite similar. Now is not the time for empty profession and hypocrisy. **The ax is already at the root of the trees** (cf. Isa. 10:34; Jer. 46:22, for the metaphor), **and every tree that does not produce good fruit will be cut down** and burned up (v. 10). The fruit that genuine repentance produces cannot be added onto the life but grows out of a basic disposition of the heart. If there is no fruit there has been no fundamental change of heart.

John looks beyond his ministry to the One for whom he is preparing the way. "My baptism," he might say, "indicates that you have repented. It is a baptism **with water**. The One who comes after me baptizes **with the Holy Spirit and with fire**." John's baptism cleansed with water; Jesus' baptism will purge with fire. The Coming One brings a large **winnowing fork** that serves to throw the grain into the air, allowing the heavy kernels to fall to the ground and the lighter chaff to be blown away. The wheat will be gathered **into the barn**, but the worthless straw will be burned **with unquenchable fire** (v. 12). Matthew repeatedly uses fire as a symbol of judgment (5:22; 7:19; 13:40, 42; 18:8; 25:41). John's baptism required repentance; Jesus' baptism tests the reality of that repentance (cf. 1 Cor. 3:13). The Coming One is so much greater than John that the Baptist acknowledges his unworthiness to untie or even to **carry** his **sandals**. In Jewish culture this responsibility fell to a servant. The disciple of a rabbi was understood to be obligated as a servant to his master. Green writes that "John is thus represented as saying that he has a disciple [One coming after him] whose disciple he is himself unworthy to be" (p. 63). The same attitude of humility is reflected in the Fourth Gospel, where John tells his followers, "He [Messiah] must become greater; I must become less" (John 3:30).

3:13–15 / Jesus travels from Galilee to the Jordan River where John was baptizing all who came out to him (cf. v. 5). This is the only direct encounter between Jesus and John the Baptist that is recorded in the Gospels. Yet because of the close relationship between Mary and Elizabeth (cf. Luke 1:39–45 and esp. v. 56), it is likely that the two boys spent considerable time together.

Those who were baptized by John would confess their sins (v. 6) and then be submerged in the waters of the Jordan (Filson thinks they probably immersed themselves at John's direction, p. 68). When Jesus stepped forward to be baptized, John immediately recognized the other's moral superiority, so he attempted to get him to change his mind (the Greek verb translated in the AV as "forbade" is taken as an "imperfect of attempted action" and rendered in other versions as "sought to dissuade" [Rieu], "protested strenuously" [Amplified]).

Schweizer's view that "John cannot have spoken the words given to him here" (p. 57) is based on the assumption that had John said what he is purported to have said he would have had to quit baptizing and become a follower of Jesus. The exchange is not at all unnatural, however, when we consider the context and pay careful attention to what Jesus said. Some question the authenticity of the exchange on the basis that it is not included in Mark's narrative. On the other hand, its inclusion in Matthew may be in response to questions that may have been raised because of Mark's failure to record it; specifically, Why was Jesus baptized? and, Does Jesus' baptism imply that he needed to repent of personal sin?

Jesus' answer to John was that by being baptized they would **fulfill all righteousness** (v. 15). The pronoun **us** refers not to John and Jesus but to Jesus and all the others who had come for baptism. Jesus identifies himself with his people in a movement of national repentance. It was required by God. Jesus' own baptism demonstrates his solidarity with the people. He was not baptized because he needed to be forgiven of sin. The **righteousness** fulfilled by the act was the ethical expectation of those who had repented of their sin and had symbolized their change of heart by being baptized.

3:16–17 / As Jesus came up out of the Jordan River, the heavens opened, and **he saw the Spirit of God descending like a dove and** resting **on him**. The opening of the heavens was a common feature of visionary experiences (cf. Ezek. 1:1; Rev. 4:1). The dove was a ceremonially clean animal used in sacrifice (Lev. 5:7; 12:6) and was the symbol of innocence. It is intriguing that Jesus, who was to baptize "with the Holy Spirit and with fire" (v. 11), is now empowered by the Spirit who descends **like a dove** (v. 16). It reflects the ministry of Jesus, who will bring health and

salvation to the repentant but judgment to those who continue
in unbelief (cf. 2 Cor. 2:16).

The synoptic accounts give no specific indication that others
saw the descent of the Holy Spirit. John's testimony, as recorded
in the Fourth Gospel, is, "I saw the Spirit come down from heaven
as a dove and remain on him" (John 1:32). That others witnessed
the event is implied by Matthew's **This is my Son, whom I love**,
as contrasted with the "You are" in Mark (1:11) and Luke (3:22).
In the Synoptics the voice from heaven is heard once again at
the transfiguration (Matt. 17:5/Mark 9:7/Luke 9:35). The only other
occurrence is in John 12:28 following Jesus' prediction of his death.
Rabbinic tradition held that, since the time when prophecy
ceased, God spoke only on occasion by a voice from heaven,
which they called *baṭ qôl* (the "daughter of the voice," that is, "the
echo of the Spirit which spoke through the prophets"; cf. Str.-B.
vol. 1, pp. 125–34).

The quotation (in v. 17) reflects several Old Testament passages. In Genesis 22:2 God says to Abraham, "Take your son, your
only son, Isaac, whom you love." Psalm 2:7 supplies the coro-
nation formula for Israel's messianic king: "You are my Son."
Speaking of the 'Ebed Yahweh, Isa. 42:1 has, "Here is my servant, whom I uphold, my chosen one in whom I delight." The
combining of these motifs at the very outset of Jesus' public ministry indicates not only that he is the promised messianic king
but that he will fulfill his ministry by taking on the role of the
suffering servant. He conquers by the power of sacrificial love.

Additional Notes   §3

3:1 / John: The name means "gift of Yahweh." It is a shortened
form of the Hebrew name "Yôhanan."

Desert of Judea: the lower part of the Jordan Valley and perhaps
the eastern slopes as well (cf. R. Funk, *JBL*, 78 [1959], pp. 205–14).

3:2 / Repent: The Jews expected a movement of national repentance prior to the inauguration of the messianic age. This translation of the Gk. *metanoeō* is unfortunately weak. *Metanoeō* does not
mean "to be sorry" but to change one's entire mental attitude and
conduct.

3:4 / **Locusts**: The popular identification with the pods of the carob tree ("St. John's bread") is without foundation.

3:6 / **Confessing**: The Gk. *exomologeomai* indicates a public (note *ex*) acknowledgment.

Baptized: For extended treatments of the character of John's baptism, see W. F. Flemington, *The New Testament Doctrine of Baptism*, pp. 13ff.; and G. R. Beasley-Murray, *Baptism in the New Testament*, pp. 31ff. For the view that John took over the practice of baptism from the Essenes (but gave it a more profound meaning), see Albright-Mann, pp. 25–26.

3:7 / The **wrath** of God is not the emotion of anger but that part of his divine holiness that actively repudiates that which is unholy in his creatures (*HDB* rev., p. 34).

3:8 / McNeile writes that the fruit of which John speaks "is not the change of heart, but the acts which result from it" (p. 27).

3:9 / **Stones . . . children**: There may be a play on words here, since in Hebrew the word for children (*bānîm*) sounds very much like the word for stones (*'ăḇānîm*).

Abraham: Edersheim notes that in Jewish tradition Abraham is pictured as sitting at the Gate of Gehenna in order to deliver any Israelite who might have been consigned to its terrors (*LT*, vol. 1, p. 271).

3:16–17 / **Voice from heaven**: the voice of God. Note that all three persons of the Godhead are mentioned in this baptismal scene.

4:1 / The baptism of Jesus, which culminated with the voice from heaven declaring divine approval, is followed immediately (Mark 1:12 has "at once") by a time of temptation. The parallel account in Luke indicates that Jesus was tempted by Satan throughout a forty-day period (Luke 4:22). Matthew describes the dramatic conclusion of this period ("after [Jesus fasted] forty days and forty nights . . . the tempter came to him," vv. 2 3). It is not at all uncommon for temptation to follow closely our times of spiritual exhilaration.

Note that Jesus is **led by the Spirit into the desert**. Times of testing (and that is the meaning of the Greek *peirazō* in this context) come from the Lord in order to strengthen and help. In the entire episode, Jesus is being put to the test. Will he, like Israel of old, disobey, or will he prove himself worthy of the messianic task assigned to him? As the author of Hebrews tells us, "Although he was a son, he learned obedience from what he suffered" (Heb. 5:8).

Although God arranges for the time of testing, it is **the tempter** who carries out the temptations. We are reminded of Job's trials, allowed by God but brought about by Satan (Job 1:8–2:10). God in his sovereignty uses intermediate agents to accomplish his will. The desert place where Jesus was tested was the rocky and barren region that lies between the high plateau east of Jerusalem and the shores of the Dead Sea. In the Old Testament it was called Jeshimon, the wasteland (cf. Num. 21:20; 1 Sam. 23:19). As the place of demons, it was an obvious choice for the conflict between Jesus and the prince of demons.

4:2–4 / Jesus spent **forty days and forty nights** in the wasteland **fasting**. Israel had wandered forty years in the desert because of unfaithfulness (Num. 14:33–34). God's purpose in this, as Moses told Israel, was "to humble you and to test you in order to know . . . whether or not you would keep his commands" (Deut. 8:2). Moses had fasted forty days and nights, without bread or water (Exod. 34:28). Now the One greater than Moses finds himself alone in the wilderness without food. There is no reason to mitigate the severity of the experience by noting that in ancient days fasting sometimes meant refraining from food during the day but not during the night.

At the end of the forty days, Jesus **was hungry**. The devil approached with the subtle suggestion that if in fact Jesus were **the Son of God**, why not use his power to turn the **stones** that lay scattered about into **bread** in order to satisfy legitimate hunger? Had not God provided manna from heaven for the grumbling Israelites (Exod. 16)? Certainly he will provide for his own Son. Besides, what good is there in having supernatural power if one doesn't use it? Perhaps the most insidious enticement of all was his request that Jesus prove in some tangible way that the voice from heaven had really spoken the truth when it said, "This is my Son, whom I love" (Matt. 3:17).

The temptation that Jesus faced was to extricate himself from a difficult situation by an act of disobedience. God had placed him there, and God would supply his need. To discover for himself whether as the Son of God he was able to take care of himself would be an act of defiance against the Father. The first Adam had failed God by disobeying; the second Adam would surrender himself to the will of God in perfect obedience. Gerhardsson suggests that this temptation and the following two correspond to the three ways of loving God as charged in the Shema (Deut. 6:4; 11:13–21; Num. 15:37–41; heart, soul, strength) and expanded in the Mishnah (*The Testing of God's Son*, pp. 71ff.).

Jesus turns to Scripture (**it is written**) for his response. God had humbled the Israelites by allowing them to go hungry in the wilderness and then supplying them with manna. His purpose was to teach them that "man does not live on bread alone but on every word that comes from the mouth of the Lord" (Deut. 8:3). True human life depends not upon the satisfaction of material wants but upon obedience to the divine will. For Jesus to have turned stones into bread would have been to place personal physical need ahead of obedience and trust in God. God calls us to a reordering of priorities that places confidence in him as the highest good.

4:5–7 / Satan's next stratagem was to take Jesus to Jerusalem and have **him stand on the highest point of the temple**. The temple was the one place in all Israel where the power and protection of God would be supreme. It may be that the **highest point** ("little wing" in Gk.) reflects verse 4 of Psalm 91 ("Under his wings you will find refuge"), from which Satan is about to quote verses 11 and 12. The very setting speaks of the protective care of God.

Now comes the temptation. **If you are the Son of God, throw yourself down**. By refusing to turn stones into bread, you demonstrated your trust in God. Now let everyone know the extent of that trust. When you throw yourself down from here you won't suffer any harm, because **"he will command his angels concerning you, and they will lift you up in their hands, so that you will not strike your foot against a stone"** (v. 6). Satan is perfectly able to use Scripture to make his point. It is, however, what Filson calls "a pious-sounding misuse of Scripture" (p. 70). What Satan omits from the verses he is quoting (Ps. 91:11–12) is the important clause in verse 11, "To guard you in all your ways." God has promised his providential care for life as we live it out daily in a normal fashion. He has not promised supernatural intervention when we decide to jeopardize life in order to prompt him to action. Satan's deceptive use of Scripture disregards context and twists the words of God so as to make them imply something God never intended. How often this same procedure is repeated today in order to provide an apparent justification for personal prejudice!

Some have interpreted this second temptation as an appeal to Jesus to appear suddenly and miraculously in the temple precincts in fulfillment of the prophecy of Malachi that "suddenly the Lord you are seeking will come to his temple" (Mal. 3:1). How much easier to establish one's messianic claims by a single miraculous act than to follow through as God has planned. But the miracle-mongers were false messiahs. Barclay mentions Theudas, who promised to split the waters of the Jordan in two; the Egyptian pretender, who would lay flat the walls of Jerusalem; and Simon Magus, who vowed he would fly through the air (vol. 1, p. 69).

Once again Jesus turns to the Old Testament for an appropriate response: **Do not put the Lord your God to the test** (v. 7). Do not presume upon the goodwill of God by demanding proof.

The words come from Deuteronomy 6:16 and refer to the time when Moses struck the rock in order to get water to satisfy the grumbling Israelites (Exod. 17:1–7). It is not our prerogative to place God on trial. Faith is simple trust, not "doubt looking for proof" (Barclay, vol. 1, p. 69).

4:8–11 / Having failed in his first two attempts, Satan now drops all pretense. He takes Jesus to a very high mountain and shows him **all the kingdoms of the world**. In a move that can be understood as nothing other than a naked power play, he offers Jesus all he can see if he will only **bow down and worship** him. Jesus is faced with the age-old temptation to act on the basis that the end justifies the means. Had not God promised, "I will make the nations your inheritance, the ends of the earth your possession" (Ps. 2:8)? The way of obedience is long and difficult. Why not come to terms with the "god of this age" (2 Cor. 4:4; cf. "prince of this world," John 12:31; 16:11)? Why not compromise just a bit and make the desired end an immediate reality?

Moses had climbed to the top of Mount Nebo, and from there the Lord had shown him the entire expanse of land that would be given to his descendants. Apocalyptic literature portrays a number of similar experiences (*2 Bar.* 76:3; *1 Enoch* 24–25). Whether or not Jesus was physically transported to some literal mountaintop should not concern us. Jesus' temptations were inner and spiritual. Their historicity is not dependent on his having been taken to a specific geographical location. This third temptation was to use the arsenal of political and worldly (diabolic) weapons to seize without delay the sovereignty that would someday be his anyway. The price of immediate possession was nothing short of the worship of Satan himself!

Jesus' response was straightforward and clear: **Away from me, Satan!** This entire affair has gone on long enough. God alone is worthy of worship (cf. Deut. 6:13). Your lust for power is blasphemous. Be gone! So the devil departed, and Jesus was ministered to by **angels** who appeared on the scene to help.

4:12–16 / The imprisonment of John the Baptist marks the beginning of Jesus' public ministry in Galilee. In chapter 11 Matthew tells of John's concern while in prison regarding the messiahship of Jesus (vv. 1–6), and in chapter 14 he records John's death at the request of Herodias (vv. 1–12). Jesus' return to Galilee was in no way a flight from danger, as some have suggested because of the way the Greek verb *anachōreō* ("to go away") is used in passages such as Matthew 2:14, 22; 12:15. Galilee, as well as Transjordania, was under the jurisdiction of Herod Antipas (the "fox" according to Luke 13:32), who had ordered the Baptist to be beheaded (Matt. 14:1–12). Jesus moved into Galilee to take over the work of John, and in a certain sense, challenged the action of Herod.

For several reasons it was appropriate for Jesus to begin his public ministry in Galilee. It was a densely populated and exceptionally fertile district in Palestine. Josephus notes that it contained a great number of villages, the smallest of which had a population of at least fifteen thousand (*War* 3.42). Galilee was not a remote back country, but a bustling and productive region through which ran two of the favorite highways of antiquity. Its population was mixed, partly because of colonists imported during the Maccabean conquest. As its name suggests (Galilee means a "ring" or "circuit"), it was surrounded by Gentiles (Phoenicians to the west, Syrians on the north and east, and Samaritans to the south). Judea was mountainous and isolated, but Galilee lay open to all sorts of contacts with the wider world. It was there in northern Palestine that Jesus began his public ministry.

Matthew says that Jesus did not stay in Nazareth (none of the synoptic writers record anything that Jesus did during that visit to his home town) but **went and lived in Capernaum** (probably Tell Hum on the northwest shore of the Sea of Galilee). Capernaum becomes the base for Jesus' Galilean ministry. In chapter 9 Matthew refers to Capernaum as Jesus' "own town" (v. 1). It was located in the district originally assigned to the tribes of Zebulun and Naphtali. In this move to Capernaum Matthew sees the fulfillment of an ancient prophecy of Isaiah. In its Old Testament setting the promise of restoration under a new and messianic king (Isa. 9:1–7) follows the devastation of the northern kingdom by the Assyrians in 733–32 B.C. (cf. Isa. 8:1–10). Matthew interprets the promise in terms of Jesus' proclamation of a spiritually redemptive message to the inhabitants of Galilee.

Galilee is described as on **the way to the sea** (the road from Damascus past the Sea of Galilee to the Mediterranean) and **along the Jordan** (that is, to the west, as it would be to the Assyrian invaders). The inhabitants of Galilee are pictured as living in the dark land of death (cf. Ps. 23:4), a Hebrew metaphor for "impenetrable darkness" (Beare, p. 115). They **have seen a great light**; a light that will dawn as the morning sun, dispelling all darkness. That great light is the message of the kingdom, which Matthew is about to describe in detail (chaps. 5–7).

4:17 / Verse 17 marks a transition. **From that time on** is a semi-technical phrase indicating a new beginning. The new beginning is the public ministry. The Greek word translated **preach** (*kēryssō*) means "to proclaim" as a herald (*kēryx*). Matthew's summary of Jesus' message parallels that of John the Baptist (Matt. 3:2): Galileans are to turn away from their sins because the long-awaited **kingdom of heaven is near**. To "repent" is not simply to feel sorry about something: it involves an active change of direction.

God's kingdom (**heaven** is a reverential substitution) is his sovereign power acknowledged by his people and actively governing their lives. Some years ago C. H. Dodd argued that the Greek *ēngiken* behind **is near** meant "has arrived," much the same as the somewhat parallel *ephthasen* in Matthew 12:28 (*The Parables of the Kingdom*, pp. 43ff.). Few today have followed Dodd on what was for his theory of realized eschatology a crucial distinction. The kingdom had drawn near in the life and ministry of Jesus, but it was not yet fully realized. That awaits the second advent (cf. W. G. Kümmel, *Promise and Fulfillment*, pp. 23ff., 105ff.).

4:18–22 / The Sea of Galilee (also called Gennesaret, Luke 5:1, and Tiberias, John 21:1) is a pear-shaped lake measuring 13 miles north to south and eight miles east to west. It lies 680 feet below sea level in a very warm climate. The surrounding countryside is fertile. Josephus reports that in the time of Christ nine cities lined its shores and its waters were crowded with fishermen.

Walking along the lake Jesus sees two brothers, **Simon** and **Andrew**, at work casting their net for fish. Simon (who was given the name "Peter" at Caesarea Philippi, 16:18) and Andrew were originally from the town of Bethsaida on the north side of the lake where the Jordan River enters (John 1:44). At this time, however, it appears that they were living in Capernaum (cf. Mark 1:29). Peter became a leader among the disciples and, along with James and John, formed an inner circle (cf. Mark 5:37; Matt. 17:1; 26:37). Jesus calls them from catching fish to a new kind of "fish-

ing"—**Come, follow me, and I will make you fishers of men** (v.
19). The call is not unlike that of Old Testament prophets (cf.
1 Kings 19:19-21). To leave one's work and quite literally "follow
after" Jesus is what it means to be a disciple (this reflects the practice of many famous teachers of antiquity). The response was immediate. Peter and Andrew leave their nets and follow Jesus.

Shortly after this another set of brothers, **James** and **John**,
were working on their nets in a boat with their father **Zebedee**.
When called by Jesus they abandon their work and follow Jesus.
The urgency of the call and the immediate response of the fishermen are worthy of note. Jesus called as his helpers not the religious leaders of Jerusalem but common people from the mixed
population of Galilee. Religious knowledge often hinders the
action required by genuine faith.

4:23-25 / Verse 23 is a summary of Jesus' ministry in Galilee. (The three parallel phrases are repeated verbatim in 9:35.) Although the population of Galilee was mixed (cf. 4:15), it was to
the **synagogues** that Jesus went in order to preach. In Matthew,
Jesus' ministry is primarily directed to the people of Israel. Custom
dictated that following the reading of the Law and the Prophets
any Jewish man over thirty was allowed to supply an interpretation. Luke records the story of Jesus taking part in the synagogue service at Nazareth (Luke 4:16-30).

Preaching differs from teaching. The Greek verb (*kēryssō*)
means "to proclaim." The **kingdom** that Jesus announced was
the long-awaited arrival of the God who would act with sovereign
power in human affairs. The healing activity of Jesus was a visible
demonstration that God's kingdom had drawn near. Sickness was
associated with sin. Sirach 38:15 reads, "When a man has sinned
against his Maker, let him put himself in the doctor's hands"
(NEB). It follows that release from sickness (the evidence of sin)
proved that One greater than Satan had arrived with the authority
and power to rule.

The news of Jesus spread everywhere. **Syria** was not simply
the Roman province bearing that name but the entire area to the
north of Galilee (with Damascus at its center). From this large
region came people with **various diseases** and **suffering severe
pain** (v. 24). Matthew refers to them as **the demon-possessed,
those having seizures** (lit., "the moonstruck"; Phillips calls them
"the insane"), **and the paralyzed**. All are healed by Jesus, who

is being followed by large crowds from all the surrounding territory. The **Decapolis** was a federation of ten Hellenistic cities that earlier had been incorporated into Judea; later they were liberated from Jewish control by Pompey (60 B.C.) and made a part of Syria. Although Jesus' teaching and preaching began in the Jewish synagogues, his fame spread rapidly throughout the gentile areas. His healing activity was by no means limited to the Jewish population. Matthew refers repeatedly (forty-nine times) to the crowds that attended the ministry of Jesus.

Additional Notes §4

4:1 / *Peirazō* is used in the sense of "to entice to evil," e.g., James 1:13 ("[God] does not tempt anyone").
Devil: See *"diabolos," NIDNTT,* vol. 3, pp. 468–72.

4:3 / **If** introduces a conditional sentence that assumes the assertion to be true and leads on to a logical conclusion based on that assumption. See Robertson, *Grammar,* pp. 1004–22, for a discussion of various conditional sentences.

4:5 / **The holy city**: Used as a designation for Jerusalem in Dan. 9:24; Tob. 13:9; Rev. 11:2; 21:2, 10; 22:19; Matt. 27:53.
Highest point: The *pterygion* (lit., "wing") of the temple could refer to Herod's portico, high above the Kidron Valley (Josephus, *Ant.* 15.11.5).

4:12 / **Galilee**: See *IDB* (vol. 2, pp. 344–47) for a concise description of the region and its culture.

4:17 / **From that time on**: In 16:21 the phrase introduces a period during which Jesus began to teach his disciples about his coming death (cf. 26:16).

4:18 / **Simon**: Simon is the Gk. form of the Heb. *šim'ôn* (English "Simeon"), a common name during NT times. There are nine different Simons listed in the NT.

4:23 / **Synagogues**: The origin of the synagogue as an institution in Judaism is somewhat obscure. It probably began some time after the dispersion of the Jewish people in 586 B.C. The synagogue served as a meeting place for community affairs, as a "house of prayer," and as a center for religious education.

Matthew's Gospel has a didactic purpose. Special emphasis is given to the message of Jesus. One of the distinct features of Matthew's Gospel is that the teaching of Jesus is collected into five sections. The Sermon on the Mount (chaps. 5–7) is the first of these blocks. The others are Instructions to the Twelve (chap. 10), Parables of the Kingdom (chap. 13), Life in the Christian Community (chap. 18), and Eschatological Judgment (chaps. 23–25). Each block closes with a formula similar to, "When Jesus had finished saying these things" (7:28; 11:1; 13:53; 19:1; 26:1).

We are not to think of the Sermon on the Mount as a single discourse given by Jesus at one particular time. Undoubtedly there was a primitive and actual sermon, but it has been enlarged significantly by Matthew (cf. Mounce, "Sermon on the Mount," *IBD*, vol. 3, pp. 1417–19). Several observations point to this conclusion. As a master teacher Jesus would not expect his listeners to be able to absorb this much ethical instruction at one time. Such a concentration of material would defeat his purpose. Certain sections are disconnected from what precedes and what follows (e.g., 5:31, 32; 7:7–11). More importantly, thirty-four of the verses in Matthew's sermon (which totals 107 verses) are not found in Luke's record of the event (Luke 6:20–49) but are scattered throughout Luke in other contexts. It is far more likely that Matthew arranged the material in a topical and orderly manner within his sermon than that Luke scattered the material and then provided new historical contexts. Furthermore, forty-seven of Matthew's verses have no parallel at all in Luke.

It is often suggested that in Matthew's five blocks of teaching we have an attempt to provide a new Pentateuch. Jesus is pictured as the second and greater Moses (cf. Deut. 18:15), who ascends the mountain, assumes the posture of authority (he sits to teach, cf. Luke 4:20–21), and delivers a new law. The idea is intriguing but not persuasive. Jesus' sermon is not a new set of laws but a description of how people who have chosen to place themselves under the reign of God are to live out their lives. The ethical requirements of the sermon are intended not to drive people to despair so they will then cast themselves upon the mercy of God, but to guide and direct those who desire to please him. It is true that the demands are stated in absolute terms ("Be perfect, therefore, as your heavenly Father is perfect," 5:48), but that is the nature of all great ethical teaching. Although we may not reach the stars, they still serve us well as reliable navigational aids.

5:1–2 / When Jesus **saw the crowds, he went up on a mountainside and sat down**, and **began to teach** his disciples. The area referred to was probably the hill country that rose to the north and west of the Sea of Galilee. Mountaintop experiences are frequently mentioned in Matthew (the third temptation, 4:8; the transfiguration, 17:1; the Great Commission, 28:16). That Luke places his sermon on "a level place" after Jesus had come down from the mountain (Luke 6:17ff.) should cause no concern. It is the sermon, not its topographical setting, that is important. Attempts to harmonize often do more mischief than good.

When Jesus sat to teach he assumed the position of authority. In Jewish synagogues the teachers sat (cf. Luke 4:20). We still speak of endowed "chairs" in the university; the pope occasionally delivers a pronouncement *ex cathedra*, "from his chair."

The question often arises as to Jesus' specific audience. The crowds mentioned in 5:1 are still there at the close of the sermon (7:28, "The crowds were amazed at his teaching"). In between these references, however, Jesus appears to be teaching his disciples (cf. 5:1b). One answer is that the disciples were the crowds (Gundry, p. 66). Another is that he was teaching the Twelve but others crowded around to listen. It seems best to understand the reference to disciples as including all who followed Jesus in order to listen to what he had to say. Obviously the Twelve were there, but the reference should not be restricted to that special group.

The Sermon on the Mount begins with a series of exclamations regarding the blessedness of those who have placed themselves under the sovereign rule of God. Albright-Mann call the Beatitudes "the spiritual charter of the Kingdom" (p. 68). The literary form employed by Matthew is common in the Old Testament, especially in the Psalms and wisdom literature (e.g., Ps.

1:1, "Blessed is the man who does not walk in the counsel of the wicked"; cf. Ps. 84:4–5, 12; Sir. 25:8–9). The Greek word for **blessed** is *makarios*. Barclay notes that Cyprus was called *hē makaria* ("the Happy Isle") because it was so fertile and beautiful that everything a person desires was to be found within its coastline (vol. 1, p. 89). Thus **blessed** describes a joy that has its secret within itself. Others have noted that Homer called the gods *hoi makares* ("the blessed ones"). What Jesus now exclaims is that it is not the rich and powerful, but the meek and lowly, who are those of whom it can truly be said, "O, the happiness of." His appraisal of what constitutes life as it was intended to be lived stands in stark contrast to conventional wisdom.

The Beatitudes are eight in number (v. 11 extends the thought of the previous verse and changes from third person exclamations to direct discourse). Some manuscripts (mostly those in Latin) transpose verses 4 and 5, presumably to bring together the "poor" in verse 3 with the "meek" in verse 5. The existing order is better: it presents four pairs of virtues dovetailed in the order A B A′ B′ C D C′ D′ (Green, p. 76). Commentators are divided on the question of whether the blessings pronounced are primarily present or future. It is unnecessary to decide for one position against the other. Although the ultimate expression of each blessing awaits the day of final vindication, the blessings themselves are to be experienced and enjoyed at the present time. The future tense in verses 4–9 emphasizes certainty rather than a necessary period of waiting.

5:3–4 / The first beatitude declares the blessedness of those who are **poor in spirit**. In Hebrew parlance the "poor" were not simply the economically disadvantaged but those who in their need had turned to God for help (Ps. 69:32; Isa. 61:1). Hill says they are the *'nwy rwḥ* in 1QM 14.7—"the humble poor who trust in God's help" (p. 111).

The Greek word for "poor," *ptōchos*, carries the nuance of extreme poverty. It is derived from a verb that means "to crouch" or "to cower" (the noun form is used of a beggar, one in abject poverty). To be **poor in spirit** means to depend totally upon God for all help (cf. Ps. 34:6, "This poor man called, and the Lord heard him; he saved him out of all his troubles").

It is often noted that Luke refers to this group simply as "poor" (Luke 6:20), whereas Matthew adds the qualifying expression **in spirit**. It is unlikely, as has sometimes been suggested, that this means "voluntarily." The promise to those who accept their absolute dependence upon God is that the kingdom of heaven belongs to them. They have entered into God's triumphal reign, established by the redemptive work of Christ and to be fully realized when he returns at the end of this age.

Blessed also are **those who mourn**—who are filled with deep regret for their own waywardness and for the evil so prevalent in the world. **Those who mourn** are not simply those who have gone through difficult times but those who understand that all the suffering in the world stems from the sinful and self-destructive human tendency to act as if God did not exist. Those who "know what sorrow means" (Phillips) are to be comforted by God himself (**they will be comforted** is a Semitic reverential paraphrase). Isaiah proclaimed the year of divine favor when the messianic king would "preach good news to the poor" (Isa. 61:1; cf. Matt. 5:3) and "comfort all who mourn" (Isa. 61:2; cf. Matt. 5:4).

5:5–6 / The third beatitude promises the earth as an inheritance for **the meek**. In the Synoptics the word for **meek** (*praus*) is used by Matthew alone, and only on three occasions. In 11:28–30 Jesus invites the weary and overburdened of this world to take upon themselves his yoke and discover that he is "gentle and humble in heart." At the close of his ministry Jesus enters Jerusalem on a lowly colt, fulfilling Zechariah's prophecy: he is "gentle and riding on a donkey" (Matt. 21:5; Zech. 9:9). Jesus carried out his messianic ministry, not as a Zealot intent on establishing by force a political kingdom, but as one who lived a life of humble and sacrificial service to God and his fellow human beings. This is the meekness to which Jesus calls his followers. It is the meek who will "inherit the land and enjoy great peace" (Ps. 37:11). "Those of a gentle spirit" (NEB), not the grasping and the greedy, receive from life its most satisfying rewards. The aggressive are unable to enjoy their ill-gotten gains. Only the meek have the capacity to enjoy in life all those things that provide genuine and lasting satisfaction.

Blessed are those who hunger and thirst for righteousness. For those who live in a world in which they can turn on the tap whenever they want water and are always able to secure some sort of food to eat, the experience of hunger and thirst is foreign. Not so in the ancient world, where so many lived constantly on the edge of starvation and often traveled through desert regions without water. Thirst as an image for spiritual longing is seen in passages like Psalm 42:1–2, "As the deer pants for streams of water, so my soul . . . thirsts for . . . God." The righteousness for which men and women long is the ability to live out one's days in conformity to God's will. This includes the final vindication of God's redemptive mission openly acknowledged by all at his triumphal return (cf. Phil. 2:10–11). The complete satisfaction of God's people is pictured as a messianic banquet (cf. Isa. 25:6; Rev. 2:17). God will satisfy them fully! Huston Smith (a well-known writer in the area of world religions) once observed that we can never get enough of what we really do not want. We were created for God and nothing short of his presence satisfies.

5:7–8 / The fifth beatitude describes the follower of Christ as **merciful** and compassionate. Behind the Greek word is the rich Hebrew term *ḥesed*, "loving-kindness" (Coverdale's translation used regularly in the RV), or "steadfast love" (RSV). To be **merciful** means to maintain the fidelity of a covenant relationship. It is not a surge of emotion but intentional kindness. It is to the **merciful** that God will show mercy. This principle of reciprocity is seen in other contexts, such as the Lord's Prayer ("Forgive us . . . as we have forgiven," Matt. 6:12; cf. 6:14–15) and James 2:13 ("judgment without mercy will be shown to anyone who has not been merciful"). Gamaliel of Jabneh (a late first-century rabbi) is quoted as saying, "So long as you are merciful, the Merciful One is merciful to you." This *quid pro quo* ethic should be taken seriously but not legalistically. Those who are genuinely forgiven cannot help but forgive.

Blessed are the pure in heart. The primary reference is not to sexual purity, although that is mentioned in 5:28, but to single-mindedness, to be freed from "the tyranny of a divided self" (Tasker, p. 62). According to James, the hypocrite needs to "purify [the] heart" (4:8). If the eye is not sound, the entire body will be in darkness (Matt. 6:23). Ulterior motives divide the heart. Jewish writers understood this inclination to moral schizophrenia as resulting from an evil *yēṣer* or impulse. What God required of those who would ascend the hill of the Lord was "clean hands and a pure heart" (Ps. 24:3–4).

The reward for complete and inward integrity is to **see God**. John writes that "no one has ever seen God" (1:18), and Paul supplies the reason: it is because he "lives in unapproachable light" (1 Tim. 6:16). To stand in God's presence is the greatest blessing conceivable. In Revelation the blessed "will see his face" (Rev. 22:4). Although the promise is primarily eschatological, it can also be realized in a spiritual sense at the present time. Genuine purity provides an immediate and profound experience of the presence and power of God. The **pure . . . see God.**

5:9–10 / The next blessedness is pronounced upon **the peacemakers.** The peace that Jesus enjoins is not a passive acceptance of whatever comes along, but an active involvement that confronts the problem and works through to a satisfactory reconciliation. "Seek peace and pursue it" is the admonition of the psalmist (Ps. 34:14). "He who practices peace," says the Jewish commentary *Sifra* (on Num. 6:26), "is a child of the world to come." The peace that we are to make is (in this context) the establishment of right relationships between members of the human family. As we work for reconciliation, we will be **called sons of God** (*hyioi theou*). This refers to those who, by acting as God acts, bear a family resemblance to their heavenly Father.

The final beatitude has to do with those who are **persecuted** for upholding by their confession and life the righteous requirements of God. To them belongs the **kingdom of heaven.** Jesus promised his followers the same hostility that he was facing (John 15:18–25). Peter often spoke of unjust suffering (1 Pet. 1:6; 3:13–17a; 4:12–19). To suffer for doing what God requires brings great consolation. Note that mention of the **kingdom of heaven** opens (v. 3) as well as closes (v. 10) the eight beatitudes. This rhetorical device, known as inclusio, is common in ancient writing.

5:11–12 / Verses 11 and 12 expand the final beatitude. Insult, opposition, and lies are all to be expected by Christ's followers. When this happens, **rejoice and be glad.** The second verb is compounded from two Greek words that mean (literally) "to leap exceedingly." The response to persecution is unbridled joy. The reward in heaven (i.e., in God's sight) is great. The prophets received that kind of treatment, and you are their true successors (cf. 23:29–36). Stendahl thinks that Jesus may be referring to his disciples as prophets in much the same way as did the Essenes (p. 776).

5:13–16 / In contrast to those who oppose the work of God in the world (cf. 5:11), the followers of Christ (**you** is emphatic in the Greek text) **are the salt of the earth**. Salt was a basic and necessary item in ancient culture. It was used as a preservative, as a purifier, and as a seasoning. In the immediate context Jesus seems to be saying that those who live out the qualities listed in the Beatitudes will permeate the world and retard its moral and ethical decay. As Tasker notes, the most obvious general characteristic of salt is its essential difference from the medium in which it is placed (p. 63). The righteous conduct of believers keeps society from turning completely rancid. If salt should somehow lose its saltiness, there is no way to make it salty again; it has become worthless and should be thrown away. Although salt does not normally lose its strength, the possibility is mentioned to stress the necessity of believers maintaining their distinctive mission in the world. Explaining how salt can be adulterated with an inexpensive white powder to increase profit is unnecessary. It is the metaphor itself, not the image it employs, that is being extended. To be **thrown out and trampled** underfoot means that unless the disciples maintain their role as salt in the world they will become useless and will be rejected.

Believers are also **the light of the world**. God said to Israel, "I will also make you a light for the Gentiles, that you may bring my salvation to the ends of the earth" (Isa. 49:6; cf. 42:6). The servant role of Israel is taken over by Jesus (John 8:12; 9:5) and passed on to his followers. Light is intended for illumination. It is for seeing. Cities built on hills cannot be hidden. How foolish it would be to light a lamp and then place it under a tub. Lamps are to be placed on lampstands; that way everyone in the house can see.

The followers of Jesus are to be like lamps on a lampstand. They are to **let** their **light shine** (aorist third person imperative) so that people will **see** their **good deeds** and give **praise** to God. Note that the **light** does not originate with believers; they are to **let** it **shine**. The light is seen in the good things they do. It is less a message directed to the intellect than a way of life lived out before others. When outsiders see that following Christ leads to a life of **good deeds**, they will **praise** not the believer but the believer's **Father in heaven**.

If the Beatitudes leave the impression that life in the kingdom is somewhat passive, the metaphors of salt and light correct such a misunderstanding. Salt permeates and performs its vital function in society. Light illumines the darkness and points people to the One who is the source of all light and life.

5:17–20 / To the pious Jew the law was perfect and unchangeable. Jesus' life and teaching appeared to many to indicate a lower view of the law. He healed on the Sabbath, failed to perform ritual duties, and was lax in observing religious feasts. It was necessary, therefore, for Jesus to point out at the beginning of his sermon the relationship of his teaching to the law.

Verse 17 is programmatic. Jesus did not come to do away with the Law and the Prophets but to bring out by word and deed the quality of life they were intended to produce. Filson correctly concludes that Jesus' freedom in interpreting and applying the law "fulfills" it by giving "the fullest expression to the divine intent in the ancient utterances" (p. 83). As the Hebrews divided their Scriptures, the **Law** consisted of the first five books of the Old Testament (the Pentateuch) and the **Prophets** included not only the major and minor prophets (as we distinguish them) but also the historical books, Joshua through 2 Kings.

Until heaven and earth disappear, not even the most insignificant detail will **disappear from the Law.** Thus Jesus displays his profound loyalty to the Judaic tradition. It was not his intention to undermine in any way God's revelation through Moses. Much has been written about what the AV calls "one jot or one tittle." The Greek text says *iōta* (transcribed in English by the letter *i*) or *keraia* ("little horn"). They are often held to represent the smallest Hebrew letter (*yod*) or the decorative serif that would distinguish similar letters in Hebrew. Beare writes that the "Law remains in force to the last dot on the last 'i' " (p. 139). The meaning is clear: the law remains *in toto*. Therefore, to break even the least significant of these commandments and lead others to do the same is to be **least** esteemed **in the kingdom of heaven.** To obey them and encourage others to do the same is to be acknowledged as **great in the kingdom of heaven.**

Jesus goes on to say that entrance into the **kingdom of heaven** requires a **righteousness** that **surpasses that of the Pharisees and the teachers of the law.** Obeying the law is important, but the way in which it is obeyed is absolutely crucial. During the exile, when Israel lost two of its essential distinctives (its land and its temple), renewed attention was given to the law (the third distinctive). A class of scholars developed who devoted their lives to the exposition and application of the law. These "scribes" were the scholars of Israel, and their aim was to spell out in rules and regulations the great principles set forth in the law. The Pharisees were a group of laymen drawn from all segments of society who had separated themselves (the name is derived from the Hebrew *paraš*, which means "separate") from all that would defile in order to carry out with precision all the regulations developed by the teachers of the law. The uprightness required by Jesus goes beyond the legalism of people like the Pharisees. What it involves is spelled out in the five antitheses that complete chapter 5 (vv. 21–48).

It is important to realize that law is an expression of the nature of God. As created beings, we have the obligation to conform to the nature and will of the Creator. That obligation is expressed in different ways at various stages of God's self-revelation. When the law was given through Moses, the responsibility was primarily, although not exclusively, external. What Jesus now teaches is that outward conformity is not enough: there must be a change within that makes external restriction theoretically unnecessary. Human beings will always be under the obligation to conform to God's nature. With the coming of Christ we now see more clearly what God is like (John 1:18; Col. 1:15; Heb. 1:3) and therefore what is required of us.

5:21–24 / Verse 20 sets forth a basic principle that is illustrated in detail by the five "antitheses" (if the teaching on divorce in vv. 31–32 is considered a separate unit, there are six) that complete chapter 5. They are called antitheses because of the recurring formula **You have heard . . . But I tell you** (vv. 21–22, 27–28, 33–34, 38–39, 43–44). Jesus does not contradict what was said but brings it into sharper ethical focus. Hill calls it "a radical intensification of the demands of the Law" (p. 119).

To the generation of Israelites who received the law through Moses came the command not to **murder** (Exod. 20:13). Those who did would be **subject to judgment**. Jesus intensifies the restriction by saying that anyone who is **angry with his brother** will answer to the court. God's **judgment** goes beyond the act to the inner attitude that produces the act. Kingdom righteousness demands the removal of any desire to harm. The anger that Jesus speaks of is *orgē*, a brooding inward anger (as compared with *thymos*, an anger that flares).

To this initial contrast Jesus adds two additional examples. Although the penalties are given in ascending order (local court, Sanhedrin, hell), it is less obvious that the offenses follow the same pattern. To call a brother *raca* (an Aramaic term of contempt) is to be answerable to the Sanhedrin. Lamsa, who translates the New Testament from Aramaic sources, says *raca* means, "I spit on you." To call a brother *mōros* ("fool") is to be "heading straight for the fire of destruction" (Phillips). The fool in Hebrew thought was not the intellectually incompetent but the person who was morally deficient. This kind of fool lived as if there were no God to whom he must account for his profligacy (cf. Ps. 14:1). Some have suggested that *mōre* (vocative: **"you fool"**) should be understood as a transliteration of the Hebrew *mōreh* ("rebel" or "apostate"; cf. Ps. 78:8). In any case, this calling into question of a brother's essential character has dire results.

The term **fire of hell** (lit. "gehenna of fire") comes from a ravine south of Jerusalem called the Valley of Hinnom—a smoldering garbage dump in the time of Jesus. Earlier it had been the place where Canaanites burned their children alive in sacrifice to Molech (cf. 1 Kings 11:7). It became a symbol for future punishment (cf. *1 Enoch* 54:1–2). Note that Jesus is dealing with relationships within the religious community (the term **brother** occurs four times in vv. 21–24) rather than laying down rules for human behavior in general.

Now for some positive advice: **If you are offering your gift** (v. 23) **at the altar** and remember a brother who has a just claim against you, go immediately and be reconciled. Then you can return and worship God. Settling a grievance with a fellow Christian takes precedence over ritual activity. The Mishnah taught that, unless an offense against a neighbor is taken care of, not even the Day of Atonement will avail (m. *Yoma* 8.9). Breaches within the fellowship are serious.

5:25–26 / Verses 25–26 continue the theme of reconciliation. The scene is of a person being taken to court. It is better to **settle** the dispute ahead of time than to be turned over to the judge, who will put you **into prison** until you pay up the last red cent. The gentile practice of imprisoning a debtor was particularly offensive to the Jews. In jail there was no way to earn money to pay the debt (Jeremias, *Parables*, p. 181). Jesus is not counseling opportunism for the sake of personal advantage. He is saying that all disputes should be taken care of without delay and that to fail at this has dire consequences. Some find in this passage an allegory of final judgment: it is important to be reconciled with God before your accuser (Satan) turns you over to the judge (God).

5:27–30 / The seventh commandment is, "You shall not commit adultery" (Exod. 20:14; Deut. 5:18). Jesus now teaches that the lustful look itself is a form of adultery. In identifying lust with action, he disregards "the well-developed distinction of the scribes between intention and action" (Stendahl, p. 776). Though the act of adultery may have far more serious social consequences (the penalty according to Lev. 20:10 is death for both parties), the intentional desire to awaken lust is equally sinful in God's sight. There is no well-marked boundary between the desire and the deed. The woman in question is probably to be taken as a married woman ("your neighbor's wife," Exod. 20:17).

So important is inward purity (cf. Matt. 5:8) that it would be better to suffer the loss of an eye or a hand and enter heaven blind or dismembered than to enter hell unscathed. Jesus is not teaching some masochistic doctrine of self-mutilation for spiritual ends, nor is he suggesting that the way to meet evil desire is to inflict radical physical surgery. The imagery emphasizes the crucial importance of taking whatever measures are necessary to control natural passions that tend to flare out of control. The **right hand** is mentioned because it corresponds to the place of honor (cf. 1 Kings 2:19; Ps. 110:1). For the same reason, it is the **right eye** that should be torn out and thrown away rather than being allowed to cause the whole body to be discarded in hell. The Greek verb translated **causes** (you) **to sin** is *skandalizō*, cognate with a noun that stands for the bait-stick in a trap that, when sprung, closes the trap and secures the animal. It is ironic that the eye, which is supposed to prevent stumbling, becomes the *skandalon* that causes one to stumble (see Gundry, p. 88).

5:31–32 / Some writers consider this section the third antithesis. The formula, however, is not the same as it is with the other five (the Gk. in vv. 21, 27, 33, 38, and 43 is *ēkousate hoti errethē*; here it is *errethē de*), nor is it clear in what way Jesus intensifies the law on divorce. It is better to take the two verses on divorce as prompted by the preceding paragraph on adultery.

Jewish law required that if a man divorced his wife he must present her with a written certificate before sending her away (Deut. 24:1). This bill of divorcement was to be delivered in the presence of two witnesses. Note that in Jewish society only a man could divorce his spouse; a woman had no such right. The written certificate was intended to protect the wife from arbitrary and overhasty action on the part of her husband. The Jews recognized that God's ideal plan was a permanent monogamous relationship. God, speaking through his prophet Malachi, put it bluntly, "I hate divorce" (Mal. 2:16).

Jesus goes beyond the Mosaic legislation, saying that **anyone who divorces his wife, except for marital unfaithfulness**, is guilty of causing **her to become an adulteress** if she marries again. In the Deuteronomy passage (24:1), the cause for divorce is said to be "something indecent about her." Rabbis differed on what this meant. The rather strict school of Shammai understood it to be unchastity and nothing else. The more liberal school of Hillel took it to be anything that might displease her husband, such as burning a dinner or being disrespectful (m. *Gittin* 9.10). It is reported that Rabbi Akiba taught that finding a woman more attractive than one's wife constituted "something indecent" and allowed divorce. Jesus agreed with the school of Shammai on this point, making an exception to permanent monogamy only for sexual impurity. The Greek *porneia* could refer to some sexual impropriety before marriage but undoubtedly refers in this context to an adulterous liaison after marriage. To divorce a wife for any other reason is to cause her to **become an adulteress** (v. 32). The marriage bond is not broken by a simple declaration (even written) of divorce. Thus the "divorced" wife who remarries is living in adultery. The responsibility for this falls upon the man who "divorced" her. Even the new husband is found to be an adulterer, because the woman he marries is still in God's eyes the wife of the other man. The requirements of the kingdom are considerably more demanding than the accepted interpretation of Mosaic law.

5:33–37 / In saying that people were formerly told not to break a promise but to carry through on every oath made to the Lord, Jesus does not quote directly from the Decalogue but summarizes a series of related passages on the subject (see Exod. 20:7; Lev. 19:12; Num. 30:2; Deut. 23:21–23). Rabbinic equivocation and deliberate ambiguity opened the door to serious misuse of vows (cf. m. *Shebuoth*). Jesus intensifies the Old Testament teaching on oaths, saying, **Do not swear at all** (v. 34). The very existence of a vow introduces a double standard. It implies that a person's word may not be reliable unless accompanied by some sort of verbal guarantee.

Jewish tradition held that oaths using God's name were binding, whereas those avoiding God's name were not. Jesus now teaches that any such practice is misguided, because God is necessarily involved in all transactions—**heaven** is his **throne, earth** is his **footstool, Jerusalem** is his **city,** and even the color of a person's hair is beyond human control (Barclay, vol. 1, pp. 159–60). What the followers of Christ are to do is simply answer **Yes** or **No** and stand by their word. Schweizer writes, "When human discourse is debased so that under certain circumstances Yes can mean No and No Yes, community is destroyed" (p. 128). To be under the rule of God (that is, in his kingdom) is to be absolutely trustworthy and transparently honest. To depart from this is to fall under the influence of the **evil one**.

Throughout the history of the church there have been those who have felt that it was wrong to take an oath of any kind. Yet Jesus allowed the high priest to put him under an oath (Matt. 26:62–64), and Paul called on God to be his witness (2 Cor. 1:23; cf. Gal. 1:20). The subject under consideration in Matthew is not so much the taking of a vow as it is the necessity of speaking the truth at all times. Jesus inevitably penetrates behind all legislation to the essential principles it intends to express. To codify his teaching is to destroy it. His "rules" reach far beyond any ability of external regulation to satisfy. They call for nothing short of complete inward surrender to God's purpose and nature.

5:38–42 / One of the oldest laws in the world was based on the principle of equal retaliation. It was called *lex talionis* and dates back as far as Hammurabi, an eighteenth-century B.C. king. It is found three times in the Old Testament (Exod. 21:24; Lev. 24:20; Deut. 19:21). The original intention was to restrict unlimited revenge. It was understood as (only) an **eye for eye** and (only) a **tooth for** a **tooth**. Further, it was never intended as an excuse for individual retaliation; it belonged in the law court and was allowed by a judge.

Jesus now changes limited retaliation to nonretaliation. Members of Christ's kingdom **do not resist an evil person** (someone who may wrong them). Like their Master, they accept unjust abuse (cf. 1 Pet. 2:21–23). Three examples of nonretaliation for personal abuse are offered. If someone should insult you with a backhanded slap to the **right cheek**, you are to **turn to him the other also** for an additional blow (v. 39). Rabbis taught that such a blow was doubly insulting and carried twice the fine as an open-handed slap. If someone **wants to sue you and take your tunic** (*chitōn*, a long, close-fitting undergarment made of cotton or linen), give that person **your cloak** (*himation*, an outer garment that served as a blanket at night) **as well**. Jewish law required that a neighbor not be deprived of his or her **cloak** (*himation*, Exod. 22:26–27) at night, otherwise, there would be no covering under which to sleep. Jesus counsels giving the aggressor not only the undergarment but the outer robe as well. Obviously this is not to be taken in a woodenly literal fashion. Jesus is not recommending that believers leave the courtroom naked!

The third illustration of nonretaliation draws from the ancient practice of armies conscripting peasants to carry their gear. The Greek verb *angareuō* ("to force") is of Persian origin (the *angaros* was a mounted courier always ready to deliver an official dispatch) and became a technical term for compulsory conscription. Simon of Cyrene was "forced" (*ēngareusan*) by the Roman soldiers to carry Jesus' cross (Matt. 27:32).

The section closes with the counsel to **give** to those who **ask** and lend to those who wish to **borrow**. Jesus' followers are not to be caught up in anxious concern about the things they possess. They are to enjoy the same freedom that led the believers mentioned in Hebrews 10:34 to endure gladly the looting of all their possessions.

5:43–48 / The final illustration of how Jesus' teaching "brings the law to perfection" (Knox) is taken from Israel's relationship to non-Jewish cultures. **You have heard that it was said, "Love your neighbor and hate your enemy."** The foundation of Jewish ethics was Leviticus 19:18; "Do not seek revenge or bear a grudge against one of your people, but love your neighbor as yourself." It is often mentioned that nowhere in the Old Testa-

ment will you find an explicit demand to hate your enemies. In
fact, some verses seem to point in quite the other direction (e.g.,
Prov. 25:21, "If your enemy is hungry, give him food to eat; if
he is thirsty, give him water to drink"). Yet many other verses
call for Israel actively to oppose its national enemies (Deut. 7:2,
"Show them [the Hittites, Girgashites, etc.] no mercy"; Deut.
20:16, "Do not leave alive anything that breathes" [among the
cities that God gives Israel as an inheritance]; Deut. 23:6, "Do
not seek a treaty or friendship with them [Ammonites and Moab-
ites] as long as you live"). This attitude is seen among the sectarians at Qumran, who were ordered to "hate all the sons of
darkness" (1QS 1.4.10). Rather than interpreting hate as a Semitic way of saying "love less," it is better to understand the teaching as directed at Israel's national enemies. The attitude reflects
God's own "hatred" of evil. David can say, "Do I not hate those
who hate you, O Lord, and abhor those who rise up against you?"
(Ps. 139:21).

Jesus now extends the definition of *plēsion* ("neighbor") in
Leviticus 19:18 to include enemies and those who persecute you.
It is helpful to remember that Jesus' ethical teaching is primarily
individual and personal rather than national and social in the inclusive sense. Within the realm of everyday relationships, there
is no category that can be labeled "enemy." Everyone we meet
(even the one who would abuse us) is a friend and therefore one
whom we are to love. Note that love is active concern: we are to
pray for those who persecute us (v. 44).

Followers of Jesus are to love their enemies as well as their
friends. In this way they show themselves to be children of their
heavenly Father. Without partiality, **he causes his sun to rise** (v.
45) on both sinner and saint and his **rain** to fall on the honest
and dishonest alike. His favor extends to all. To be children of
God requires that we meet moral conditions. To be like God we
must show our favor not simply to those who are ready to love
in return. There is no reward for loving those who love us. Even
the despised **tax collectors** do that. And if we show courtesy only
to our friends, there is nothing out of the ordinary in that. What
God requires is that his children **be perfect, therefore,** just as he
is perfect (v. 48).

This last statement (v. 48) has often been misinterpreted.
It has served as a basic text for the doctrine of Christian perfec-

tionism, which requires of the Christian absolute moral impeccability, but it often ends up reclassifying sin as something less serious than it is. The perfection to which Jesus calls his followers has just been defined by the context. Perfect love is an active concern for all people everywhere, regardless of whether or not they receive it. To do this is to imitate God and demonstrate that we are his children (v. 45). It is to display a family likeness. The Greek work *teleios* ("perfect") means "having attained the end/purpose." Since human beings were made in the image of God (Gen. 1:26), they are "perfect" when they demonstrate in their lives those characteristics that reflect the nature of God.

Additional Notes §5

5:4 / Metzger notes that if vv. 3 and 5 had originally been together, with their rhetorical antithesis of heaven and earth, it would have been unlikely that any scribe would have inserted v. 4 between them. It is easier to assume that a second-century copyist brought the two verses together to produce the antithesis and to put *ptōchoi* ("poor") and *praeis* ("meek") in a closer relationship (*TCGNT*, p. 12).

5:5 / **Meek**: In its secular use, *praus* ("gentle") described outward conduct between people; in the NT it describes an inward quality and relates primarily to God (cf. Vincent, *WSNT*, vol. 1, p. 37).

5:8 / **Pure in heart**: Albright-Mann note that the theme of purity of heart is well attested in rabbinic literature and quote *Midrash Rabbah* on Gen. 40:8, "The Holy One, blessed be He, loves everyone who is pure in heart" (p. 47).

5:13 / **Salt**: For an interpretation of salt as indicating productivity rather than preservation, cf. E. P. Deatrick, "Salt, Soil, Savor," *BA* 25 (May 1962), pp. 41–48.

5:15 / **Bowl** is *modios* (a Latin loanword), a container used for measuring grain. It held about one peck.
Lamp: normally, a shallow open vessel filled with oil on which floated a wick. See *IBD*, vol. 2, pp. 871–73.

5:20 / **Righteousness**: See C. Brown's article "Righteousness, Justification" in *NIDNTT*, vol. 3, pp. 352–77.

5:22 / **Raca**: A. B. Bruce (p. 107) notes that *raca* expresses contempt for a person's head ("you stupid!"), whereas *mōre* expresses contempt for a person's character ("you scoundrel").

5:38 / McNeile, noting that the principle of an eye for an eye was restrictive rather than permissive, writes: "It limited revenge by fixing an exact compensation for an injury" (p. 69).

5:39 / The insult offered may be that given to a person held to be a heretic (see Jeremias, *The Sermon on the Mount*, p. 27).

5:41 / **Forces**: See "Aggareuein: The Word of an Occupied Country," in Barclay, *A New Testament Wordbook*, pp. 15–17.

§6 Sermon on the Mount: Prayer and Anxiety (Matt. 6:1–34)

6:1 / The three most prominent religious obligations of Jewish piety were almsgiving, prayer, and fasting. The first eighteen verses of chapter 6 deal with these acts of religious devotion. In each case there is a wrong way and a right way. The followers of Jesus are to avoid all ostentatious display and to quietly fulfill the obligations in an unobtrusive manner. In carrying out religious duties they are not to make a public display in order to attract attention to themselves. That approach would deprive them of their heavenly reward.

Some scholars find a contradiction between this charge and the earlier advice (in 5:16) that believers are to let their light shine before others "that they may see your good deeds." The contexts, however, are distinct. In the earlier case, the temptation was to keep one's religious commitment private in order to avoid persecution; in the later, the tendency is to call attention to one's act of devotion for personal gain. The biblical doctrine of rewards holds that, since God is absolutely and perfectly just, he must punish evil and reward what is good (cf. Prov. 24:12; 2 Thess. 1:5–10). It need not be thought of in some crassly material way: the reward for holiness is holiness itself.

6:2–4 / The first example related to the giving of alms. To give money for the poor was one of the most sacred duties of Judaism. Tobit says, "It is better to give alms than to treasure up gold. For almsgiving delivers from death, and it will purge away every sin" (12:8b–9a). The Hebrew word ṣᵉdāqâ means both "righteousness" and "almsgiving." Followers of Jesus are not to give to the needy in the manner of the hypocrites who sounded a trumpet to call attention to their benevolence and thus receive the praise of other people. They are rather to make it a very private transaction, and God, who is fully aware of all that takes place, will provide the proper reward.

The NIV translates, rather literally, **Do not announce it with trumpets.** The expression should be taken metaphorically, although there is evidence that the ram's horn announced public fasts during times of drought when almsgiving might be expected. The GNB takes the clause as a figure of speech and paraphrases, "Do not make a big show of it." That is what the **hypocrites** do in the synagogues and on the street corners. Matthew is fond of the term "hypocrite" (he uses it thirteen times to Luke's three and Mark's one), which is derived from the theater and means "play-actor." To be a hypocrite is to pretend to be someone you are not. It is easier to pose as a righteous person than to actually be one. One second-century rabbi declared that nine-tenths of all the hypocrisy in the world was to be found in Jerusalem.

Those who give to be seen and admired have already **received their reward in full** (v. 2). No further compensation remains. They got what they bargained for. The Greek *apechō* was a technical commercial term that was often used in the sense of payment in full, complete with a receipt. Schweizer mentions that only in acts of charity (within Judaism) was there sometimes hope of receiving both honor in this life and a heavenly reward later—the capital remaining invested in heaven while the interest is enjoyed on earth (p. 144).

Rather than calling attention to one's acts of charity, one should not even let the left hand know what the right hand is up to. It is unnecessary to conjure up some image of how such a transaction might take place in a literal sense. (Gundry makes the interesting suggestion that it may mean to slip in the gift unobtrusively with the right hand alone rather than to use both hands in a manner designed to catch the attention of others, p. 102.) God will see the kindness and provide the proper reward at the proper time.

6:5-6 / A second important religious duty among the Jews was prayer. In the morning and in the evening the devout Jew would recite the Shema (three short passages of Scripture from Deuteronomy 6 and 11 and Numbers 15), and at nine in the morning, noon, and three in the afternoon he would go through the Shemoneh Esreh (the Eighteen Benedictions). Acts 3:1 notes that Peter and John went to the temple "at the time of prayer—at three in the afternoon." According to Jewish custom, if you were in the streets at this time it was proper to stop, turn toward the temple, and pray (cf. the Moslem practice even today). Apparently the hypocrites would plan their day so as to be in some conspicuous place when it was time to pray. On busy **street corners** or in the square, they would lift their hands to God and display their "devotion" to all who were passing by. Like those who called attention to their acts of charity, these "playactors" have been paid **in full** (cf. v. 2).

Jesus tells his followers that when they wish to pray they are to **go into** some private place (the Gk. *tameion* may refer to a "storeroom," the only room in the house with a door, and therefore private) and **close the door** (cf. 2 Kings 4:33; Isa. 26:20). There they may pray to their Father "who is there in the secret place" (NEB), and he will provide the appropriate reward.

6:7–8 / Do not keep on babbling like pagans. They are wrong in thinking that God hears them because of the length of their prayers. God does not need to be instructed by lengthy prayers, because he already **knows what you need before you ask him.** The word used to describe the prayers of the pagans is *battalogeō*, which occurs nowhere else in the New Testament or in secular literature of the day. It is probably an onomatopoietic word constructed by way of analogy with the better known *battarizō*, "to stammer or stutter" (Delling, *TDNT*, vol. 1, p. 597). Behind the word is the practice of the heathen who developed long lists of divine names, hoping that by endless repetition they would somehow invoke the name of the true god and receive what they wished. To know and pronounce correctly the name of a god was thought to provide the power to manipulate that god.

6:9–10 / Matthew now expands his teachings on prayer by adding what has come to be known as the Lord's Prayer. The same prayer, in a somewhat shorter form, is found in Luke 11:2–4 where Jesus responds to his disciples' request to teach them to pray as John had taught his disciples. The differences between the two accounts argue that the prayer was intended as a guide rather than a liturgical chant to be memorized. Matthew's version contains three petitions that relate to God and his kingdom followed by four requests for the life of believers here and now. Many scholars interpret the entire prayer in an eschatological setting (Stendahl calls it an "extended Maranatha," p. 779), the **daily**

bread being the messianic banquet and the **temptation** a reference to the time of severe persecution at the end of the age (cf. Matt. 24:22). It is better to take the first three petitions as bearing upon the future consummation and the next four as related to God's action in our lives at the present time (cf. Beare, p. 175). Whatever the primary focus, however, each petition has implications for both the present and the future.

In form, the Lord's Prayer opens very much like an Aramaic liturgical prayer known as the Kaddish. This prayer speaks of hallowing the name of God, of the coming of his kingly rule, and of the creation of the world according to his will. When Jesus says to pray, **our Father**, he reveals a dramatic new relationship made possible between God and human beings. The Aramaic *'abbā* that stands behind the Greek *patēr* ("father") was an intimate and affectionate title that children used when speaking to their father. It became so embedded in the minds of first-century Christians that the Aramaic lingers in the compound "Abba, Father" found in Mark 14:36, Romans 8:15, and Galatians 4:6. That we pray to **our Father** reminds us that the Christian faith is essentially a family affair.

The first petition asks that the **name** of God be revered and held in honor. God's **name** stands for his character as revealed in history. To hallow God's **name** is to treat with high and holy regard the person of God himself. This petition is followed by an urgent request that God will establish in a full and final sense his rule on earth. Although the **kingdom** came in the life and ministry of Jesus, it awaits the second advent to be complete and final (cf. 1 Cor. 15:28). We live now in those days between the beginning of the age to come and the end of the age that is present. God's sovereign rule is realized in the hearts of his followers, but it will one day be openly acknowledged (cf. Phil. 2:10–11).

The heart of the prayer is that God's **will** may **be done** here **on earth** as well as **in heaven** (v. 10). When the two clauses of verse 10 are taken as parallel, we learn that God's kingdom comes whenever his will is done. Perfect obedience to his will awaits the final arrival of the King. In the meantime, those who follow Christ can experience his sovereign rule by living lives of obedience. Some writers take the final clause (**on earth as it is in heaven**) as qualifying all three of the preceding petitions.

6:11–13 / In the second half of the prayer, we find the focus shifted to matters of everyday concern. The first request is for **bread**. The Greek adjective *epiousios* (**daily**) is not found outside the Lord's Prayer in the New Testament. With the possible exception of one place where *epiousi* may have been intended to be completed as *epiousion*, it occurs nowhere in secular literature. Any technical commentary will list the possible derivations of the word and suggest various meanings. Foerster is convincing when he argues that *epiousios* indicates measure rather than time (thus ruling out the sense "for the coming day/tomorrow") and offers the rendering, "The bread which we need, give us to-day [day by day]" (*TDNT,* vol. 2, p. 599). The background is God's daily provision of manna that could not be stored (except on Friday) for a future day (Exod. 16). God responds to our needs day by day.

The next petition is for forgiveness (v. 12). Since we owe God complete obedience, every failure puts us in debt to him. Behind the Greek *opheilēma* ("debt/one's due") is the Aramaic *ḥôbâ,* which was used figuratively of sin as a moral debt. The request for forgiveness is based upon our willingness to forgive others. The person who does not forgive is unable to receive forgiveness.

Lead us not into temptation (v. 13) means do not let us fall into a trial so difficult that we will fail. The Greek *peirasmos* means both **temptation** and "trial." When God "tempted" (AV, Gen. 22:1; *epeirase,* LXX) Abraham by telling him to offer his son Isaac, the clear meaning is that he put him to the test. James's word on temptation (as seduction to evil) is that "each one is tempted when, by his own evil desire, he is dragged away and enticed" (James 1:14). The two meanings of "tempt" should be kept separate. For interpreters who understand the prayer eschatologically, the period of trial is the intensely difficult time of suffering that immediately precedes the second coming of Christ—"the hour of trial that is going to come upon the whole world to test those who live on the earth" (Rev. 3:10; cf. Matt. 24:22). We have already opted to interpret the final petitions as related to the believer's life now. Lest anyone misunderstand the first clause of verse 13 as somehow involving God in seducing human beings to evil, Jesus adds **but deliver us from the evil one**; he is the one who tears down and destroys. The Greek *ponēros* can be translated "evil" or **the evil one**. Since in Hebrew thought Satan is not designated as "the evil one," many interpreters prefer the former meaning (i.e., those difficult circumstances that often plague our lives).

Readers of most modern-speech versions will note the omission of any doxology at this point. ("For thine is the kingdom, and the power, and the glory, forever. Amen.") It is commonly recognized that this is a later liturgical addition. It is not found in any Greek manuscript before the fifth century. Apparently it was a Jewish practice to end every prayer with a doxology even when there was nothing of that nature in the text (cf. Jeremias, *Unknown Sayings of Jesus*, p. 28). The doxology reflects the major strands of David's prayer in 1 Chronicles 29:10–13.

6:14–15 / To round off the teaching on prayer, Matthew adds a saying of Jesus to the effect that God's forgiveness as it relates to us depends upon our willingness to extend forgiveness to others (cf. Mark 11:25). It expands the concept expressed in the fifth petition of the Lord's Prayer. It should not be taken as a quid pro quo arrangement in which God keeps tabs on our relations with others and withholds his forgiveness until we have merited it, but as a way of saying that forgiving others who have wronged us follows naturally from our having been forgiven by God.

6:16–18 / A third highly esteemed religious duty among the Jewish people was fasting. In addition to the fast on the Day of Atonement (Lev. 16:31 is interpreted in this way), there were fasts connected with mourning (e.g., 1 Sam. 31:13), with times of distress (e.g., Ps. 35:13), with preparation for a theophany (e.g., Deut. 9:9), and with other times of special significance. Fasting was thought to strengthen prayer by demonstrating how serious was the supplicant's approach. According to the *Didache*, the "hypocrites" (by the second century A.D. this derogatory title had become a standard epithet for the Jews) fasted Mondays and Thursdays (market days!), and therefore Christians were to fast Wednesdays and Fridays (8:1).

The hypocrites are said to **disfigure their faces to show men they are fasting**. The Greek verb *aphanizō* ("to disfigure") means to make invisible (the *a* negates *phainō*, "to shine/appear"). In this context it suggests that the hypocrites made themselves unrecognizable by putting ashes on their heads that would fall onto their faces and into their beards, thus disguising their identity. It is ironic that in their desperate attempt to be recognized for piety they end up being unrecognizable.

Jesus instructs his followers to fast in such a way as to call no attention to themselves. They are to **wash** their **face** and be sure that their general appearance does not reveal that they have gone without food. The hypocrites have been paid **in full** right now (they want the admiration of others, and they get it). Jesus' disciples, however, are to practice their religion in private; they will thus be rewarded by their Father who is aware of all that takes place **in secret**.

6:19–21 / The natural human tendency is to store up material possessions here on earth. Jesus advises laying up **treasures in heaven**, where the uncertainties of life cannot affect them. Where people put their **treasure** reveals where their hearts really are. Unless "moth and eating" (the NIV follows Tyndale's translation of *brōsis* as **rust**, which lacks support from the LXX) is a grammatical expression meaning "eaten by moths," we have three ways in which earthly possessions are destroyed. In the ancient East elaborate clothing was viewed as part of a person's treasure. Such material was easily devastated by moths. "Eating" could refer to the gnawing of mice and other vermin (McNeile, p. 84) or in a more general sense to what Weymouth calls "wear-and-tear." Since houses were normally made of mud brick or baked clay, it was relatively easy for a thief to dig through (*dioryssō*; NIV, **break in**) and **steal** possessions. Very little protection existed in the ancient world; this highly contrasts the security of treasures laid up in heaven.

6:22–23 / Throughout chapter 6 Jesus draws a series of comparisons (between the conduct of the hypocrites and that of his own followers in almsgiving, prayer, and fasting; between treasures stored on earth and those stored in heaven; and, in the section yet to come, between the two masters, God and money). Here he contrasts the good eye, which provides light for the entire body, and the evil eye, which leaves the body in darkness.

In the physiology of Jesus' day **the eye** was thought of as a window that brought light into the body. An eye could be *haplous* ("single") or *ponēros* ("evil"). The contrast is usually presented in one of two ways: one, "sound" in the sense of clear, able to see distinctly, and "not sound" (RSV), unable to focus clearly; and two, "generous" and "stingy." The first (and less probable) option notes that *haplous* in the LXX represents the Hebrew verb *tam*, which carries the idea of "singleness of purpose" (Hill, p. 142). This would make the saying an expansion of "blessed are the pure in heart" (Matt. 5:8). The second option points out that the "evil eye" is a Semitic metaphor for greediness or a grudging spirit (cf. Matt. 20:15) and takes *haplous* as it is commonly used, to signify "generous" (cf. Rom. 12:8; James 1:5). In this case Jesus is saying that a generous spirit brings moral health and wholeness, whereas a mean spirit prevents a person from seeing what is really important. This interpretation follows naturally after the words on laying up treasure in heaven and leads on to the mention of money as a master that cannot be served at the same time as God (v. 24). If all the **light** a person has is **darkness**, "how intense must that darkness be" (TCNT).

6:24 / Jesus has just taught his disciples that treasures should be stored in heaven, not on earth. This could lead to concern regarding adequate provisions for daily life. Don't be anxious about these things, says Jesus, because nature itself teaches that God will provide. Make his kingdom your highest priority; tomorrow will take care of itself.

One of Jesus' most memorable statements is the radical truth that **no one can serve two masters**. Knox translates verse 24: "You must serve God or money; you cannot serve both." *Māmôn* is an Aramaic word that means "wealth/property." It is probably derived from a root that means "that in which one trusts" (Hauck in *TDNT*, vol. 4, p. 388). Although the word itself is neutral, it came to be used in a derogatory sense. In the Targums (Aramaic paraphrases of the Old Testament) it was used for dishonest profit gained by selfishly exploiting another person. The "mammon of unrighteousness" (AV) of Luke 16:9 corresponds exactly to an Aramaic phrase meaning "possessions acquired dishonestly" (*TDNT*, vol. 4, p. 390). In *Paradise Lost*, Milton personifies Mammon as a fallen spirit who even in heaven admired the golden streets more than the divine and holy.

Slavery requires complete devotion to one owner. It is impossible to be a servant of God and still serve Mammon. A choice must be made. The love–hate contrast does not refer to an emotional relationship but should be taken in the sense of faithful service as opposed to disregard.

6:25–34 / Since serving God rules out serving money, the logical conclusion is that followers of Christ should not be anxiously concerned about food and clothing. God takes care of the birds who neither plant nor gather a harvest into barns. He also dresses the flowers of the field in garments more beautiful than Solomon with all his wealth could secure. Children of the kingdom are certainly of greater value than birds! And wild grass is here today and gone tomorrow. When you worry about such things not only are you like the pagans but you dishonor God as well. He is fully aware of your needs. Worry is practical atheism and an affront to God.

In this passage we see Jesus drawing upon nature for analogies that will illumine and strengthen spiritual truth. Birds rely upon God's providential care. They do not busy themselves with anxious human pursuits. Flowers do not spin garments for themselves. They just grow, and God adorns them with color and beauty. The argument is from the lesser to the greater: if God does all this for birds and flowers, won't he also take care of you?

Several specific items need to be mentioned. For Matthew's more general term **birds of the air** (*peteinon*, v. 26) Luke has "ravens" (*korakas*, Luke 12:24). "Raven" in Aramaic is masculine, and "lily" is feminine. Laboring in the field was a man's work and spinning at home a woman's.

In verse 27 Jesus asks whether by **worrying** about it anyone can add a single cubit to his or her stature. *Pēchys* ("cubit") was originally a forearm, then a measure of about eighteen inches. Since *hēlikia* ("stature") normally means "age" and *pēchys* can be used metaphorically as "a span of time," it is best to take the phrase to mean "to prolong life by even a short period of time" (v. 27; NIV has **add a single hour to his life**).

Jesus' disciples are to examine with care (*katamanthanō*, a compound in which the prefix *kata* intensifies the verb *manthanō*, "to learn") **the lilies of the field** (v. 28). The flowers are perhaps the purple anemone, whose color would lead naturally to a comparison with the royal purple of Solomon (cf. the "purple garments worn by the kings of Midian," Judg. 8:26).

Jesus chides his disciples, calling them "you 'little-faiths' "(v. 30, Phillips). The word used, *oligopistos*, occurs only five times in the New Testament, four of which are in Matthew. It describes the believer whose actual confidence in God falls short of what we could reasonably expect. The **pagans** of verse 32 are probably those unbelievers outside the circle of the disciples. Anxiety is pagan, in that, apart from a knowledge of the true God, there is ample reason to be anxious about many things.

Instead of nervous anxiety about those basic physical necessities that God in his providence is perfectly able to supply, the disciple is to seek God's kingdom and that righteousness of life that demonstrates obedience to the divine will (v. 33). These are the genuinely important issues of human existence, not "What's for dinner?" or "What can I wear?" God will supply all those things when needed. The chapter closes with two proverbial statements that counsel "living in the present instead of crippling the present by fear of the imagined future" (Filson, p. 102). A note of irony runs through the verse: each day provides its own share of anxieties; why add tomorrow's problems to those we already have today? Things are bad enough as they are. The American essayist and critic Joseph Wood Krutch observes, "Anxiety and distress, interrupted occasionally by pleasure, is the normal course of man's existence" (*The Twelve Seasons*).

Additional Notes §6

6:1 / **Reward**: God's rewards express his character. They are an integral part of his covenantal relationship and therefore are affected by human obedience. The doctrine of rewards was sometimes misunderstood to imply automatic material return for righteous acts and inevitable suffering for sin.

6:2 / **Hypocrites**: For a milder view, see Albright-Mann (pp. cxv–cxxiii). They translate *hypokritēs* as "overscrupulous" and say that "nothing can justify the continued use of the word 'hypocrite' in our English versions" (p. 73).

Give: Rabbinic views on charity are set forth in Montefiore and Loewe, *A Rabbinic Anthology*, pp. 412–39; also Str.-B., vol. 4, pp. 536–58.

Some have suggested that the image of **trumpets** may have come from the thirteen trumpet-shaped containers in the temple treasury into which worshipers placed their contributions (cf. Luke 21:1).

6:9 / For a convenient summary on the form of the Lord's Prayer, see *NIDNTT*, vol. 2, pp. 869–77. See also Jeremias, *The Prayers of Jesus*; E. Lohmeyer, *"Our Father."*

6:12 / **Debts**: Gk. *opheilēmata*. An appropriate translation; "trespasses" is a mistranslation made common by the Church of England Book of Common Prayer.

6:13 / The doxology, which was appended for liturgical purposes, may have been composed on the basis of 1 Chron. 29:11–13.

6:14 / **Sin against**: Gk. *paraptōmata*. It stresses a conscious violation involving guilt.

§7 Sermon on the Mount: By Their Fruits (Matt. 7:1–29)

7:1–5 / Human nature encourages us to pay far more attention to the shortcomings of others than to our own faults. We tend to evaluate others on the basis of a lofty standard of righteousness that somehow is not applicable to our own performance. Jesus says, **Do not judge.** The Greek construction (*mē* plus the present imperative) carries with it the idea of ceasing what you are now doing. Williams translates, "Stop criticizing others." Judging, in this context, implies a harsh and censorious spirit. If you insist on condemning others, you exclude yourself from God's forgiveness. Although it is psychologically true that a critical spirit receives from others a harsh response, Jesus is here speaking of final judgment. The NIV correctly translates, **or you too will be judged.**

The admonition not to judge is often taken incorrectly to imply that believers are not to make moral judgments about anyone or anything. That this is not what was intended is clear from verses 15–20, which warn of false prophets who can be known by the fruit they bear. Jesus does not ask us to lay aside our critical faculties but rather to resist the urge to speak harshly of others. The issue is serious in that God will judge us by the same standard we apply to others. This rather frightening truth should change the way in which we tend to view other people's failings.

Verses 3–5 present the ludicrous picture of someone with a long beam or rafter (MM refer to *dokoi* as heavy beams used in the building of the temple, p. 168) protruding from his eye trying to extract a tiny chip of dried wood (or perhaps a speck of dust) from the eye of another. Obviously we are dealing with Eastern hyperbole (cf. Matt. 19:24, with its scene of a camel going through the eye of a needle!). How hypocritical to be concerned with the minor fault of another in view of one's own personal failure. Based on the account of the two debtors in Matthew 18:23–

35, some have seen here the enormous offense of our own failure before God in comparison with the minor offenses between people. In any case, the **plank** is to be removed from our own eye before we indulge in removing the **speck of sawdust** from the eye of another. Taken in an unqualified sense, this would put a complete stop to helping others with their moral difficulties. Undoubtedly it is intended to restrict hypocritical correction of others rather than to prohibit all helpful correction.

7:6 / Verse 6 is proverbial and difficult to interpret in its present context. **Dogs** and **pigs** are derogatory terms applied to the Gentiles. Some think that in the present context they refer to all who are not disciples of Jesus. Not giving what is holy to the dogs would be instruction directed against the mission to the Gentiles (cf. 10:5), and not throwing pearls in front of pigs would relate to restricting admission to the Eucharist (cf. *Didache* 9.5). Probably the words should be understood in a more general way as counsel against sharing spiritual truth with those who are unable and unwilling to accept it.

Because **what is sacred** is not parallel with **pearls** it has been suggested that the Greek word for **sacred** mistranslates an Aramaic original that meant "earring." The text is acceptable as it stands. It would be unthinkable to take sacred food and give it to dogs or valuable pearls and feed them to pigs. Finding pearls unpalatable, pigs will trample them underfoot, and dogs will turn and attack those who fed them. In other words, use discretion as you share the truth of God with others.

7:7–11 / Earlier in the sermon (6:5–15) Matthew brought together a portion of Jesus' teaching on the subject of prayer. Now he expands it by stressing how important it is for believers to be persistent in prayer. The present imperatives, "keep on asking," "keep on seeking," and "keep on knocking" (Williams) indicate that prayer is not a semi-passive ritual in which we occasionally share our concerns with God. In Luke, the narrative is immediately preceded by the story of the man awakened from sleep at midnight by an importunate neighbor who needs bread to feed a guest (Luke 11:5–8). Prayer requires stamina and persistence. It is those who keep on asking that receive and those who keep on seeking that find. God opens the door to those who keep on knocking. Divine delays do not indicate reluctance on God's part.

In the time of waiting we learn patience, and the intensity of our desire is put to the test. God, through Jeremiah, told the exiles in Babylon, "You will seek me and find me when you seek me with all your heart" (Jer. 29:13). It is those who "hunger and thirst for righteousness" that are satisfied (Matt. 5:6).

Jesus now reasons that since earthly fathers who are less than perfect will not mock a child who asks for food, does it not follow that God will give good things to those who ask? Should his son ask for **bread** a father will not hand him a **stone**. Should he ask for a **fish** he will not be given a **snake** (the reference is to some eel-like fish without scales that, according to Lev. 11:12, was not to be eaten). **Though you are evil** (v. 11), says Jesus, you know how to provide your children with what is best for them. **How much more** will God, the heavenly Father, who is perfect in righteousness and love? Schweizer writes that "human maliciousness is here simply presupposed" and that this runs counter to the "widespread romantic belief that man is innately good and need only be left to himself with as few restrictions as possible for everything to improve" (pp. 173–74). Jesus is not making a theological statement about absolute human goodness but is drawing a comparison between parents' natural acts of kindness toward their children and the perfection of God's generosity toward those who seek his favor.

7:12 / Verse 12 is commonly called the Golden Rule. In its negative form it is found in many ancient cultures. Confucius said, "What you do not want done to yourself, do not do to others." In the fourth century B.C., the Athenian orator Isocrates said, "Whatever angers you when you suffer it at the hands of others, do not do it to others." Hillel states the same principle in response to a request that he teach the entire law while standing on one foot (b. *Shab.* 31a). Apparently it never was stated in the positive form (**Do to others what you would have them do to you**) by anyone before Jesus. Some writers hold that the shift from negative to positive is without any particular significance. However, in its negative form the Golden Rule could be satisfied by doing nothing. The positive form moves us to action on behalf of others; it calls us to do for others all those things that we would appreciate being done for us. Now we have moved from justice to active benevolence. This kind of outgoing and dynamic concern for others sums up the Law and the Prophets (cf. Weymouth). It is "the essence of all true religion" (Phillips). The Golden Rule brings into focus the ethical intent that lay behind all the Old Testament legislation on matters of interpersonal relationships. The law of love is the ultimate expression of the ethical teaching of both law and prophetic injunction (Matt. 5:17).

7:13–14 / In one sense the Golden Rule represents the high point of the sermon. The four paragraphs that follow contrast the two ways (vv. 13–14), the two kinds of fruit (vv. 15–20), the two kinds of followers (vv. 21–23), and the two kinds of builders (vv. 24–27). In each case there is a sharp distinction drawn between true discipleship and mere religious activity. Jesus brings his sermon to a close with a clear call for action.

The idea of two ways is found throughout secular literature. Hesiod (the ancient Greek poet) warns that the way of wickedness is "smooth and near to hand," whereas the path to virtue is "long and steep and rough to begin with" (*Work and Days*). Jeremiah represents Jewish thought when he records God's message, "See, I am setting before you the way of life and the way of death" (21:8; see also Deut. 30:19; *Didache* 1.1).

Matthew's use of the figure is a bit ambiguous in that it combines both gates and roads. Does one enter through a gate onto a road (v. 13), or does a road lead ultimately to a gate (v. 14)? Most writers hold that Matthew has conflated two sayings, one referring to a door or gate (cf. Luke 13:24) and the other to two ways. However that may be, the essential idea is relatively clear. One way is broad and easy. It is the way of self-centeredness, and the majority travel that road. The other way is narrow and hard to find. Only a few travel the road of personal commitment and discipline. One road leads to **destruction** and the other to eternal **life**. The saying is primarily eschatological, although it speaks as well of life here and now. It describes two ways to live: two ways that separate and lead to two distinct destinies. The choice is clear: follow the crowd with its characteristic bent toward taking the path of least resistance, or join the few who accept the limiting demands of loyalty. The easy way will turn out hard (it ends in **destruction**), whereas the hard way will lead to eternal joy (**life**).

7:15–20 / For several hundred years before the time of Christ it was generally believed that prophecy had ceased. The period between the two Testaments is sometimes called the silent years. With John the Baptist the prophetic voice returned, and in early Christianity prophecy flourished. To the crowd that gathered on the Day of Pentecost, Peter explained that the phenomenon of tongues was the fulfillment of Joel's promise that in the last days God would pour out his Spirit on everyone, so that young men would see visions, old men would have dreams, and both men and women would proclaim his message (Acts 2:17-18; cf. 1 Cor. 14:29-31).

As the church grew, the problem of false prophets became acute. Jesus had warned against the rise of false prophets who would deceive the people (Matt. 24:11, 24). John also warned his followers (1 John 4:1-3; Rev. 2:20). How were the Christians to recognize a false prophet? In earlier days a prophet was discredited if what he proclaimed in the name of the Lord did not come true (Deut. 18:20-22). The *Didache* had some simple tests to identify a false prophet (if he stays more than two days or asks for money, 11.5-6). It is "from his behavior, then, [that] the false prophet and the true prophet shall be known" (*Didache* 11.8).

Jesus warns against **false prophets**. They come **in sheep's clothing** (that is, they appear to be one of the believing flock; cf. Num. 27:17 and Ps. 100:3 for the figure; in addition, prophets often wore garments made of skins of animals, Zech. 13:4; Matt. 3:4), **but inwardly they are ferocious wolves** (all their activity is prompted by personal greed, and they will tear and destroy others for their own gain). To come dressed as a prophet was to claim the office. At first their teaching appeared to be true, but when the way they lived was examined they were found to be **wolves** (false prophets; cf. Ezek. 22:27; Zeph. 3:3).

False prophets are recognized **by their fruit**. In a day when God was still revealing his will through the prophetic office, it was more difficult to validate a message on the basis of its theological acceptability. False prophets could be identified more simply by the way they lived. **Do people pick grapes from thornbushes, or figs from thistles?** If there are no **grapes** you do not have a grapevine. If the **fruit** is bad, you do not have a healthy tree. Likewise, if the life of the prophet does not measure up to the claim, then you are dealing with a false prophet. "Like root, like fruit" is the ancient saying. Good theology must produce ethical uprightness. Conduct reveals character.

7:21-23 / Since what people do reveals who they really are, it follows that simply calling Jesus Lord is not enough. On the day of judgment false prophets will protest that in the name of Jesus they prophesied, drove out many **demons**, and worked **many miracles**, only to be declared **evildoers** unknown to the Lord. Only those who do what God desires will enter the **kingdom of heaven**. Judgment is based upon living out the will of God, not on claims of apostolic activity.

Lord was a common form of polite address (much like our "sir"), although the present context (final judgment) reflects its later use as a reverential title. The earliest Christian creed was "Jesus is Lord" (1 Cor. 12:3). It implied that he was accepted as master and that his teaching was therefore binding. To claim allegiance (**Lord, Lord**) does not secure entrance to the kingdom of heaven (the final state, when God's sovereign reign is perfectly realized). Only those who do **the will of my Father** may enter.

On that day (v. 22) refers to the day of judgment (cf. Mal. 3:17-18; the "day of the Lord," Joel 2:1; Amos 5:18; etc.). At that time false prophets will make all sorts of claims regarding what they did on earth. Some will have invoked the name of Jesus to perform exorcisms. The seven sons of Sceva are an example of this (Acts 19:13-16). The use of a name in this connection implies full authority of the one named. Peter commanded the lame man at the Beautiful Gate to get up and walk "in the name of Jesus Christ of Nazareth" (Acts 3:6).

Jesus does not deny that the false prophets could have performed "miracles" (cf. Rev. 13:13-14). It is not true however that they could have had anything to do with him. Thus he will send them away as having never known them (that is, having not commissioned them or in any sense regarded them as his own). In spite of all appearance to the contrary, they "traffic in wrongdoing" (Knox) and have "worked on the side of evil" (Phillips). Gundry, however, feels that the reference is not to Hellenistic libertines but perhaps to Jews or Gentiles who Judaized their Christianity in order to escape persecution (pp. 132-33).

7:24-27 / Jesus has just taught that false prophets can be detected by what they do (v. 16) and that it is action, not rhetoric, that provides entrance into the kingdom of heaven (v. 21). This principle of judgment based on deeds is now applied to everyone. Jesus pictures two builders: one builds a house on a rock and the other chooses a sandy location. Later, when the rain pours down, causing a flash flood of the river over its banks, the first house withstands the storm and the other house is swept away. The imagery comes from climatic conditions in Palestine. The country is dry most of the year, but following the autumn rains, sudden torrents may rush down dry ravines and carry away anything in their path.

The purpose of the parable is to warn those who have listened to the sermon that wisdom calls for action. The **wise man . . . hears** and **puts** [Jesus' words] **into practice**: the **foolish man . . . hears** and **does not put them into practice** (vv. 24, 26). The storm is final judgment. Although both houses may look very much alike, only one will withstand the final testing. The wise not only hear the teachings of Jesus (**these words of mine**, v. 24) but make a concerted effort to live out in their daily lives all that the teaching implies. The foolish may have built a well-structured theology, but it is the foundation, not the house, that determines what happens in the last days. "Obedience to his [Jesus'] teaching is the one solid basis for withstanding the future crisis" (Filson, p. 108).

7:28-29 / Verses 28 and 29 form a transition from the teaching of Jesus to a section recording a number of his miraculous deeds (8:1-9:34). It opens with a formula (*kai egeneto*) that is found at the juncture of each of Matthew's blocks of teaching and the narrative that follows (11:1; 13:53; 19:1; 26:1) but nowhere else in his Gospel.

When Jesus finished his teaching, **the crowds** (see commentary at 5:1) **were amazed** at the **authority** with which he taught. Unlike the scribes, who based their opinions on the explanations offered by all the rabbis who preceded them, Jesus had a self-authenticating ring of authority to his words. It was the same authority that led him to forgive the sins of the paralyzed man (Matt. 9:6) and that he gave to his disciples so that they could drive out demons and heal the sick (Matt. 10:1). It was an expression of who he was (cf. Matt. 28:18) and was recognized immediately. There was no need for his teaching to be buttressed by philosophical argument or persuasive rhetoric. It validated itself to the human conscience.

Additional Notes §7

7:6 / **What is sacred**: The picture is that of a priest taking meat offered on the altar and throwing it to one of the many dogs that wandered the streets of ancient cities. Dogs were "unclean" in the sense that they scavenged food wherever they could find it with no attention to ceremonial taboos. For information on pigs and dogs, see the article "Animals" in *IBD*, vol. 1, pp. 55–57.

7:10 / **Snake**: Fish were a regular part of the Palestinian diet. A water snake could easily be passed off as a fish.

7:15 / **False prophets**: Cf. Matt. 24:24; Acts 13:6; 2 Cor. 11:13ff.; 1 Tim. 4:1; 2 Pet. 2:1; 1 John 4:1.

7:22 / *Ou . . . eprophēteusamen* (**did we not prophesy?**) expects an affirmative answer. Those who asked in this way were self-deceived and not a little arrogant.

7:23 / **I will tell**: The Gk. is *homologeō*, which in this context means to make a legal pronouncement (as it does in Matt. 10:32; 14:7; John 9:22; 1 John 4:15).

7:24–26 / Vincent says the contrast is not between two different sites on which to build houses, but between two ways of laying a foundation. Drawing on Luke 6:48 (which speaks of digging deep and building on a rock) and the practice in Arab lands of going down through the sand to bedrock, he finds the contrast to be between one who carefully chooses and prepares a foundation and one who builds haphazardly (*WSNT*, vol. 1, p. 51).

7:28 / *Kai egeneto* occurs frequently in the LXX as a literal rendering of the Hebrew *wayhî*, translated in the AV by the familiar "and it came to pass."
Amazed: *ekplēssō* means (lit.) "to be struck out of one's senses." The imperfect tense pictures Jesus' hearers as spellbound as he finishes his address.

§8 A Ministry of Healing (Matt. 8:1–34)

Matthew summarized the public ministry of Jesus as teaching, preaching, and healing in chapter 4 (v. 23; repeated in 9:35). In chapters 5–7 we were introduced to the teaching ministry of Jesus. In chapters 8–9 we will learn of his ministry in deeds. This second main section of the Gospel comprises three series of acts of miraculous power. Each series has three miracles—one in the realm of nature (calming a storm, 8:23–27) and the other eight connected with some form of sickness. Between each set of three is a paragraph or two of material not about miracles (8:18–22; 9:9–17).

By isolating the account of the woman suffering from severe bleeding from the middle of the story of the Jewish official's daughter who had just died (9:18–26; see vv. 20–22), some count ten miracles. It is then suggested that Matthew has put together these two chapters in such a way as to parallel the ten plagues of Moses in Egypt. The conjecture is unlikely. It is true, however, that Matthew has brought together material that is scattered throughout the other Synoptics. Six of the miracles are also found in Mark, but located in chapters 1–10. By recording the miracles in a form more concise than Luke's, Matthew makes the statements of Jesus stand out more distinctly.

8:1–2 / As Jesus came **down from the mountainside** where he had been teaching, he was followed by a large group of people. **A man** suffering **with leprosy** approached Jesus and, falling to his knees, acknowledged Jesus' ability to cure him. True leprosy (caused by Hansen's bacillus) would probably have kept the man away from the crowd that surrounded Jesus. According to Jewish law, lepers lived in isolation and warned all who approached by crying out "unclean! unclean!" (Lev. 13:45). The Greek word refers to any sort of inflammatory skin disease, such as psoriasis or ringworm (cf. NIV text note; GNB aptly translates, "a dreaded skin disease"). In any case, the condition made the person ceremonially unclean (Lev. 13–14).

The reverent faith of the leper is seen both in his approach (he **knelt**; *proskyneō* regularly describes the act of prostrating oneself before a person of eminence) and in his address to Jesus (**Lord** is rendered by the GNB as "Sir," but in this context it is more than a polite title: Matthew uses it only of those who believe in Jesus; cf. 15:22; 17:15; 20:30–31). Jesus responded by reaching out and touching the leper—an act that, according to Leviticus 5:3, would not only make a person ceremonially unclean but also guilty (Lev. 5:5–6 describes the penalty and how atonement must be made). According to rabbinical practices, it was illegal even to greet a leper in an open place. Priests often ran and hid themselves upon seeing a leper in the distance.

8:3–4 / Jesus' response to the leper's **if you are willing, you can make me clean** was, "Of course I want to" (Phillips) "be clean again" (NEB). Immediately (*eutheōs*, v. 3) the leprosy was gone. Then Jesus charged the man not to say a word to anyone. Wilhelm Wrede (in 1901) was the first to suggest that this command to silence was a creation of Mark, who felt it necessary to explain why Jesus was not more widely recognized as the Messiah during his earthly ministry. It is far better to accept it as historical and understand it as Jesus' precaution against the rapid rise of a movement that did not understand the nature of his messiahship. Popular excitement would arouse Roman opposition and make it even more difficult to carry out a messianic ministry that was not national and militaristic but universal and sacrificial.

Jesus tells the cleansed leper to **go, show yourself to the priest** for the prescribed examination and **offer** the proper **gift** (Lev. 14:10ff.) This will serve **as a testimony to them** (*eis martyrion autois*). This rather difficult phrase may mean "as evidence of your cure" (TCNT) or may perhaps be an indication that Jesus had no intention of setting aside the law (cf. 5:17). The plural **them** could be either the crowds that observed the healing or the priests (the "ecclesiastical ministers of public health,") who would learn about it when the cleansed leper appeared at the temple to offer his sacrifice.

8:5–9 / Matthew's second miracle story has as its main point the remarkable faith of a Gentile. It foreshadows the ultimate inclusion of non-Jews in the kingdom of heaven and warns the nonreceptive Jews that they may find themselves excluded.

The account is found in a longer version in Luke (7:1–10) but not in Mark (a related story occurs in John 4:46–53). The major difference between the two is that in Matthew the centurion himself comes to Jesus, whereas in Luke he first sends a delegation of Jews from the local synagogue and subsequently a group of friends. It may be that Matthew in his shorter version passes over the original contact and that Luke does not bother to say that the centurion went with his friends to meet Jesus just outside Capernaum. The first-person discourse in Luke (7:6–8) certainly implies that the centurion went out to meet Jesus.

The Roman officer was probably not an official centurion (*hekatontarchos*: the commander of a hundred men), because in Jesus' day Galilee was not under Roman military occupation. That began after the death of Herod Agrippa in A.D. 44. Schweizer calls him a "Syrian Gentile in the service of Rome" (p. 213).

The officer met Jesus with the urgent request that he come and heal his **servant**, who was suffering from a painful form of paralysis. Since the Greek *pais* can mean "boy," some have taken the sick child to be the son of the centurion (as in John 4:49–50). The parallel in Luke's account (*doulos*, "servant") makes this less probable. Verse 7 is more likely an emphatic statement than a question (which would be, "Am I [a Jew] to come [into the house of a Gentile] and heal him?"). Jesus had just reached out and touched a leper: he would not hesitate to enter the house of a Gentile, an action that, though considered defiling by the rabbis, was not prohibited in the Old Testament.

The officer protested Jesus' decision to go to his house, saying that it was unnecessary for him to actually be there. If Jesus would simply give the order, the sickness would leave. As one who understood the role of authority, he acknowledged that the command alone would achieve the desired result. The *kai* in verse 9 should be translated "even" rather than "also" (ASV) or **myself** (NIV). The officer is arguing that even he, a subordinate authority, can accomplish his desire with an order. How much more can Jesus, the ultimate authority, perform a healing with no more than a word of command.

8:10–13 / Jesus is astonished at the faith of the centurion. He turns to those who are following and says, **I tell you the truth, I have not found anyone in Israel with such great faith** (v. 10).

The faith of which he speaks is absolute confidence in Jesus' power to speak the word and heal from a distance.

In Judaism, as well as in many of the Hellenistic mystery cults, the banquet was a symbol of great blessedness. To share a formal meal indicated close fellowship and a sense of solidarity. Jesus speaks of an eschatological messianic banquet attended not only by the renowned patriarchs of Israel but by **many** Gentiles **from the east and the west**. Isaiah spoke of the last days, when all the nations would stream into Zion (Isa. 2:1–5). Israel cherished this hope (Tob. 13:11; 1 Enoch 90:30–36) but saw it as an enhancement of its own nation and its glory. Jesus now says that those who should be in the kingdom of heaven will be cast out into outermost darkness. The contrast is between the brightly lit banquet hall and the blackness that prevails outside. In that place of eternal darkness where the faithless are **there will be weeping and gnashing of teeth**. To be excluded from what was considered a national destiny and to have Gentiles take their place was a shocking revelation to the Jewish religious establishment. They would never be able to accept as true the scenario that Jesus laid before them.

Jesus tells the officer to return home. On the basis of the centurion's faith, the servant is to be restored to wholeness. Matthew records that precisely at that moment the servant was indeed healed. Although the incident centers on a miraculous healing, the major emphasis is on the remarkable faith of the centurion. It parallels the previous account of the leper, who was fully convinced that Jesus could make him clean if he wanted to (8:2).

8:14–17 / From John 1:44 we know that Peter came from the town of Bethsaida (a fishing village on the north shore of Galilee just east of the Jordan). Mark 1:29 places the home of Peter in Capernaum, and 1 Corinthians 9:5 tells us that Peter was married. Jesus entered the home of Peter and found Peter's mother-in-law **in bed with a fever**. The fever was probably connected with malaria, which was common in that region.

Jesus reached out and touched the woman's hand; immediately she was restored to health. This is the only incident in Matthew in which Jesus takes the initiative in healing. Elsewhere there is a request of some sort. To touch a person with a fever was prohibited by Jewish law, but in Jesus the kingdom of God was actively invading the realm of Satan's control. The woman rose and began ministering (*diēkonei* is an inceptive imperfect) to Jesus (and the others as well, according to Mark 1:31).

When evening came (v. 16) the people brought to Jesus a great number of those who were possessed by demons and were suffering from various diseases. He **healed** them **all**. The sequence of events in Mark 1:21–34 and the clause "that evening after sunset" (v. 32) places the healing activity of Matthew 8:16 on the evening following the Sabbath (Jewish days begin at sunset the night before). To have brought the sick to Jesus during that day would have been to violate the prohibition against working on the Sabbath. Jesus simply speaks the **word** (as he did in the case of the centurion's servant, vv. 8, 13), and the sick are restored. Since exorcisms and the healing of disease are mentioned separately, it would appear that they are to be distinguished.

We have already encountered the formula quotation on several occasions (1:22–23; 2:5–6; 17–18, 23; 4:14–16). We now meet the first formula quotation within the public ministry of Jesus. Matthew quotes from the Hebrew text of Isaiah 53:4 using either his own translation or that of a non-LXX text that followed the Hebrew closely (the LXX spiritualizes, "He bears our sins and is pained for us"). He applies the text to the healing activity of Jesus in the physical realm (**He took up our infirmities and carried our diseases**). Elsewhere in the New Testament the Isaiah passage is used to support the vicarious and redemptive nature of Christ's ministry. Matthew's application of the prophecy of Isaiah to the healing ministry of Jesus is striking.

8:18–20 / Jesus' healing ministry in Capernaum had attracted a great many people. Seeing the **crowd around him**, Jesus orders his disciples to cross over to the eastern side of the lake. A scribe approaches Jesus and declares that he will follow him wherever he goes. Gundry lists five factors that favor identifying the scribe as a disciple rather than a professional teacher of the law (pp. 151–52), although elsewhere in Matthew those who address Jesus by the title teacher are nondisciples (12:38; 19:16; 22:16, 24, 36). Stendahl observes that the scribes who taught in the synagogues were not automatically enemies but potential and actual disciples (p. 781). To follow Jesus in this context means both to follow him across the lake (as a symbol of committed discipleship) and to follow his teaching (as a way of life). Physical following became a symbol of a new spiritual and ethical orientation.

Jesus' answer (v. 20) sounds very much like a general proverb adapted to this circumstance. Some have suggested that the **foxes** represent Herod and those who sided with him (Luke 13:32 calls him "that fox") and the **birds of the air** Gentiles, but the conjecture is unlikely. Jesus is simply pointing out that those who follow him will feel homeless. Schweizer notes that to follow Jesus is "to step forth into insecurity" (p. 219). Miracles create enthusiasts who need to learn the difficulties connected with discipleship before they start on the journey.

This is the first place in Matthew where Jesus designates himself **Son of Man**. The title represents the Aramaic *bar nāšā*, signifying "man." Most scholars trace its use by Jesus back to the apocalyptic figure in Daniel 7. This "one like a son of man" who comes with the clouds of heaven is both individual (Dan. 7:13–14) and corporate (Dan. 7:27). Within the Gospels the term is used exclusively by Jesus as a self-designation (twenty-nine times in Matthew alone). At times it is used in connection with the sufferings of Jesus during his earthly existence; elsewhere it is found in passages that emphasize the glory of his triumphant return at the end of the age.

8:21–22 / The first man said he would follow Jesus but he needed to be reminded of the cost. Now a second disciple says that he will follow Jesus but first must return home and **bury** his **father**. That the first would-be follower called Jesus "Teacher" (v. 19) and the second calls him "Lord" (v. 21; Gk. *kyrios*) does not help us identify the two with any precision. Both titles were polite ways of addressing Jesus as a recognized leader. Nor is it necessary to discover whether the man's father was in fact dead, on the point of dying, or would die sometime in the future. In ancient cultures the obligation to bury one's parents was a weighty responsibility. For the Jews it was a filial duty implied by the fifth commandment (cf. Tob. 4:3; 6:14).

Jesus' response to the hesitant disciple was, **Follow me, and let the dead bury their own dead** (v. 22). This enigmatic statement is often interpreted to mean that the task of burying the physically dead is to be left to the spiritually dead (those not responding to the urgency of the kingdom message). It is probably better to take it in a more general way as indicating that the ordinary priorities of this life are to give way to the demands of Christian discipleship. (In Luke 14:25-33 one cannot be a disciple without placing Christ above family ties, carrying one's own cross, and giving up everything one has.)

8:23-27 / Jesus now gets into a boat with his disciples and starts across the Sea of Galilee. This pear-shaped lake (eight miles wide and thirteen miles from north to south) lies 680 feet below sea level. The high hills that surround it are cut with deep ravines that act like great funnels drawing violent winds from the heights down onto the lake without warning. The boat carrying Jesus is caught in one such **storm** (*seismos* literally means "earthquake"). Waves rise and crash over the deck. Some writers note that the boat is "covered" (AV, v. 24; Gk. *kalyptō*), in the sense that it appeared to sink in the troughs between the waves. But this would scarcely be enough to frighten seasoned sailors (cf. v. 25). Gundry holds that the storm posed no threat to the disciples, but, in correspondence with Matthew 28:2, it was a sign of Jesus' majesty (p. 155). Interpretations of this sort have made the prior decision that the evangelist is a literary artist rather than a reliable narrator.

The imperfect *ekatheuden* (**was sleeping**) and the emphatic pronoun *autos* contrast Jesus with the terrified disciples. They wake him up with the cry, **Lord, save us!** "We are going down" (Williams). Jesus first chides them for their lack of faith (*deilos* means "cowardly") and then rebukes the storm. The personal nature of the verb (**rebuked**) suggests that he treats the violent forces of nature as demonic (cf. Job 38:11). Immediately there is a great calm. The disciples are amazed and exclaim, **What kind of man is this?** The response is less a question than an exclamation. Jesus' mastery over the elements of nature leaves them dumbfounded. Due to the use of the plural **men** (*anthrōpoi*) in verse 27, some have thought that the amazement belonged to those who later were told the story. Though the accounting of the miracle would undoubtedly produce that effect, the immediate reference is to those who experienced the sudden stilling of the storm.

8:28-29 / The story of Jesus casting out demons and sending them into a herd of swine who then rushed down a steep bank and into the lake (vv. 28-32) is held by many interpreters to be an example of ancient people misunderstanding insanity in terms of demon possession. Filson comments, "Obviously the story uses patterns of thought not satisfactory to modern men, who would call these demoniacs mentally deranged" (p. 116). Rather than arguing questions such as whether demon possession was a primitive explanation of eccentric behavior or whether it was morally right for Jesus to destroy a large herd of pigs, it is better to hear the story as it was told and to come to grips with what it intends to tell us about the authority of Jesus over all the powers of the supernatural realm.

The event took place in the **region of the Gadarenes**. The city of Gadara (one of the cities of the Decapolis, a federation of ten Greek cities in central Palestine) lay some five miles southeast of the Sea of Galilee. Jesus is met by **two demon-possessed men** who were so violent that no one dared to travel the road near the **tombs** where they lived. In ancient times graves were associated with the world of demons and unclean spirits. That the accounts in Mark and Luke speak of one demoniac rather than two causes no particular problem. Each synoptist tells the story in a way that emphasizes what he wishes to get across.

Suddenly the demons cry out, objecting to Jesus' arrival before the appointed time. They know Jesus as **Son of God** (one possessed by divine power) and recognize that their own destiny is punishment. Their objection is that Jesus has advanced the time of their torture. Intertestamental literature describes the final doom of fallen angels (cf. *1 Enoch* 15-17). Their knowledge of the supernatural world is reflected in James 2:19, "Even the demons believe that [there is only one God]—and shudder."

8:30-34 / The presence of a **herd of pigs** in the vicinity indicates that the event took place in non-Jewish territory (according to b. *Baba Kamma* 7, the Jews were not allowed to raise pigs). The demons beg that if they are cast out they be allowed to enter the swine. Jesus tells them to go. They enter the pigs, and the entire herd immediately rushes down the steep bank and into the sea. The Greek text of Matthew (v. 32) makes it clear that it was the demons who **died in the water** (*apethanon* is plural, whereas *he agelē*, the **herd**, is singular), although it is assumed that the pigs were drowned as well. The entire episode would be a vivid demonstration to the demoniacs and to all observers that Jesus possessed authority over the realm of evil spirits. Sympathy for the pigs and their owners overlooks the priority Jesus puts on the value of the individual made in God's image. When the people of the nearby town learn what happened they flock out to meet Jesus, but upon seeing him they urge him to **leave their region.** They were unnerved not by the financial loss but by an awareness of Jesus' supernatural authority. They had come out for the purpose of seeing a person who had power to exorcise evil spirits, but upon actually meeting him they were anxious to get him away from their area.

Additional Notes §8

8:8 / **Under my roof:** The Mishnah says, "The dwelling-places of Gentiles are unclean."

8:11 / **Take their places:** Gk. *anaklinomai* means "to recline." See Str.-B. vol. 4, pp. 618f. for the Jewish practice of eating while reclining at the table. Leonardo da Vinci's *Last Supper,* picturing the disciples sitting at a table, is misleading.

8:12 / **The darkness:** Cf. 22:13 and 25:30 for other occurrences of this uniquely Matthean expression.
Gnashing of teeth: The expression is found six times in Matthew 13:42, 50; 22:13; 24:51; 25:30) and only once in Luke (13:28). It is a vivid Eastern metaphor for sorrow and remorse.

8:14 / **Peter:** Clement of Alexandria (a second-century convert to Christianity) wrote that Peter and his wife suffered martyrdom together (*Miscellanies* 7.6).

8:16 / **Spirits . . . and . . . all the sick:** The Phillips translation ("Indeed, he healed all who were ill") tends to blur this distinction.

8:17 / This verse is a basic proof text for those who believe that physical healing as well as spiritual healing has been provided by the atoning death of Jesus.
To fulfill: Stendahl holds that the formula quotations originated with a school led by a converted rabbi who applied Jewish methods of teaching to a new cause (p. 770).

8:20 / **Son of Man:** Albright-Mann translate *hyios tou anthrōpou* with "the Man," on the basis that it emphasizes the representative character of Jesus' ministry as Matthew sees it and is more faithful to the original Hebrew/Aramaic (p. 95). For the extensive literature on the subject, see *NIDNTT* vol. 3, p. 665.

8:28 / **Gadarenes**: Some early manuscripts read "Gerasenes" or "Gergesenes" rather than **Gadarenes**. Gerasa, however, was about thirty miles from the sea, and Gergasa (near the lake?) may have entered the manuscript tradition as a correction posed by Origen (Metzger, *TCGNT,* pp. 23–24).

8:29 / **Before the appointed time**: According to *1 Enoch,* evil spirits proceeding from the giants "afflict, oppress, destroy, attack, do battle, and work destruction . . . until the day of the consummation, the great judgment" (15:11–16:1).

9:1–8 / Jesus leaves the region of Gadara on the east shore of Galilee and returns by boat to Capernaum (cf. Mark 2:1). There, some men bring to him a **paralytic, lying on a mat**. In Jesus' day most people slept on mattresslike pads on the floor. Thus the **mat** would be a sort of pallet or stretcher that could be carried without undue difficulty. When Jesus saw their **faith**, that is, their confidence that he could restore the paralyzed man to health, he said, **Take heart, son; your sins are forgiven.**

In the ancient world there was a widespread belief that sickness was the result of sin. Barclay cites Rabbi Chija ben Abba as representative of this point of view: "No sick person is cured from sickness, until all his sins are forgiven him" (vol. 1, p. 327). In John 9 Jesus' disciples ask concerning the blind man, "who sinned, this man or his parents, that he was born blind?" (v. 2). Note that Jesus makes no necessary connection between sin and sickness. He responds, "Neither this man nor his parents sinned" (John 9:3).

Since it was widely accepted that only God could forgive sin (cf. Isa. 43:25), the point of view of the scribes seemed irrefutable. Jesus, in declaring that the sins of the paralyzed man were forgiven, was **blaspheming** (v. 3). The only alternative would be that Jesus was a divine being, and that was a conclusion they chose not to accept. As the official exponents of the law it was their duty to be on the lookout for heretical teaching. The punishment for blasphemy was stoning (m. *Sanh.* 7.4).

Jesus perceived their inward reasoning and proposed a test. Since they accepted the premise that sickness was the result of sin, if a person had the power to heal, then his authority to forgive the sin that caused the sickness would have to be accepted. Jesus therefore says, **But so that you may know that the Son of Man has authority on earth to forgive sins . . .** (v. 6). It is noteworthy that nowhere else except in Luke 7:48 is Jesus pictured as forgiving sins. He was named Jesus because he would "save

his people from their sins" (Matt. 1:21), but this forgiveness would
come as a result of his atoning death (26:28), not from a ministry
of absolution. Jesus' reference to himself as the **Son of Man** is
more than a simple substitute for "I." It contains overtones of
supernatural authority and celestial dignity.

Jesus turns to the paralyzed man and orders him to rise,
take up his **mat and go home**. The moment of truth has come.
The man "sprang to his feet" (Phillips) and headed for home.
Those who witnessed the miracle were struck with awe and
praised God that **such authority** was given **to men**. Some commentators see in this statement a reference to later Christians, who
would declare sins forgiven and perform miraculous cures to sub-
stantiate that pronouncement (Gundry, p. 165). Others take it as
an indication that the crowd understood **Son of Man** (v. 6) in the
sense of "man" (Tasker, p. 96).

9:9 / As Jesus leaves Capernaum (cf. Mark 2:1), he sees
a man named Matthew sitting at the tax collector's booth alongside the road. In Jesus' day heavy taxes were levied upon the
people for all sorts of things. In addition to the three main taxes
(ground tax, income tax, and poll tax), duty was imposed upon
all imported goods. Every caravan that used the main roads and
the ships that came into harbor were taxed. Matthew was one
of a widely despised group who collected taxes from the Jewish
people and turned them over to Herod Antipas, tetrarch of Galilee and Perea. His booth was probably along the great highway
that led from Damascus to the sea. Some writers, perhaps because of Mark 2:13-14, put his place of business near the sea, in
which case he would collect duty on goods shipped in from the
territory under the jurisdiction of Philip. Although tax gatherers
were not necessarily ceremonially unclean, their involvement with
pagan currency and their reputation for dishonesty caused law-
abiding Jews to keep their distance.

In both Mark (2:14) and Luke (5:27) Matthew is named
Levi, although this latter name occurs in none of the listings
of the twelve apostles (Matt. 10:3; Mark 3:18; Luke 6:15; Acts
1:13). Either **Matthew** is the name given to Levi when he became a disciple or both names belonged to the same person
from the beginning. When Jesus says to the tax gatherer, **Follow
me**, Matthew immediately leaves his place of business and follows the Lord.

9:10–13 / We next see Jesus as host to a number of **tax collectors and "sinners."** These were common people who paid little or no attention to the strict requirements of ceremonial law. The NIV places the affair **at Matthew's house** (as suggested in the Lucan parallel, 5:29), although the Greek text of Matthew simply says "in the house" with Jesus as the probable antecedent. However, for Jesus to have a house would run counter to his statement in Matthew 8:20 that "the Son of Man has no place to lay his head." While they were reclining at dinner (a style popular in the Greco-Roman world and copied by wealthy Jews) **the Pharisees** came and asked Jesus' disciples why their teacher ate with "irreligious people" (Goodspeed). They intended to undermine the faith of the disciples.

Jesus overheard their query and answered ironically that it was not those in good health but the sick who require the help of a doctor. The **healthy** were the Pharisees who saw themselves as having no need, although their true condition was quite the opposite (cf. Rev. 3:17–18). The **sick** were the outcasts, who recognized their need for healing. Green (p. 104) quotes a similar saying attributed to Diogenes (a fourth century B.C. Cynic philosopher): "Neither does a physician who is capable of giving health practice among those who are well."

Jesus counsels the Pharisees to go and learn (a common rabbinic formula) what the Scripture means when it says that God desires mercy, not sacrifice. The quotation is from Hosea 6:6. Jesus' ministry to the ceremonially unacceptable is an act of mercy, and this pleases God more than the Pharisees' fastidious attention to sacrificial offerings. **Mercy** translates the Hebrew *ḥesed*, a word rich in meaning and conveying the idea of strong covenant faithfulness and love. Jesus then interprets his earlier statement by adding, **I have not come to call the righteous, but sinners** (v. 13). The pronouncement reveals a consciousness of having come to this world from a heavenly sphere. There is no reason to assign this insight to the faith of the early church (as some do), unless one begins with the assumption that Jesus was no more than a man or that he was unaware of his divine origin.

9:14–17 / Jesus is still at table with tax collectors and "sinners" (v. 10) when a group of followers of John the Baptist come and ask him why his disciples do not **fast.** Pharisees apparently fasted twice a week (cf. Luke 18:12; *Didache* 8), and John's

disciples fasted as well. In the previous paragraph the question
was whether Jesus should be eating with outcasts; now the question is whether he should be eating at all! (Hill, p. 175). His failure to satisfy the religious scruples of sectarians would become
a continuing irritant.

Jesus answers with a reference to the Jewish wedding feast.
In that setting it would be inappropriate for the guests to mourn
while [the bridegroom] is with them (v. 15). Later, when **the
bridegroom** was **taken from them**, there would be time for fasting. In this figure Jesus is the **bridegroom**, and his disciples are
the **guests**. The Old Testament often pictures the relationship of
God and his people as a marriage (Hos. 2:16-20; Isa. 54:5-6; cf.
2 Cor. 11:2; Rev. 21:9f.). The messianic wedding feast is under
way: now is the season for joy, not mourning. The reference to
a day when the bridegroom will be taken away anticipates the
death of Jesus. Some modern commentators feel this reveals the
point of view of the early church (Filson, p. 140; Green, p. 104).
The argument is only as strong as one's conviction that Jesus
would not have been able at this point in his ministry to predict
his own demise.

Two illustrations from everyday life point up the essential
discontinuity between the old forms of worship in Judaism and
the new spirit of the messianic age. No one takes a piece of un-
shrunk (Gk. *agnaphos*) cloth to patch a hole in an old garment,
because upon washing it would shrink and tear away, leaving the
hole worse than ever. Likewise you do not put fresh wine in old
wineskins, because as it ferments the pressure will break the hardened skins and both wine and wineskin will be spoiled. In context, the new cloth and fresh wine represent the joyous spirit of
the new age. Old garments and hardened wineskins are the restrictive forms of previous worship. In Romans 7:6 the same two
Greek words are used to compare the "old [*palaiotēti*] way of a
written code" and the "new [*kainotēti*] way of the Spirit." Gundry
notes that Matthew emphasizes the preservation of the wineskins,
which points up Matthew's stress on the coming of Jesus to fulfill the Law and the Prophets rather than to destroy them (p. 171).

9:18-19 / As Jesus continues to teach, **a Jewish ruler**
comes to him in behalf of his **daughter** who **has just died**. Kneel-
ing before Jesus, he declares that if Jesus will but come and touch
her she will be restored to life. This **ruler** of the synagogue (as

Mark and Luke both identify him) was an important person in the Jewish community. To seek the help of one who would be considered a dangerous heretic by the orthodox indicated how desperate he was. His faith in the power of Jesus to perform such an act suggests that those in the synagogue were fully aware of the activity and claims of Jesus. Jesus' response is immediate. He rises from the table and, accompanied by his disciples, starts toward the home of the **ruler**.

It is often noted that Matthew's accounts are considerably shorter than Mark's. This narrative is only one third the length of Mark's. Differences between the accounts are often mentioned. However, since it is not the primary purpose of this work to comment on the relationships among the Synoptics, our discussion will focus on the account as it occurs in Matthew.

9:20–22 / While Jesus was on the way to the ruler's house, a **woman** who had for **twelve years** suffered with chronic bleeding approached Jesus from behind and touched the border of his robe. The **edge** (*kraspedon*) of Jesus' robe may refer to one of the tassels, which, according to Numbers 15:37–41 (cf. Deut. 22:12), were to be worn on the four corners of the outer garment. The tassels would remind the people of the commandments of God. The woman's flow of blood made her ritually unclean (Lev. 15:19–33), which accounts for her coming to Jesus from **behind**. She kept saying (*elegen* is imperfect) to herself that if she were able to touch his robe she would be healed.

Jesus turns and says, "Cheer up; your confidence in me has brought you healing." The perfect tense (*sesōken*) suggests that the woman was healed even before Jesus spoke. Yet it was Jesus' presence and power, not the woman's faith, that effected the cure. Faith plays the vital role of releasing the divine activity (Tasker, p. 100).

9:23–26 / Following this "miracle within a miracle" Jesus continues to the house of the Jewish official. Upon arriving, he finds the characteristic disturbance created by professional mourners, which included **flute players** (Gk. *aulētai*). The Talmud indicates that even the poor were expected to provide two flute players and one wailing woman (b. *Ketub.* 46b). In ancient times, because of the rapid decomposition of the body, it was important that the corpse be buried within a few hours of death.

Jesus orders everyone to leave, declaring that the girl is **not dead but asleep**. That the people understood his words literally is seen in their reaction—"They laughed derisively at Him" (Berkeley). Although the figure of sleep is used in both the Old and New Testaments for death (Dan. 12:2; 1 Thess. 5:10), the Greek verb here (*katheudō,* "is sleeping") is not found elsewhere in the New Testament in that sense. Thus Barclay, for instance, understands the girl to be in a coma, from which state Jesus brought her back and thereby kept her from being buried alive (vol. 1, p. 345). It is far more likely that she had in fact died and that Jesus, the giver of life, raised her from the dead.

9:27–31 / Isaiah 35 tells of a coming day when God will open the eyes of the blind and unstop the ears of the deaf (v. 5). Matthew's account of Jesus as the giver of sight says, in effect, that the day of messianic deliverance has arrived.

As Jesus walks along, **two blind men** follow him and call for mercy. The title they apply to him, **Son of David**, was messianic, but in the popular mind meant little more than wonder-worker. Jesus apparently paid scant attention to their cries and went inside. Seeing them follow him inside, he asks if they believe in his power to heal their blindness (v. 28), a common malady in the ancient world. Lack of sanitary conditions made blindness from infection widespread.

In response to their affirmative answer Jesus **touched their eyes**, and **their sight was restored**. Moffatt translates, "As you believe, so your prayer is granted." The attitude of faith allows the giver of sight to pronounce the authoritative word. Jesus now sternly warns them (*embrimaomai* suggests strong emotion; in some early texts it was used of the snorting of horses) not to tell anyone. It would hinder the true messianic work of Jesus should he gain undue fame as a healer. The blind men, however, not being able to contain themselves, **spread the news** everywhere.

9:32–34 / Matthew alone records this next unit about the healing of the demoniac who could not speak, although the statement in verse 34 about **the prince of demons** (Beelzebub) is found in Mark 3:22 and in Luke 11:15. It fulfills the promise of Isaiah that "the eyes of the blind [will] be opened and the ears of the deaf unstopped" (Isa. 35:5).

As Jesus and the others left the house where the two blind men had been healed, Jesus was met by a group who brought to him a mute. The Greek (*kōphos*) can mean either deaf or unable to speak (or both) but in this context stresses the inability to speak. The man's condition was the result of a **demon**. When Jesus drove out the demon the man began to talk, and everyone was astonished. They exclaimed, **Nothing like this has ever been seen in Israel**. The reaction of the religious leaders was quite different. Instead of acknowledging the power of God at work, they decided that it was by the power of the prince of the demons that Jesus had performed the exorcism. The contrast in how the healing was perceived is Matthew's major point.

9:35-38 / From 9:35 through 10:42 we have Matthew's second large collection of sayings. Verse 35 is virtually equivalent to 4:23, which introduced the previous collection, chapters 5-7 (since there were no chapter divisions in ancient manuscripts, writers used other methods to indicate internal structure). Once again Jesus' itinerant ministry is described as teaching, preaching, and healing (v. 35).

As Jesus looked out on the surrounding crowds, he was deeply moved with compassion. They appeared as **sheep without a shepherd**, "distracted and dejected" (Weymouth). The Greek *errimmenoi* means **helpless**. The image of shepherdless sheep occurs repeatedly in the Old Testament. Micaiah tells the king of Israel, "I saw all Israel scattered on the hills like sheep without a shepherd" (1 Kings 22:17: cf. Num. 27:17). It was used by Jesus (John 10:1-18) and the early church (1 Pet. 2:25) as well.

In the helplessness of the crowd Jesus sees an opportunity for the proclamation of the kingdom. So he tells his disciples to pray that the Lord of the harvest will send workers to gather in the lost. Since the figure of the harvest often occurred in connection with judgment (Isa. 17:11; Matt. 13:30), some feel that the summons to the disciples was to warn people of approaching doom and to call them to repentance. The context suggests the more positive note of the approaching kingdom (see 10:7-8).

Additional Notes §9

9:2 / **Forgiven**: Gk. *aphientai* is present passive, indicating that the sins of the paralyzed man were either "in a state of remission" or were "at [that] moment remitted" (McNeile, p. 115).

9:10 / **Tax collectors**: For the role of tax collectors in the time of Christ, see *TDNT*, vol. 8, pp. 88–105.

"Sinners": Albright-Mann translate *hamartōloi* with "nonobservant [Jews]" and note that they were considered sinners primarily because they "had to handle currency with pagan inscriptions and pagan iconography" (p. 105).

9:13 / **Go and learn what this means**: "Go and learn" was a common rabbinic formula used to encourage the pupil toward understanding (Str.-B., vol. 1, p. 499).

9:15 / **Guests of the bridegroom**: Gk. *hyioi tou nymphōnos* means (lit.) "sons of the bride chamber" (*nymphōn* is a wedding hall). It is a Hebrew idiom for wedding guests.

9:16–17 / Though these verses are usually taken as teaching the difference between the Christian community and Judaism, Albright-Mann understand them as a judgment by Jesus on the position taken by the followers of John the Baptist. The messianic kingdom had come, and there could be no room for a competing community who remained loyal to John (pp. 108–9).

9:23 / In the Near Eastern world grief was expressed toward God by silent and reverent submission (cf. Job 1:21). Toward friends and neighbors, it took the form of open and tumultuous wailing. At the moment of death a shrill wail summoned others to the home of the deceased to join in the mourning. Professional mourners were hired as part of the tradition, and the entire ritual followed a pattern.

9:25 / Parallel stories are connected with Elijah (1 Kings 17:17–24), Elisha (2 Kings 4:17–37), and Peter (Acts 9:36–41).

9:34 / This verse is omitted by a number of manuscripts, but most textual scholars accept its inclusion. Metzger notes that the evidence for the shorter text is exclusively Western and that the passage seems to be needed to prepare the reader for 10:25 (*TCGNT*, pp. 25–26).

10:1–4 / Jesus called together his **twelve disciples** and **gave them authority to drive out evil spirits and to heal every disease and sickness**. The distinction between exorcism and healing suggests that they are two different functions. This is the first mention of the twelve disciples in Matthew. He assumes they are known to the reader. That there are twelve disciples follows from the fact that they represent the new Israel: the twelve tribes of Israel find their counterpart in the twelve disciples. Interestingly, there were twelve members in the Qumran council as well (1QS 7.1ff.).

The disciples are here (v. 2) called **apostles** (the only occurrence of the word in Matthew). An apostle was one who was "sent on a mission" (Gk. *apostellō*). Beare holds that the title denoted a charismatic function rather than a specific office and that it was not limited to the Twelve (p. 240). In 1 Corinthians 15:5, 7, there is a distinction between the Twelve and "all the apostles."

The names of the disciples are also listed here and in Mark 3:16–19, Luke 6:13–16, and Acts 1:13. The order varies somewhat, although Simon Peter heads each list and Judas Iscariot is always last (obviously, he is not listed in Acts). All lists have as the first four the two sets of brothers, **Peter** and **Andrew**, **James** and **John**. Matthew's designation of Peter as **first** (v. 2) probably means first and foremost rather than first in the list. Since Mark wrote his Gospel as it came to him through Peter, it is understandable that this reference would be missing in his list (Mark 3:16). After listing James and John, Mark adds "to them he gave the name Boanerges, which means Sons of Thunder" (Mark 3:17).

The second set of four names in each list includes: **Philip and Bartholomew; Thomas and Matthew. Bartholomew** is a patronymic (*Bar Talmai*, son of Talmai; cf. 2 Sam. 13:37) rather than a name. He is commonly identified with Nathanael of John 1:46. The name **Thomas** means "twin," as does the Greek *didymos* (Didymus; cf. John 11:16). Only in the Gospel of Matthew is Matthew called **the tax collector**. It reflects the author's amazement that Jesus would call into his service one who had served in such a disreputable occupation.

In the final set of four only the infamous **Judas Iscariot** is well known. **James son of Alphaeus** is so named in order to distinguish him from James the brother of John. **Thaddaeus** (some manuscripts have Lebbaeus) is called "Judas son of James" in both Luke and Acts. It is conjectured that Judas was his original name but, after stigma was attached to the name by Judas Iscariot, he changed it to Thaddaeus (meaning "warmhearted"). The NIV's **Simon the Zealot** interprets the Greek *simōn ho kananaios* ("Simon the Cananaean"), not in a geographical sense, but as derived from a Hebrew root meaning "zealous." Whether this described his energetic character or referred to a former relationship with the Zealot party is uncertain. If **Judas Iscariot** means "Judas, man of Kerioth" he would be the only non-Galilean among the disciples. But "Kerioth" is of uncertain derivation.

It is noteworthy that only Peter, James, and John play any role in the Book of Acts. The disciples were all Jewish by ancestry and probably remained with that branch of Christianity after the church became increasingly Gentile in the second half of the first century. For that reason, our knowledge of their later lives comes primarily from tradition.

10:5–10 / The twelve apostles (*apostoloi*) are now sent out (*apesteilen*) to proclaim the message of the kingdom. They are not to go **among the Gentiles** or into any of the towns of Samaria. Galilee was surrounded by pagan lands on all sides except the south. In that direction lay Samaria, a country in which Israelites not deported to Babylon had intermarried with the occupation forces. The Twelve were commissioned to take the message to **the lost sheep of Israel** (v. 6). A common critical opinion is that this injunction could not have originated with Jesus but "emanated from those circles of the early church which were opposed to such an extension of the mission" (Beare, pp. 241–42). There was no need, so the argument goes, to warn the disciples against something that never would have been in their minds to do. The instructions of Jesus, however, are consistent with the New Testament emphasis that God has directed his redemptive efforts to the Jew first and then to the Gentile (cf. Rom. 1:16; 2:9, 10). Rieu translates, "Do not stray into the pagan lands." First of all, the message goes to God's ancient people. Later, the disciples will be commissioned to "go and make disciples of all nations" (Matt. 28:19).

In sending the Twelve to the lost sheep of the people of Israel Jesus was, according to some views, directing his disciples to the *'am hā'āreṣ* ("the people of the land," those who did not follow all the ceremonial prescriptions of Judaism). It is more likely that the reference was to all of Israel. Like sheep that have wandered from the fold (cf. 9:36), they are spiritually scattered and in need of help. This regathering would be the dawn of the messianic age.

The message to be proclaimed is that the **kingdom of heaven** has drawn **near**. The long-awaited reign of God is about to break into human history (in concert with the realized eschatology of C. H. Dodd, Phillips translates, "has arrived"). That is why the **sick** will be healed, **demons** will be driven out, and the **dead** will be raised to life. A number of Greek manuscripts (mostly later) omit the reference to raising the dead, although the editors of the UBS text do not question its originality (cf. Metzger, *TCGNT*, pp. 27–28). Commentators uncomfortable with the apparent intention of the phrase (**raise the dead**) suggest that it should be taken metaphorically to mean the restoration to life of those who are dead in trespasses and sins.

The punctuation of the Greek text connects the two final clauses of verse 8 with what precedes. It is better to take them with the instructions that follow. They have freely received, so they are to give freely. There is no need to take along money or extra provisions, because a worker should receive those things from the people served. The NIV mention of **belts** or "girdles" (*zōnai*), refers to the ancient custom of tucking money into the waistband.

In addition to starting out without **gold or silver or copper**, the Twelve are not to take a knapsack for carrying food, an **extra tunic, or sandals or a staff**. In Mark's account they are allowed to take a staff and wear sandals but not to take an extra garment (Mark 6:8–9). Luke prohibits a staff (Luke 9:3). These discrepancies have been explained in different ways. The simplest way to understand Matthew's divergence from Mark is to take the "two" (or **extra** as the NIV has it) with **sandals** and **staff** as well as **tunic**. It would hardly be reasonable to understand Matthew as saying that the Twelve are to travel barefoot and without a staff for protection against snakes and wild animals. They are to travel unencumbered and allow their hearers to take care of their daily needs.

10:11–15 / Verses 11–15 instruct the Twelve regarding their entrance into towns. Upon arriving at a **town or village** they are to find lodging with a family willing to put them up and to stay there until their work is done. They are not to change lodging in search of more comfortable accommodations. Gundry holds that the **worthy** (v. 11) host would be a fellow disciple and that the charge is to stay, not where they find hospitality, but "where the proclamation of the Kingdom has already found a favorable reception" (p. 188).

As the disciples enter a house, they are to give the Semitic **greeting** (v. 12) "peace be with you." If the family in the home is **deserving** (Lamsa, "trustworthy") the greeting of **peace** is to **rest on it**; if not, it is to **return** to the disciples. In ancient days a pronouncement of this sort was thought to have an objective existence. It could be taken back as well as given. In Isaiah 55 God's word is said to go out and accomplish that which he desires (Isa. 55:11). Whenever the disciples are refused hospitality, they are to leave and **shake the dust off** their **feet**. This gesture indicates they have nothing in common with those who reject the message and that the town or house is delivered to divine judgment (cf. Pilate washing his hands, Matt. 27:24). The act itself is a way of saying that one is standing on what must be considered "heathen" soil that must not be carried back to the Holy Land. So serious is the judgment that on Judgment Day God will show greater mercy to the people of the notoriously wicked **Sodom and Gomorrah** (Gen. 19; cf. Luke 17:29; 2 Pet. 2:6) than to those who reject the disciples and their message.

10:16–20 / The Twelve were pictured in the previous paragraph as normally received in a fairly friendly manner. In the verses that follow there await rejection and persecution. Since verses 17–22 parallel closely the apocalyptic discourse in Mark 13:9–13, most commentators understand that Matthew is here looking beyond the immediate mission of the disciples to the future evangelistic ministry of the church. In Mark, suffering is a sign of the approaching end (13:29); in Matthew, it is an unavoidable part of missionary activity. There is no particular rea-

son that words uttered by Jesus must be restricted to a single setting. His sayings have manifold application and were undoubtedly repeated on many occasions.

The Twelve are sent out **like sheep among wolves** (v. 16).
They are without defense against the ferocious attacks of their
opponents. Therefore they must be as prudent (the LXX at Gen.
3:1 uses *phronimos* of Satan in the guise of a snake) as serpents
and as harmless or **innocent** (*akeraios* means "unmixed," thus here
"with purity of intention") **as doves**. Paul gives similar advice in
Romans 16:19, "I want you to be wise about what is good, and
innocent about what is evil."

The disciples are going to be opposed both by Jewish leaders (v. 17) and by gentile authorities (v. 18). Their "fellow men"
(TCNT) will betray them to local councils, where they will be
whipped (*mastigoō* is used in John 19:1 of the scourging of Jesus).
In Jesus' day the Roman government had delegated to the Sanhedrin (the Jewish high council) ultimate authority in legal affairs
as well as in religious matters, as long as they did not encroach
upon the authority of the Roman procurator (BAGD, p. 786).
Deuteronomy 25:1–3 outlines the procedure for giving a guilty
man up to forty lashes (see Acts 22:19; 2 Cor. 11:24). The disciples will also be dragged before **governors and kings** (v. 18).
The immediate reference would be to Roman provincial governors
and puppet kings like the Herodian princes (who were actually
tetrarchs). However, God has a purpose in opposition such as this.
It is to the end (Gk. *eis*) that the disciples will be **witnesses** to
both Jew and Gentile (the antecedent of **them** in v. 18 is the group
identified in v. 17). The disciples' testimony is not "against" (AV)
but **to** their opponents. Their purpose is primarily to convince
the unconverted, not convict their adversaries (Green, p. 110).

Jesus instructs his disciples not to worry about what they
are to say or how they are to speak when they are brought to
trial. When the time comes they **will be given** (that is, God will
tell them) **what to say**. The words that they speak will not be their
own. It will be **the Spirit of** their **Father** (the Holy Spirit) who
will speak through them. Unfortunately, this verse has provided
too many preachers an excuse for not adequately preparing the
Sunday sermon. Spurgeon, the nineteenth-century English Baptist, always put his sermon together on Saturday evening, but he
had spent the entire week in reading and preparation.

10:21-25 / The prophet Micah spoke of the day of God's visitation as a time when "a man's enemies [will be] the members of his own household" (Mic. 7:6). In *1 Enoch* 56:7 we read, "A man shall not know his brother, nor a son his father or his mother, till there be no number of the corpses through their slaughter." Faithful witnesses will meet opposition not only from Jew and Gentile but also from members of their own families. **Brother will betray brother**, and **children** will have **parents . . . put to death**. Disciples of Christ will be the object of universal hatred because they bear the name Christian (cf. 1 Pet. 4:14). Some take the phrase **because of me** (lit., "on account of my name," v. 22) to mean the use of Jesus' name (as in Matt. 7:22) for exorcisms and healings. Those who hold out in the face of persecution until the coming of the Son of Man will be saved. Obviously, they are not spared persecution; rather, they are shielded against spiritual harm and delivered into the coming kingdom. Holding out to the end (v. 22) does not mean remaining in those towns where they are being persecuted. Being wise as serpents (v. 16) means moving on to other villages. There is no particular virtue in unnecessary martyrdom.

Verse 23 is difficult. A straightforward reading of the text indicates that before the Twelve finish their mission to the towns of Israel the Son of Man will come. Albert Schweitzer based his entire scheme of thoroughgoing eschatology on this verse. He held that Jesus thought that the mission of the Twelve would bring in the kingdom. He was disappointed when it did not turn out that way. Later Jesus attempted to bring in the kingdom by his own vicarious suffering. That was his final disappointment (Schweitzer, *The Quest of the Historical Jesus*, pp. 358-63). Others have suggested that verse 23b originated at a later period and is an argument against the church's mission to non-Jews, on the grounds of an imminent Parousia. Barclay explains it by suggesting that Matthew, who writes at a time later than Mark, reads into a promise of the coming of the kingdom (cf. Mark 9:1) a promise of the second coming of Christ (vol. 1, p. 382). Others hold that the "coming" is a coming of judgment on Israel.

One thing we do know is that by the time Matthew wrote, the mission of the Twelve was history and the Parousia had not taken place. This points to a different understanding of what it means for the Son of Man to come. Gundry holds that in writing

verse 23 Matthew "implies a continuing mission to Israel alongside the mission to Gentiles" (p. 194). This explanation involves
considerable subtlety. Tasker is of the opinion that the verse is
best understood "with reference to the coming of the Son of Man
in triumph after His resurrection" (p. 108). Unless Matthew is putting words that reflect a later situation into the mouth of Jesus,
or Jesus was simply mistaken (as Schweitzer holds), this explanation is the most satisfactory.

Verses 24–25 argue that followers of Christ should not be
surprised if they receive the same treatment as their teacher and
master. If the head of the family is called **Beelzebub** (or Beelzebul, "the prince of demons," 12:24; cf. 9:34), how much more
will be slandered those of his household. The exact origin of the
name Beelzebub is uncertain, although many commentators connect it in some way with Baal-Zebub, the god of Ekron (2 Kings
1:2, 6). The Greek *oikodespotēs* ("head of the house") is a pun on
the name Beelzebub.

10:26–31 / Three times in this paragraph Jesus counsels
his disciples against fear. First, they are not to be **afraid of** people
(v. 26). The day is coming when everything that has been hidden from public scrutiny will be openly displayed. The secret
plans will be known to all. As far as the disciples' ministry is concerned, that time is now. What Jesus has told them in comparative privacy they are to proclaim publicly. Those things they have
learned in personal conversation must now be announced to the
whole world. **Roofs** regularly functioned as platforms for important public announcements. It is often noted that Jesus' words
about the disclosure of hidden things are used by Luke to warn
against hypocrisy (Luke 12:1–3), whereas in Matthew they call
for a public declaration of the message the disciples have learned
in private. The proverbial nature of the statements of Jesus makes
them applicable to many situations.

Second, the disciples are not to fear those who may **kill
the body** but are powerless to **kill the soul** (v. 28). Rather, they
should fear God, who is able to destroy **both soul and body in
hell** (*geenna*, the Valley of Hinnom, a ravine south of Jerusalem
whose fires symbolized the punishment of the wicked). Beare
notes that among the Greeks it was commonly held that the soul
was dissolved upon the death of the body (p. 247). Gundry adds,
"Despite much current opinion to the contrary, Jews as well as

Greeks regarded physical death as separation of the soul from the body" (p. 197). In context the **soul** is a person's true self. Opponents may put the messengers of God to death, but they are unable to separate them from the source of true life. Senior writes, "Paralyzing fear should not be an ingredient of Christian ministry" (p. 109). Only God can kill the soul. If there is to be fear, let it be fear of God.

The prospect of martyrdom is anything but pleasant. But throughout the New Testament it is taught that God's faithful people will suffer (cf. John 15:18–21; 2 Tim. 3:12). Scripture has never painted a chimerical picture of a sentimental deity. So, **don't be afraid** (the third reference, v. 31) of whatever could happen. Sparrows are seemingly insignificant and inexpensive, but not one of them will die (**fall to the ground**) **apart from the will of your Father**, and **you are worth more than many sparrows** (Semitic literature often uses "many" to mean "all"). In fact, God "takes every hair of your head into his reckoning" (Knox). The *assarion* (**penny**) was a Roman copper coin worth one sixteenth of a denarius (a day's wages for a manual worker). Sparrows were the least expensive living things sold in the market and were used for food by the poor; a penny would buy two sparrows. In Luke's account (12:6), five sparrows go for two cents—perhaps the fifth is thrown in for a bargain.

Some have suggested that the Greek for **fall** (**to the ground**) translates an Aramaic word meaning "to light or land upon" (e.g., Barclay, vol. 1, p. 389). But this removes the idea of martyrdom that is central to the section. Others note that the Greek of verse 29 says "without your Father"—it does not have the additional word "knowledge" (TCNT), "permission" (Beck), or "consent" (GNB). If we are not to complete the phrase in this way, the idea would be that even in death sparrows and faithful witnesses are not deprived of the presence of God. As the well-known hymn has it, "Be not dismayed whate're betide; God will take care of you."

10:32–33 / Stendahl gives the gist of this next paragraph as "the only thing worth fearing is not to be found on Jesus' side by failure to confess him before men" (p. 783). Those who acknowledge **before men** that they belong to Jesus will be openly acknowledged by him before God. **Before men** in this context probably means "in earthly courts of law," and **before my Father**

means "in the heavenly court where God sits as the ultimate Judge." To Eli, God said, "Those who honor me I will honor, but those who despise me will be disdained" (1 Sam. 2:30). Verse 33 adds the obvious corollary—whoever disowns Jesus will be rejected by him in the final reckoning. At the final judgment Jesus will speak for or against a person on the basis of whether that person has been a fearless advocate or a silent witness. One's involvement in spreading the message of the kingdom has eternal consequences.

10:34–39 / The prevailing Jewish opinion was that when Messiah came he would usher in a time of universal peace. Not so, says Jesus. I have come, but not to **bring peace to the earth**. I bring not peace **but a sword**. In this context the sword symbolizes that which divides a family against itself. Jesus' statement that he came to bring strife is the normal Semitic use of consequences as though they were intentions. Amos asks, "When disaster comes to a city, has not the Lord caused it?" (Amos 3:6).

Malachi tells of the coming day of the Lord when the prophet Elijah will appear and "turn the hearts of the fathers to their children, and the hearts of the children to their fathers" (Mal. 4:6). For now, however, the lament of Micah over the moral breakdown of Israel is more to the point (Mic. 7:6): **a man** turns **against his father** and **a daughter against her mother. A man's enemies will be the members of his own household** (v. 36). Especially in gentile families, where every member played some role in the local cult, would the gospel bring division. The challenge of total commitment has always brought division, even within the bonds of a family relationship.

It follows that to love members of one's own family more than God disqualifies a person for discipleship. Luke, who perhaps translates literally from an Aramaic source, has it that one must "hate" his own family in order to become a disciple of Jesus (Luke 14:26). The issue is one of priorities: our commitment to Christ must be greater than to anyone else. Jesus is not counseling his followers to ride roughshod over family affection or responsibility. The point is that when a person pledges solidarity with Christ and his mission, nothing—not even the love of a family member (understood as unsympathetic to the Christian faith)—must be allowed to stand in the way.

If placing family before Christ disqualifies a person for discipleship, so also does putting self in the same position. To be worthy of discipleship a person must **take his cross and follow** (v. 38) in the path of the Master. To "take up the cross" means to consider oneself already sentenced and on the way to execution. It is complete self-denial. Whether this means bearing the shame and loneliness of being a social outcast or actually being ready to suffer a martyr's death is incidental. Some have found incongruity in the fact that it is not until chapter 16 (vv. 21-23) that Jesus first predicts his crucifixion. This method of execution was well known in Palestine, and the image would have been easily understood by Jesus' disciples.

Verse 39 is the most frequently recorded saying of Jesus in the New Testament. It is found six times in the Gospels (cf. Matt. 16:25; Mark 8:35; Luke 9:24; 17:33; John 12:25). If a person seeks to preserve his own life he will **lose it,** but if for the sake of Christ he lets it go he will **find it.** That self-seeking is self-defeating (Filson, p. 134) is the central paradox of Christian living. In the context of cross-bearing it would appear that "gaining one's life" may refer to escaping martyrdom by denying the faith. It has been historically true that in times of persecution some professing Christians have come to terms with the world by renouncing their faith. Such action forfeits the true life of the soul. On the other hand, willingly to accept martyrdom for Christ's sake is to gain the higher life (**life** in v. 39 is used in a double sense—physical, and true or spiritual). The saying of Jesus is also true in a more general sense; to pursue selfish interests is to lose out on what life is all about, whereas to devote oneself to Christ brings deep and lasting satisfaction.

10:40-42 / At the end of the discourse Matthew once again emphasizes the mission setting. Jesus instructed the Twelve to stay in homes and towns where they were welcomed in verses 11-14. Now he adds that those who extend hospitality to the itinerant evangelists actually entertain both Jesus and the Father. Later in a parable dealing with final judgment, Jesus will teach that to minister to the needs of the hungry and oppressed is to minister to God himself (25:31-40). In the context of persecution (v. 23), hospitality could involve harboring at considerable risk those who are wanted by the authorities. Therefore, to provide shelter for a prophet in the role of a messenger of God is to share in the

prophet's reward (that is, the reward that a prophet receives; cf. 5:12; 6:1).

Jesus here refers to his disciples in three ways: they are prophets, righteous men, little ones. The **righteous** (*dikaios*) **man** is a believer whose life is marked by righteous conduct. Hill's suggestion that this designation may refer to a group of teachers within the church (p. 196) assumes that the verse originated at a later period. Gundry holds that the **little ones** are disciples who do not hold positions of leadership in the church (p. 203).

It is often observed that Matthew gives no account of the mission journey itself (both Mark and Luke record the return of the Twelve, Mark 6:30; Luke 9:10). The normal critical explanation is that for Matthew the "disciples" symbolize Christian believers of his own time, and the mission charge is a set of instructions for the outreach of the church in the later part of the first century. Nothing is said about the completion of the missionary journey because it is still under way and will be completed only when the Son of Man returns (cf. Beare, p. 252).

Additional Notes §10

10:2 / **Apostles**: See D. Muller's article "Apostle," in *NIDNTT*, vol. 1, pp. 126–35; also Rengstorf in *TDNT*, vol. 1, pp. 407–45; S. Freyne, *The Twelve: Disciples and Apostles*.

10:4 / **Judas Iscariot**: Kepler (in *HDB* rev. pp. 535–36) lists other possibilities: "the man of Issachar" (making Judas a Samaritan), "the carrier of the scortea" (a leather moneybag), "the liar" (from Aramaic), and "dagger-man" (from the Latin *sicarius*) and therefore a Zealot. Since in later iconography Judas is regularly depicted as red-haired, Harald Ingholt concludes that "Iscariot" derives from the Aramaic root *sqr*, which means reddish-brown or ruddy (see reference in Albright-Mann, p. 118). Thus he would be known as "Judas the redhead."

10:13 / **Peace**: The Gk. *eirēnē* has the same broad range of meaning as the Hebrew *šālôm* (wholeness, health, and security). In epistolary salutations " 'peace' comprehends the sum of blessing experienced, as 'grace' the sum of blessing bestowed" (*HDB* rev., p. 743).

10:14 / **Shake the dust off your feet**: In Acts 13:51 Paul and Barnabas shake the dust from their feet in protest against the Jews of Pisidian Antioch. Paul shakes out his clothes in Acts 18:6 (cf. Neh. 5:13) in protest against the Jews of Corinth and says, "Your blood be on your own heads! I am clear of my responsibility." For the Jewish custom, see Str.-B., vol. 1, p. 571.

10:15 / **Sodom and Gomorrah:** Sodom is the most often mentioned (thirty-six times) of the "cities of the valley." It became the symbol of wickedness, and its destruction, along with that of Gomorrah, is held out as a warning of the punishment that will fall on those communities that willfully sin against God. See Gen. 19:1–29 for the account of its destruction by a rain of burning sulfur.

10:25 / **Beelzebub:** See the articles "Baal-zebub" in *IDB*, vol. 1, p. 332, and "Beelzebul" in *ISBE* rev., vol. 1, pp. 447–48.

10:38 / **Cross:** Crucifixion was well known in Palestine. One of the Maccabean rulers crucified eight hundred Pharisees, and the Roman general Varus broke up a Jewish revolt, crucifying two thousand Jews along the roads leading into Galilee.

§11 Jesus' Words About John the Baptist (Matt. 11:1-30)

11:1-6 / Verse 1 of chapter 11 marks the transition to a new section in Matthew's Gospel. Once again we find the same formula that was used at the end of the Sermon on the Mount (*kai egeneto hote etelesen ho Iēsous*; cf. 7:28). Up to this point the public ministry of Jesus has met with success. Now the atmosphere changes, and hostility begins to manifest itself. Having finished giving instructions to the Twelve, Jesus departs (apparently alone) to **teach and preach** in nearby towns. From this point on, healings are less frequent (cf. Matt. 4:23).

Jesus began his ministry in Galilee following the imprisonment of John the Baptist (Matt. 4:12). Josephus records that Herod confined John in the fortress of Machaerus on the east side of the Dead Sea (*Ant.* 18.116-119). Matthew supplies the details in chapter 14 (vv. 3-12;). **In prison** John hears about the public ministry of Jesus and sends some of his disciples to inquire whether or not Jesus is the expected Messiah. John is normally pictured as languishing in prison and riddled by doubts about Jesus. On the banks of the Jordan he had fearlessly proclaimed the coming of one who would baptize with fire and whose winnowing fork would separate the chaff to be burned with unquenchable fire (Matt. 3:11-12). But Jesus' messianic ministry had not measured up. Perhaps he was not the Messiah after all. Would not Messiah secure the release of his courageous forerunner?

Although psychological reconstructions are by nature conjectural, there is little doubt that John was confused by all that was happening. Luke says that John sent two (Gk. *dyo*) of his disciples to question Jesus (Luke 7:18), a reading that is found in some manuscripts of Matthew as well (instead of *dia*, "through"). The title "the Christ" (*ho Christos*) reflects the perspective of Matthew rather than John. **What Christ was doing** includes the healings and exorcisms of chapters 8 and 9. It is not obvious why learning of Jesus' miraculous deeds should engender doubt on John's part. Some hold that John's inquiry reveals the beginning of faith rather than expressing doubt (e.g., Fenton, p. 175).

John's disciples ask, Are you the Coming One **or should we expect someone else?** Although the title "the Coming One" (*ho erchomenos*) is not found in Jewish texts as a messianic title, it does reflect verses such as Isaiah 59:20 ("The Redeemer will come to Zion") and Psalm 118:26 ("Blessed is he who comes in the name of the Lord"). That Matthew uses *heteron* rather than *allos* (**someone else**) suggests that John was expecting a Messiah of a different sort.

Jesus sends the inquirers back to John with instructions to tell him what they **hear and see** (v. 4). It is up to John to grasp the appropriate messianic implications. Schweizer writes, "Faith must always be a man's own personal response and can never be the mere mechanical repetition of what has just been said" (p. 257). Verse 5 is poetical in structure, consisting of three pairs of parallel clauses. This arrangement may reflect early Christian hymnody. The material is taken from three passages in Isaiah (29:18-19; 35:5-6; 61:1) and corresponds to the kinds of ministry carried out by Jesus in chapters 8 and 9 (the curing of the blind, the lame, the mute, etc.). The **poor** are those who fully realize their spiritual poverty. Those who take no offense at Jesus' messianic activity and accept him for who he obviously is are said to be **blessed** (the beatitude of v. 6 corresponds to those in 5:3-11).

11:7-15 / As John's disciples are leaving, Jesus turns to the crowds and asks, What were you expecting **to see** when you went **out into the desert? A reed swayed by the wind?** Of course not. John was no weak and vacillating person blown about by every contrary wind of opinion. This inference could have been drawn by some because of Jesus' warning concerning stumbling (v. 6). A second question follows: What then did you go out to see? A man dressed "in silks and satins"? (Williams). No: people who dress like that belong in the courts of kings. John wore the rough garment of camel's hair held in place by a leather belt (Matt. 3:4). *Malakos* (v. 8) means "soft," and in 1 Corinthians 6:9 it suggests effeminacy. There is irony in Jesus' comparison of the fearless prophet with the courtiers of King Herod.

Then why did you go out? It was to see a prophet, was it not? And that is what you saw. John was **more than a prophet**

(v. 9), not because he held some higher office but because he had the privilege of announcing the fulfillment of all prophetic dreams. He stood on the threshold of the coming kingdom. He is the one of whom Scripture says, **I will send my messenger ahead of you who will prepare your way before you.** The quotation is from Malachi 3:1 and reflects the LXX of Exodus 23:20. Jesus changes "before me" in the original to "before you" and in so doing refers the passage to himself as Messiah.

I tell you the truth, continues Jesus, that there has not risen among mortals anyone greater than John the Baptist. Yet the humblest member of the kingdom of heaven is greater than he. John was not greater in personal achievement or professional stature, but his role as the messianic herald placed him in a position of prophetic honor. Because he would die a martyr before the new age would be secured, he would not be privileged to enjoy the blessings of even the lowliest of those who would be in the kingdom. It is unlikely that **he who is least in the kingdom** is a reference to Jesus as servant (Matt. 20:28) and that the point of the saying is that Jesus is greater than John (cf. 3:11).

The interpretation of verse 12 has been discussed at length. One's approach turns on whether *biazetai* is passive ("has suffered violence") or middle ("has been coming violently"). Because the noun *biastai* (**forceful men**) that occurs in the parallel clause is used in a negative sense (the cognate verb *biaō* means "to defraud, cheat, or overpower"), it is better to take *biazetai* as passive and translate "has been enduring violent assault" (Weymouth). Jesus is saying that ever since the days of John the Baptist the kingdom of heaven has been under assault by violent men who are trying to overcome it by force. These men are sometimes identified as Zealots who want to force the kingdom's arrival. More likely they are like Herod, who imprisoned John, and the Jewish antagonists of the gospel.

Up **until** the time of **John**, the Prophets and the Law spoke about the coming kingdom. With the appearance of John, the kingdom is actually under way. John is "the 'Elijah' who must come before the Kingdom" (Phillips). Prediction has given way to fulfillment. John is the prophet of the new order who stands on the threshold of the promised coming age. Schweizer correctly notes that the point is not so much that John is Elijah as it is that with John the crucial turning point in history has arrived (p. 263).

Those with insight will understand. **He who has ears** that can hear should listen carefully.

11:16–19 / Jesus searches for a way to illustrate Israel's lack of acceptance of the kingdom. **To what can I compare this generation? They are like children sitting in the marketplaces** who refuse to take part in either the wedding game (**flute . . . dance**) or the funeral game (**dirge . . . mourn**). In Luke's account there are two groups calling to one another (Luke 7:32). The girls play the flute, but the boys will not dance (men danced at weddings). The boys sing a dirge, but the girls will not mourn (women were professional mourners at funerals). In Matthew's account one group of children complain to their playmates that they will neither **dance** nor **mourn**.

The interpretation follows. John came fasting (Matt. 9:14) and drinking no wine (Luke 1:15), and they said he was demon-possessed. Jesus came eating (Matt. 9:15), and drinking (John 2:1–10), and they reviled him as a man "given to gluttony and tippling" (Weymouth)—**a friend of tax collectors and "sinners."** Like children who refused to play either game, they rejected the asceticism of John and the way of freedom offered by Jesus.

Green understands the verses in a slightly different way. The children who sit in the market place and call to others are the Jewish people, who demand activity from others and then blame them for not responding and thus spoiling games that they themselves had never meant to join into. They neither repent with John nor rejoice with Jesus (p. 117).

Jesus concludes with the observation that the **wisdom** of God (his way of doing things) is vindicated by the **actions** it produces. The works of Christ demonstrate conclusively that in him the kingdom has arrived. Its rejection by the self-righteous cannot impair the evidence.

11:20–24 / Although the crowds listened to Jesus gladly (Mark 12:37b), there followed no serious change of heart. They rejected the austerity of John and the open-mindedness of Jesus. The very towns where Jesus had performed most of his miracles had neither recognized him as the Coming One (11:3) nor turned from their sins. Thus, instead of blessing (11:6), they are to receive **woe** (v. 21). That the three cities mentioned in verse 21–23 lie relatively close to each other just to the north of the Sea of

Galilee suggests that Jesus himself (in contrast to the Twelve, who
were sent throughout Galilee) stayed rather close to home.
The pronouncement **woe to you** (v. 21) occurs frequently
in Matthew (esp. in chap. 23). Although it warns of final judgment, it is an expression of grief rather than anticipated vengeance. **Korazin** is unknown apart from its mention here and in
a single Talmudic reference (b. *Menahoth* 85a), an illustration of
how much of Jesus' activity is unrecorded in the New Testament
(cf. John 21:25). It is identified with the ruins at Khirbet Kerazeh
about two and a half miles north-northwest of Capernaum. A later
tradition that the Antichrist would come from Korazin may rest
upon the words of Jesus recorded here. **Bethsaida** was located
on the north shore of the Sea of Galilee just east of the Jordan.
It was the home of Peter, Andrew, and Philip (John 1:44; 12:21).
Jesus declares that if **Tyre and Sidon** had witnessed the demonstrations of God's power that these cities had, **they would have
repented long ago in sackcloth and ashes**. Tyre and Sidon were
famous Phoenician cities regarded by the Old Testament prophets
as centers of wealth and power (Isa. 23; Amos 1:9–10). Most of
the oracles are directed against Tyre, because Sidon declined in
importance after it was destroyed by the Assyrians in 67 B.C. The
use of **sackcloth and ashes** as the appropriate garb for repentance
is seen in passages such as Esther 4:3 and Jonah 3:5–6. In the
day of coming judgment these pagan cities will fare better than
the towns in Galilee that witnessed the many miracles of Jesus.
Judgment is related to privilege.

Jesus now singles out his own home town, **Capernaum** (cf.
4:13). Drawing upon Isaiah's prophecy against Babylon (Isa. 14:13–
15), Jesus says, Will you exalt yourself even to heaven? **No, you
will go down to the depths**. (v. 23). If Sodom had seen the miracles that you have seen it would still be around today. Schweizer
speculates that the pride of Capernaum may have resulted from
the fact that Jesus the famous prophet was living there (p. 267).
But pride leads to destruction, and in the day of judgment the
wicked city of Sodom (in which not even ten righteous men could
be found, Gen. 18:32; 19:24) will be shown more mercy than
Capernaum, which shall be cast down to Hades (the abode of
the dead).

11:25–26 / The final section of chapter 11 (vv. 25–30)
comprises three rather separate utterances: a thanksgiving, a

soliloquy, and an invitation. The major question raised by commentators regarding these verses has to do with authenticity. It is commonly held that the high Christology of the passage, combined with similarities to Gnostic thought, places its origin at a later period. Beare comments, "This meteorite from the Johannine heaven (von Hase) is undoubtedly a theological (christological) composition from the hand of an unknown mystic of the early church" (p. 266). The following discussion holds (with Green) that the material is integral to Matthew and to its context (p. 119).

Jesus gives thanks to his heavenly Father for revealing to the childlike what is hidden from the proud. The opening of his prayer of thanksgiving, **Father, Lord of heaven and earth** (v. 25) resembles Ben Sira's prayer, "I will give thanks to thee, O Lord and King" (Sir. 51:1). The **wise and learned** are the scribes and Pharisees, the official guardians of Israel's wisdom. Paul speaks disparagingly of the "scholars" and "skillful debaters of this world," noting that according to the Scripture, God will "destroy the wisdom of the wise and set aside the understanding of the scholars" (1 Cor. 1:19–20, GNB). The **little children** ("babes," AV) are the followers of Jesus who, unimpeded by preconceived ideas of how God should act, respond with simple faith to Jesus and his mighty works. It is paradoxical but true that study can separate a person from truth as well as bring a person to truth. It is the attitude of the learner that determines the result. It has always been God's gracious will (v. 26) to resist the proud but give grace to the humble (James 4:6).

11:27 / Verse 27 records several remarkable claims by Jesus: God has **committed to** him **all things**; he himself is known only by **the Father**; and the Father is known only by him and **those to whom** he has chosen **to reveal him**. The authenticity of the verse is regularly questioned because of its Johannine ring (cf. John 3:35; 10:15). Other obstacles are the absolute use of the title **the Son** and the claim of mutual personal knowledge, which suggests Gnostic and Hermetic influence. Bultmann calls the passage a "Hellenistic revelation saying" (*History of the Synoptic Tradition*, p. 159). Similarity, however, does not prove dependence. Until it is conclusively proven that the Fourth Gospel is a later stage in christological thought, we need not be surprised if at places the words of Jesus in the Synoptics sound somewhat like his words in John. The absolute use of "the Son" in Mark 13:32 (hardly a copyist's emendation, in that it claims ignorance of the time of the Parousia on the part of Jesus) answers one problem, and the emphasis on knowledge in the Dead Sea Scrolls answers the other. Jeremias points out a number of Semitisms that argue an early date and thus strengthen the case for authenticity (*New Testament Theology,* vol. 1, pp. 57–59). It is unnecessary to take the definite article in the titles as generic, thus making the verse a parable about the mutual relationship between a father and son.

11:28–30 / The invitation to come to Jesus and, by taking up his yoke, to find rest, occurs only in Matthew, although it is cited independently in the Gospel of Thomas. Applied in a general sense, it is a favorite passage of all who find themselves from time to time weighed down with the responsibilities of life and burdened with cares. The promise of rest is to those who have found the ceremonial obligations of the law (especially as extended by scribal tradition) too difficult to keep. Matthew denounces the scribes and Pharisees as those who "tie up heavy loads and put them on men's shoulders" (23:4). Elsewhere in the New Testament the law is presented as an intolerable burden (cf. Acts 15:10; Rom. 7:10, 24–5). It is to these who would approach God in the simplicity of personal trust that Jesus promises rest. Rest, of course, does not mean inaction; the following verse indicates that it involves a yoke.

It is commonly noted that the language of this section bears some resemblance to the words of Ben Sira, who taught that zeal for the study of the law brought him rest. By taking up the yoke of wisdom one receives instruction: rest is found with a minimum of labor (Sir. 51:27–29). Although the language is similar, there is no real agreement in thought. The yoke that Jesus offers is a way of life quite distinct from Ben Sira's suggestion.

Gundry finds in the structure of these verses an attention to literary detail that leads him to assign the passage to Matthew rather than the spoken word of Jesus (pp. 218–19). Yet sayings often repeated develop a rhythmic quality that can become highly artistic. The **yoke** that Jesus offers is a way of life characterized by gentleness and humility. It stands over against the "yoke of the law," which is strict obedience to all the precepts and commandments. Schweizer thinks the yoke is probably to be understood not as an ordinary yoke placed across the shoulders of a worker but as the yoke imposed by the victor on the vanquished (Jer. 28:10–14). It is not labor that leads to rest, but following after the one who is as gentle as if humbled—not after a conqueror but after one who appears conquered (p. 273). Although the *hoti* in verse 29 is usually translated "because," it is also possible to take it in the sense of "that"—**Learn from me** that **I am gentle and humble in heart** (v. 29). This is the lesson that leads to rest of spirit and soul. Although the requirements of the kingdom are great (5:17–20), they appear in a different light when seen as expressions of loving obedience rather than demands for religious achievement.

The Greek word in verse 30 for **easy** is *chrēstos*, which can mean "well fitting." Thus Norlie translates, "For My yoke fits so easily that My burden is light." The yoke of Christ fits comfortably on those who place themselves under it. The **burden** he asks us to bear **is light** in that it is not obedience to external commandments but loyalty to a person.

Additional Notes §11

11:5 / Jewish tradition held that physical healing would accompany the arrival of the Messiah (cf. Str.-B., vol. 1, pp. 593–94).

11:7 / **See**: Gk. *theaomai* means "to look at" or "behold," in the sense of gazing at a show or demonstration. Our English word *theater* is derived from the Greek.
Reed: Gk. *kalamos*, "reed/stalk/measuring rod." Reeds flourished along the banks of the streams and lakes of Galilee, some growing as high as twenty feet.

11:11 / The Greek text of v. 11 begins with *amēn*, a solemn affirmation of truthfulness.

11:12–15 / Albright-Mann take these verses as coming from a circle of John the Baptist's disciples. Matthew felt compelled to include them because they had become firmly rooted in oral tradition outside the gospel tradition proper (pp. 137–39).

11:16 / **Marketplaces**: The Gk. *agora* was first of all a place of assembly (from the verb *ageirō*, "to bring together"). Since commerce took place wherever people had gathered, the word came to be used in that sense.

11:16-17 / For further information on children's games, see E. F. Bishop, *Jesus of Palestine*, p. 104.

11:27 / For helpful discussions of the critical issues, see A. M. Hunter, *NTS*, vol. 8, pp. 241-49; and I. H. Marshall, *Interpretation*, vol. 21, pp. 91-94.

Knows: Gk. *epiginōskō*, "to know exactly, completely, through and through" (BAGD, p. 291).

11:28 / **Weary and burdened**: The perfect passive participle (*pephortismenoi*) expresses a state of weariness from having carried a heavy load.

11:29 / **Yoke**: A symbol of obligation and subjection (cf. Moore, *Judaism*, vol. 1, p. 465). In *Pirke Aboth* (3.6) the law is described as a yoke.

Humble: In classical literature the idea of humility was generally held to be a vice. The Gk. *tapeinos* means "undistinguished/subservient." The Christian virtue of humility (*tapeinophrosynē*) is an outgrowth of the gospel. Since true greatness is holiness, we are "lowly" because we are sinful (cf. Vincent, *WSNT*, vol. 1, pp. 68-69).

§12 Opposition Mounts (Matt. 12:1–50)

In chapter 12 Matthew relates a number of incidents that reveal the basis for Pharisaic opposition to Jesus and his ministry. Jesus vindicates his disciples' plucking grain on the Sabbath (vv. 1–8), restores a paralyzed hand on the Sabbath (vv. 9–14), moves away when he hears of a plot against him (vv. 15–21), refutes the Pharisees' claim that he drives out demons by the power of Beelzebub (vv. 22–32), calls his antagonists "snakes" who will be held accountable on the day of judgment (vv. 33–37), and refuses to perform a miracle for the "wicked and adulterous" people of his day (vv. 38–42). Small wonder that the unrepentant religionists rose up against him! So strong is the opposition that some writers have decided that the material belongs to the Jewish-Christian controversies that arose at a later time. However, without such opposition during the lifetime of Jesus, the crucifixion would remain an enigma.

12:1–2 / Although Matthew does not mention the return of the Twelve, we find them back with Jesus as the narrative resumes with chapter 12. Walking through the grain fields, they become hungry, so they pick some heads of grain and begin to eat. In Jesus' day cultivated fields were laid out in long narrow strips with paths in between. The season would have been late spring, when the grain was ripe. That the disciples were not stealing is clear from Mosaic legislation, which says, "If you enter your neighbor's grainfield, you may pick kernels with your hands, but you must not put a sickle to his standing grain" (Deut. 23:25).

When the Pharisees saw what Jesus' disciples were doing, they objected, saying that such activity on the Sabbath was unlawful. Had not God said, "Six days you shall labor, but on the seventh day you shall rest" (Exod. 34:21)? In order that the Torah not be broken, the scribes and Pharisees had developed a precise code of regulations. Thirty-nine different kinds of work were prohibited on the Sabbath (m. *Shab.* 7.2). According to the Book of Jubilees a man is to die if on the Sabbath he goes on a journey, farms, lights a fire, rides a beast, travels by ship, kills a beast, or catches a fish (50:12). From the Pharisaic perspective, the disciples had unlawfully reaped (pluck the grain), winnowed (rub it between the hands), threshed (separate the chaff), and prepared a meal (eat the grain).

12:3–8 / Jesus responds to the Pharisees by asking whether they had read about when **David** and **his companions** entered the house of God and ate the consecrated bread, although it was against the law for anyone except the **priests** to eat it. The story is recorded in 1 Samuel 21:1–9. Although the Jewish leaders knew the story well, they had failed to grasp its spiritual lesson, that is, human need must take precedence over ceremonial technicalities. The **bread** that David received from the priest was from the twelve loaves that were placed every Sabbath on a table of pure gold in the house of God. When they were replaced with new bread, they could be eaten by the priests. The hunger of Jesus' disciples (v. 1) parallels the hunger of David's men and points up a comparison between David and the "Son of David." What was permissible for the lesser is even more appropriate for the greater.

Jesus draws his second illustration from the practice of the temple priests, who break the law every Sabbath and yet are not guilty. The priests "profane" the Sabbath by changing the consecrated bread "regularly, Sabbath after Sabbath" (Lev. 24:8), and "on the Sabbath day" making a double burnt offering (Num. 28:9). If Sabbath laws can be set aside in the interests of temple service, it follows that they can be set aside for something or someone **greater than the temple**. And Jesus declares that that is exactly the situation. The Greek comparative *meizon* is neuter (a few manuscripts have the masculine) and has caused most writers to interpret the "something greater" as the kingdom that Jesus inaugurates. Gundry is persuaded that Matthew's high Christology argues for a reference to Jesus, and he explains the neuter as stressing "the quality of superior greatness rather than Jesus' personal identity" (p. 223; for other views, see Hill, p. 211).

Once again Jesus quotes the prophet Hosea (6:6) in support of actions that run counter to Jewish restrictions (cf. 9:13). He states that his opponents would not have been so quick to condemn the innocent if they had grasped the real meaning of

the Scripture that said, **I desire mercy, not sacrifice**. The Greek
eleos translates the unusually rich Hebrew *ḥeseḏ*, which connotes
God's faithful and merciful help that flows from a covenant relationship binding the two together (cf. *TDNT*, vol. 2, p. 480). It
is not Jesus' purpose to compare the ceremonial law unfavorably
with the moral law. The point is that acts of kindness take precedence over religious rites when one must choose in a given situation. The kingdom of God is of greater importance than the
ceremonial legislation that prepared the way for its arrival. If the
Pharisees had understood this principle, they would not have criticized the disciples for plucking grain on the Sabbath. That **the
Son of Man is Lord of the Sabbath** should not be difficult to
grasp. The title has eschatological overtones: it is not simply a
way of saying "man," as if what is being taught is the humanitarian lesson that physical needs are more important than religious prescriptions. As Messiah, Jesus has the authority to
override Sabbath ordinances when appropriate.

12:9–14 / Jesus has just declared that the moral obligation to show kindness takes precedence over the ceremonial responsibility to fulfill ritual duties (vv. 1–8). The incident that
follows demonstrates the same ethical priority. Jesus moves on
from there and enters a synagogue. **Their synagogue** refers to the
synagogue of the Pharisees (cf. v. 2). It does not reveal a later period in history when Jewish Christians were no longer welcome
in local synagogues. There he encounters a man with a withered
hand. The apocryphal Gospel According to the Hebrews identifies
him as a stonemason who sought healing so he could work with
his hands and not have to beg for food (cf. M. R. James, *The Apocryphal New Testament*, pp. 4–5). Both Mark and Luke say that those
in the synagogue "watched him carefully" (Gk. *paratēreō*) to see
if Jesus would heal on the Sabbath so they could accuse him
(Mark 3:2; Luke 6:7). In Matthew they ask Jesus the leading question, **Is it lawful to heal on the Sabbath?** The implication of course
is that healing is work and would therefore violate the Sabbath
ordinance (cf. Exod. 20:8–10).

Though rabbinic law permitted medical help to a person
whose life was in danger (m. *Yoma* 8.6; *Mek. Exod.* 22:2; 23:13),
it was obvious that in the case of a shriveled hand the cure could
wait until the next day. It is important to realize how precise Jewish custom was when it came to keeping the Sabbath. It was the

reason Pompey was able to conquer Jerusalem; he built up his offensive position outside the city on Sabbaths, when the Jews simply looked on but would do nothing to stop him (Josephus *Ant*. 14.58–63). It was not the purpose of those who baited Jesus to get a theological answer to their query but to goad him into action that they assumed was against the law.

Jesus counters their question with another question (a normal gambit in rabbinic debate). If you have a **sheep** that **falls into a pit on the Sabbath** (v. 11), will you not lay hold and help it out? Is it not taken for granted that any reasonable person (even the most conscientious Pharisee) will lend a hand in such a case, even on the Sabbath? Some have noted that this premise would not have been accepted universally: the Essenes at Qumran prohibited the rescue of even a newborn animal on the Sabbath (CD 11.13–14). The people to whom Jesus was speaking would not hesitate to help an animal in need, otherwise Jesus' argument would be without force. What angered Jesus (cf. Mark 3:5; he looked around *met' orgēs*, "with anger") was that they would come to the aid of livestock on the Sabbath but would deprive one of their own countrymen of the miracle of healing.

Jesus goes on to point out the obvious: **How much more valuable is a man than a sheep** (v. 12), and therefore it is perfectly appropriate to perform this act of mercy on the Sabbath. He then tells the man to stretch out his hand. The man **stretched it out**, and it was made as sound as the other hand. Instead of rejoicing over an act of human kindness, the Pharisees withdrew to plot how they might be able to do away completely with Jesus. The Pharisees were beginning to realize that not only was their prestige at stake but also their basic understanding of true religion. The freedom with which Jesus acted was a serious threat to their traditional point of view. What they could not grasp was that freedom from ritual commandment need not lead to moral chaos but within the kingdom of God imposes a responsibility far greater than any law could demand. Jesus' person was so authoritative and his reasoning so persuasive that those who would not agree had but one option—get rid of him. What began as name-calling (e.g., 9:34) ended in crucifixion.

12:15–16 / When Jesus learned that the Pharisees were plotting to take his life, he moved on to another area. Matthew's use of *ginōskō* rather than *oida* (as in v. 25) suggests that he received a report of their intentions rather than knowing it by intuition. **Many followed him, and he healed all their sick**. There is no particular reason to conclude that since he healed them **all**, the **many** who followed him were all sick people needing help (see Filson, p. 148).

Why Jesus would warn his followers not to make him known has been the subject of considerable scholarly debate. Matthew records five occasions on which Jesus commanded silence (8:4; 9:30; 12:16; 16:20; 17:9). It may have been that he wanted to avoid further trouble with the Pharisees. No sense in antagonizing those who are already bent on doing you in. Some have felt that Jesus wanted to direct attention away from himself and to his message. Phillips translates, "that they should not make him conspicuous by their talk." Many have explained the injunctions to silence as a way of discouraging a following based on misguided messianic enthusiasm. He came as Messiah but not the kind of nationalistic messiah they had chosen to expect.

In Mark's parallel account, the order not to make him known is directed to the unclean spirits who fell before him confessing that he was the Son of God (Mark 3:11-12; cf. Luke 4:41). This, along with other observations, led Wilhelm Wrede around the turn of the century to develop a critical view known as the "messianic secret." He held that belief in Jesus as Messiah came as a result of the church's post-Easter faith. The church then put out the story that Jesus had secretly told his disciples of his messiahship and charged them not to let it be known. Thus the "messianic secret" is an attempt to read back Jesus' messiahship into the life of Jesus (see the article by Colin Brown in *NIDNTT*, vol. 3, pp. 206-11). Tasker says of this theory, "It is one of the more pervasive features of a certain type of modern Gospel criticism that it regards these injunctions of Jesus to keep silent about Himself as a literary device of Mark, followed by Matthew and Luke, to explain why Jesus was not more widely recognized as Messiah in His lifetime" (p. 126).

12:17-21 / Matthew himself states why Jesus charged those whom he had healed not to tell others about him. He says, **This was to fulfill what was spoken through the prophet Isaiah**. Then follows a quotation from chapter 42 of the prophet Isaiah, verses 1-4 (the first of the Servant Songs). The quotation is the longest of Matthew's formula quotations and diverges from not only the Hebrew and the Septuagint, but also from any of the known Targums (Aramaic paraphrases). Green (p. 124) suggests that the alterations are due to apologetic use in the church (Lindars), to the work of the "school" of interpretation behind Matthew (Stendahl), or to the editorial work of Matthew himself (Barth). Though the original reference may have been to Cyrus, the Persian king who conquered the Near Eastern world of his day, the passage is messianic and points forward to the coming Redeemer. The quotation itself summarizes the ministry of God's Servant, who came quietly to carry out his assigned role and ultimately to bring about universal justice.

The first two lines of the quotation are connected with the voice from heaven at both the baptism of Jesus and his transfiguration (3:17; 17:5). He is God's **servant** (Gk. *pais*, "child" or "son"), **chosen** and loved by the Father and anointed by the **Spirit** to **proclaim justice to the nations**. The Greek verb in v. 19a (*erizō*, "to argue or wrangle") does not come from the Isaiah text but serves to explain Jesus' quiet withdrawal from controversy with the Pharisees (v. 15) The Greek verb for **cry out** (v. 19) can be used for the barking of a dog. That his voice is not heard **in the streets** could perhaps be intended to contrast with the hypocrites who pray standing in open public areas (cf. 6:5). The **bruised reed** and the **smoldering wick** refer to those who have been worn down by the difficulties of life. Jesus comes as a gentle Messiah (cf. 11:29). He will continue "until the time when he crowns his judgment with victory" (Knox), and in him the nations of the world will rest their hopes. Matthew's universal hope for the gospel is nowhere seen more clearly than here.

12:22-24 / A demoniac who was blind and unable to speak was brought to Jesus, who restored him to health. This brief narrative repeats a healing also recorded in chapter 9 (vv. 32-33). In the earlier account the man's blindness was not mentioned. The purpose of the story is not to call attention to Jesus' miracle but to emphasize two widely differing responses to the person and work of Christ. **All the people** that pressed around to see the miracle were dumbfounded at what Jesus had done (*existamai* means "to be beside oneself"; in Mark 3:21 the same word is used of Jesus by his family: "He is out of his mind"). They kept saying (*elegon* in v. 23 is imperfect), "This man could not possibly be the Son of David, could he?" The Greek construction expects a negative response but allows for the possibility that the answer could be yes.

Matthew uses **Son of David** eight times as a title for Jesus. It has solid roots in the Old Testament (2 Sam. 7:13-15; Amos 9:11) and had become a popular messianic title by the time of Christ. The title is quite often connected in the Gospels with healings and exorcisms. Howard Marshall suggests that this connection could have resulted from the title's being understood particularly in terms of the character of Solomon, who had a reputation for power over evil spirits (*NIDNTT*, vol. 3, p. 651).

When the Pharisees heard the crowds entertaining messianic ideas about Jesus, they said, with scorn, "This man expels demons only because **Beelzebub** the ruler of the demons gives him the power. He can control demons in others only because he himself is controlled by the chief of demons."

12:25-28 / Jesus is well aware of their way of thinking. It is incredible that learned men, trained in the art of skillful debate, would not realize the full implications of their position. Jesus points out that kingdoms divided are bound to collapse, and that if demons are cast out by the power of Beelzebub then their own disciples are as demonic as he is (vv. 25-27). The argument is called *reductio ad absurdum* (showing that the consequence is impossible or absurd when carried to its logical conclusion). Kingdoms engaged in civil war are on the way to destruction. Cities and households divided by internal conflict cannot stand. So if one part of Satan's kingdom is expelling another, there soon will be nothing left.

The second part of the argument (vv. 27-28) is even more damaging. Let us say for the sake of argument that I cast out demons by Beelzebub's power. Tell me, by what power do your disciples do the same? What your own followers do proves you are wrong.

Jewish exorcists were widely known in the first century. Acts 19:13-20 relates the story of the seven sons of the Jewish high priest Sceva, who, attempting to cast out demons in the name of Jesus, were attacked by the man with the evil spirit. Josephus supplies information about how the Jewish exorcists went about their trade (*War* 7.178-189).

Jesus continues: if, on the other hand, it is by the Spirit of God that I drive out demons, then it follows that God has taken up his reign in your midst. Luke's use of "the finger of God" in the parallel passage (Luke 11:20) reflects the term as it is used in the Old Testament for such things as the plague of gnats (Exod. 8:19) and the writing of the Ten Commandments on tablets of stone (Deut. 9:10). Only here and in 19:24; 21:31, 43, does Matthew use **kingdom of God** rather than kingdom of heaven. Perhaps this particular saying was so well established in the tradition that he was hesitant to rephrase it. A great deal has been written on *ephthasen* in verse 28 (cf. G. E. Ladd, *The Presence of the Future*, pp. 138–45). It is best to take it to mean that the kingdom has arrived but not necessarily in its fullness.

12:29 / Verse 29 is a short parable that makes the point that in order to rob a **strong man's house** it is necessary first to tie him up. This is normally interpreted to mean that Satan (the **strong man**) has been overpowered by Jesus and is therefore unable to prevent him from plundering his goods (exorcizing those possessed by demons and thereby belonging to Satan). According to popular Jewish thought, Satan would be bound in the end times (*Ass. Mos.* 10.1; *Test. Levi* 18.1; cf. Rev. 20:2). Jesus' miraculous deeds prove that Satan is powerless to resist, and therefore the eschatological kingdom has begun. Gundry holds that Matthew turns the saying to another end. Jesus is the "strong man," and his "goods" are his disciples. Since Satan cannot bind Jesus, those who would persecute Jesus' disciples will not prevail (p. 236). The argument is not persuasive.

12:30–32 / With the Pharisees in mind, Jesus says that all who are not **with** him (helping to gather the lost sheep of Israel; cf. 10:6) are **against** him (they scatter the sheep; cf. 10:16). The saying does not contradict Mark 9:40 ("For whoever is not against us is for us"), which was Jesus' response to his disciples concerning a man casting out demons in Jesus' name. In that case, it can be properly said that those who do mighty works in Jesus' name are not able afterwards to speak evil against him (Mark 9:39). In the situation referred to in Matthew the religious opponents of Jesus are guilty of blasphemy (12:30–32). The exorcism of verse 22 that cured a blind mute elicited from the Pharisees the charge that it had been done by the power of Beelzebub. Jesus now responds with the harshest words in the Gospels. To blaspheme against the Spirit is different from any other kind of sin—

it will **not be forgiven**. Even speaking **against the Son of Man will be forgiven** but not speaking **against** God's **Holy Spirit**.

There has been a great deal of speculation about the "unpardonable sin." Some have been haunted by the possibility that they have committed this sin and are therefore no longer able to be forgiven. Jesus is saying to his antagonists that to attribute to Satan that which has been accomplished by the power and Spirit of God is to demonstrate a moral vision so distorted that there is no longer any hope of recovery. It would be possible to speak against the Son of Man and be forgiven because at that time in Jesus' ministry there was a hiddenness about his person. Not so with the mighty works wrought by the Spirit. They were clear demonstrations that the kingdom (power and reign) of God was present in the world. Denial of this was not the result of ignorance but of a willful refusal to believe. Therefore it is unforgivable. The only sin that God is unable to forgive is the unwillingness to accept forgiveness. Thus the "unforgivable sin" is a state of moral insensitivity caused by continuous refusal to respond to the overtures of the Spirit of God.

12:33–37 / Four centuries before Christ the Greek dramatist Menander noted that a person's character reveals itself in the spoken word. Jesus put the same truth in the image of a tree and its fruit. A good tree bears good fruit, but a diseased tree bears unusable fruit. The quality of the fruit tells you what kind of tree you have. Matthew applies the saying of Jesus to the Pharisees who have just claimed that Jesus has exorcized a demon by the power of Beelzebub. People show by the fruit they produce what they are really like. Verse 34 indicates that Jesus denounces the Pharisees for their evil conclusions regarding his activity. A few writers suggest that Jesus is calling upon the Pharisees to be consistent in their judgment about him: that is, either he is used by the Spirit to do a good work in casting out demons or he is in league with the devil and his deeds are evil. In other words, "Make up your mind." Phillips translates, "You must choose between having a good tree with good fruit and a rotten tree with rotten fruit." The problem with this interpretation is that the Pharisees had already decided what kind of a "tree" Jesus was.

When John the Baptist saw the religionists of his day coming out to be baptized, he called them a "brood of vipers" who thought they could escape the coming judgment by joining the crowd (3:7). Jesus applies the same designation to the Pharisees who now oppose him. **You brood of vipers**, how would it be possible for **you who are evil to say anything good?** What the mouth speaks flows from the heart. Good people have stored up goodness, and evil people have stored up evil. Thus when they speak they cannot but disclose what they are. In New Testament terminology **the heart** stands for the inner person, thus **the mouth** in this case simply expresses what a person is really like. No amount of religious pretension can conceal that those who have aligned themselves against Jesus are basically evil.

On the day of judgment people will have to account for every idle word they have spoken (v. 36). The Greek *argos* ("idle") is a compound that means "produce nothing" (*ergon*, "a deed," and *a*, an alpha privitive). A **careless word** is one that would have been better left unspoken. Offhand remarks serve the purpose of judgment in that they are better indicators of character than carefully designed statements. Plummer notes that carefully spoken words may be a "calculated hypocrisy" (p. 181). Rabbinic tradition held that not only a person's deeds but also his or her words were recorded in a heavenly record (Str.-B., vol. 1, pp. 639–40). Out of our own mouths will come the words that condemn or acquit us.

12:38–42 / Some of the scribes and Pharisees respond (the Greek verb in v. 38 is *apokrinomai*, "to answer") to Jesus by challenging him to demonstrate in some conclusive way that he has the power and authority he claims. "**Teacher** (the title normally used in Matthew by those who were not followers of Jesus), let us see some spectacular sign," they request. The Greek *sēmeion* occurs regularly in the Fourth Gospel, with the meaning of a "miracle of divine origin" (BAGD, p. 748). In the Synoptics, miracles are *dynameis*, "mighty works." What the Pharisees wanted was something like the signs performed by Moses to convince Israel that God had appointed him to his mission (Exod. 4:1–9). They had witnessed his healings and exorcisms, but now they wanted irrefutable evidence that defied natural explanation. Paul speaks of exactly that attitude in 1 Corinthians 1:22, "Jews demand miraculous signs." Such an attitude does away with faith. It originates not in a desire to know but in the decision not to believe.

You are a wicked and adulterous people, responds Jesus. You insist (the NIV's **ask** does not do justice to the intensive compound *epizēteō*) on a miraculous sign as a prerequisite for believing. The only one you will get is the **sign of the prophet Jonah.** Just as he spent **three days and three nights** in the belly of the sea monster (following the LXX; Hebrew has "large fish"), so **the Son of Man will be three days and three nights** in the realm of the dead (**heart of the earth** is not a specific reference to the tomb; cf. Eph. 4:9). Commentators differ on what the sign actually is. Hill says the death of the Son of Man is the only sign given (p. 220). Most believe that the sign refers to the resurrection of Jesus. Tasker remarks that there was to be no sign except the supreme sign, the resurrection, which was the Father's unmistakable vindication of his Son (p. 131).

The term **adulterous generation** takes the adjective in a metaphorical sense to mean "unfaithful" or "apostate." Ezekiel speaks of Israel and Judah as two women (Oholah and Oholibah) who "became prostitutes in Egypt" (Ezek. 23:1ff.; cf. Isa. 57:3; Hos. 2:2–13). The Jews of Jesus' day had broken their covenant relationship with God and were therefore "unfaithful in marriage." Associating the **three days and three nights in the heart of the earth** with Jesus' death and resurrection has troubled some. He was crucified on Friday and rose on Sunday—three days counting inclusively, but not three nights. To press the time frame is to misunderstand the nature of a recognized figure of speech. Mention of **Jonah** leads to a comparison of the Jews of Jesus' day with the pagan city of Nineveh (v. 41). Jesus says that in the final judgment the repentance of the Ninevites when they heard the **preaching of Jonah** will rise to accuse those who have been privileged to hear someone even greater. The neuter gender of *pleion* has led some to take the word to mean "something greater," but Gundry is correct in saying that it emphasizes quality as distinct from personal identity (p. 246; as NIV: **one greater**). The reference is to Jesus. The **Queen of the South** (cf. 1 Kings 10:1–13) will join with the Ninevites in leaving the Jews "without excuse" (Knox), because she came all the way from Arabia to listen to the wise teaching of Solomon, whereas Jesus' opponents have refused to accept the word of **One** who is **greater** than Solomon. It is not Jesus' purpose to praise the heathen as much as to shame the Jews. Advantage carries responsibility. Later, Paul speaks favorably of the Gentiles, who sometimes "do by nature things required by the law" (Rom. 2:14).

12:43–45 / Jesus now tells the parable of an **evil spirit** who returns from wandering in the desert and, finding its former house put back in order, moves in again with **seven other spirits more wicked than itself**. Jesus concludes, "And that is just what will happen to this evil generation" (v. 45c, Phillips).

The verb *exerchomai* ("to go out") does not necessarily mean "to be cast out." Why the unclean spirit leaves is not stated, although it travels through the wilderness in search of a resting place (in Matt. 11:29 *anapausis* has the sense of "deep satisfaction/refreshment"). It was commonly held that the arid regions of Palestine were favorite haunts of demonic spirits (cf. Tob. 8:3, where the demon fled to "the remotest parts of Egypt"). It was while Jesus was in the desert that he was tempted by the devil (4:1ff.).

Finding no rest in the desert, the demon returns to its house. There was nothing to harm or destroy in the desert, so it might as well go home. Upon arriving, it discovers its house swept clean, redecorated, and standing empty. So it invites seven other demons (and these worse than itself) to move in with it. Little wonder that the man (the house) was worse off than before!

The parable has to do with the spiritual condition and destiny of Jesus's hearers. Jesus had come to his people with the message of messianic deliverance (cf. Luke 4:17–19). The kingdom of heaven had come, and the power of evil was being broken. In the parable this is the time when the demon was elsewhere looking for rest. But the repentance of Israel was far from complete. The house was swept and set in order, but the new resident (the Spirit of God) had not been invited to move in. Reformation without regeneration is fraught with danger. So the forces of evil return, and the final state of the nation is worse than at first (Heb. 6:4–6 is somewhat parallel). The reference is not simply to final judgment: it describes the existing condition of the Pharisees in Jesus' day.

12:46–50 / While Jesus is still talking with the crowds, his **mother and brothers** arrive and try to get through to speak to him. Mark 6:3 names the four brothers as James, Joseph, Judas, and Simon. Although one segment of scholarship has held from about the fourth century on that Jesus' brothers were either half-brothers (sons of Joseph by a previous marriage) or cousins (sons of a sister of Mary), it is best to take the Greek *adelphos* in the normal sense of a regular brother. In Mark's account, Jesus' mother and brothers had come to take charge of him because they thought that he had gone mad (Mark 3:21). John 7:3–5 clearly indicates that his brothers did not believe in him. The absence of any reference to Jesus' "father" Joseph supports the conjecture that he was an older man when he married and had probably died by this time. Not only the Jewish religionists but Jesus' own family as well failed to grasp his mission and message.

Verse 47 is missing in a number of the older and better manuscripts of the New Testament (Sinaiticus, Vaticanus, earliest Latin and Syriac versions), probably because an early scribe skipped from the final word of verse 46 (*lalēsai*) to the same word where it also completes verse 47 (scholars call this homoeoteleuton). It supplies a transition from verse 46, which tells of the arrival of Jesus' family, to the **he replied to him** of verse 48.

To the message that his family is outside wanting to talk with him, Jesus responds with the rhetorical questions, **Who is my mother, and who are my brothers? Pointing to his disciples,** he declares, **Here are my mother and my brothers.** On what basis? **Whoever does the will of my Father in heaven is my brother and sister and mother.** Doing God's will is accepting the mighty deeds of Jesus as heralding the arrival of the messianic kingdom. The author of Hebrews writes that, since all those purified from their sins have the same Father, "Jesus is not ashamed to call them brothers" (Heb. 2:11).

Additional Notes §12

12:1 / **Grainfields**: Gk. *ta sporima* ("fields of grain") belongs in the word group that includes *sperma* ("seed") and *speirō* ("to sow"). The grain is probably wheat.

12:4 / **Consecrated bread**: Lev. 24:5–9 describes the preparation of the consecrated bread. The twelve loaves are placed on the table in two rows of six each. The number twelve is associated with the twelve tribes of Israel and suggests that the offering is a pledge to maintain the covenant relation.

12:24 / **Beelzebub**: See commentary on 10:25 for Beelzebul/ Beelzebub (and cf. NIV text note here). No Greek manuscript has **Beelzebub**, which is a transliteration of the derisive nickname given to the god of Ekron, Baal-zebub, "Lord of Flies," rather than "Master of the House."

12:27 / For the practice of exorcism in Judaism, see Acts 8:7; 19:12–13; see also Mendelsohn's article in *IDB*, vol. 2, pp. 199–200.

12:28 / **Kingdom of God**: Albright-Mann hold that in the Matthean tradition the term kingdom of God applies to God's reign that follows final judgment (p. 155). It is not clear, then, why the kingdom is here said to have already come upon them.

12:31 / For further discussion, see O. E. Evans, "The Unforgivable Sin," *ExpT* 68, pp. 240–44; see also the article *"blasphēmeō," NIDNTT,* vol. 3, esp. pp. 341–42.

12:35 / **Brings**: The Greek *ekballō* means "to throw out" more or less forcibly. Vincent says that the issues of the heart are thrown out "as if under pressure of the abundance within" (*WSNT*, vol. 1, p. 72).

12:42 / **Queen of the South**: The name of the queen is not given in the account in 1 Kings 10. A variant of the biblical story is found in the Koran (*Sura* 27.22–45), which provides the name Bilqis and suggests Marib as the capital city.

12:43 / **Evil spirit**: A demon is "unclean" (NIV text note; Gk. *akathartos*) in the sense that it defiles everything it is associated with.

§13 Parables of Jesus (Matt. 13:1-58)

In chapter 13 we come for the first time to Jesus' favorite method of teaching, the parable. The seven parables recorded in this chapter form Jesus' third discourse as arranged by Matthew. There are in the first three Gospels about sixty separate parables. In the LXX the Greek *parabolē* almost always translates the Hebrew *māšāl*, which denotes a wide variety of picturesque forms of expression, including the proverb, metaphor, allegory, illustrative story, fable, riddle, simile, and parable proper. All forms of the Hebrew *māšāl* except the riddle are found in the New Testament, primarily in the Synoptic Gospels.

The parable is a simple story taken from daily life that illustrates an ethical or religious truth. William Scott observes, "Disinclined as he was to discursive exposition, the Semite practised the art of persuasion by thus skillfully appealing to the imagination" (*HDB* rev., p. 725). For many years the church allegorized the parables, ignoring the obvious meaning and finding support for theological positions. It was Adolf Jülicher's famous *Die Gleichnisreden Jesu* (1888-99) that convinced interpreters to abandon the allegorizing approach and accept parables as didactic stories that made one essential point. The parable is an effective teaching method because it calls upon the hearer to discover the truth. It was not uncommon for rabbis to use the parable in controversy so as to veil the answer to the public and then explain it later to their followers (Daube, *The New Testament and Rabbinic Judaism*, pp. 141ff.). Many modern commentators have given up any attempt to find what a particular parable may have meant in its original setting and have concentrated on what it probably meant to the Gospel writer. Others believe that, although the parable is useful for teaching in a variety of settings, the Gospel writers have transmitted to their readers the meaning Jesus intended when he used the parable.

13:1-9 / Leaving the house, Jesus went and sat beside the sea. So many people crowded around him that he went aboard a small boat (probably one used for fishing) and sat down to teach. **All the people stood on the shore**. (Contrary to today's practice, teachers in Jesus' day normally sat down to teach.) He taught them many truths by means of parables. His first parable drew upon the agricultural life of Palestine. A sower went out to plant a field. **As he was scattering the seed**, some fell **along the path** worn through the field by villagers. Since plowing followed sowing (cf. Jer. 4:3), seeds that fell along the path would be easy prey for hungry birds (cf. *Jubilees* 11:11). Seed that fell on **rocky places** (in Palestine much of the soil is no more than a thin layer of earth over an underlying limestone shelf) quickly sprouted but, without an adequate root system, withered when the sun rose. Other seed fell among the brambles (*akantha* is a thorn plant; cf. Jesus' "crown of *akanthōn*" at 27:29), which sprang up and choked the young plants.

Some of the seed, however, fell onto rich soil and yielded a harvest up to a **hundred** times as great as the seed that was sown. Although seven- to tenfold was considered average, a hundredfold was not impossible (Isaac's crops reached that level "because the Lord blessed him," Gen. 26:12; cf. *Sib. Oracles* 3:63–64). Here the figure probably has a touch of Near Eastern exaggeration. Jesus concludes with the admonition to think about what he has just said; there is more than appears on the surface (v. 9). A few verses later (vv. 18–23) Jesus will provide his disciples with an explanation of the parable of the sower. Writers who take this explanation as originating in the early church normally interpret the parable in its primary setting to mean that the kingdom, although experiencing considerable opposition and failure, will in the long run produce a rich harvest beyond all expectation (cf. Hill, p. 225; Stendahl, p. 785). As always, conclusions depend upon basic assumptions regarding the nature of the biblical text.

13:10–17 / When Jesus finished the parable of the sower, his disciples came to him with the question, **Why do you speak to the people in parables?** This question would be hard to understand if parables served to clarify truth by simple illustration. A different explanation is in order. Jesus answers their query by indicating that the privilege of understanding the secrets of the kingdom belongs to his followers but not to those who refuse to believe. In Jewish apocalyptic literature the "mystery of the kingdom" was the counsel of God disclosed only by revelation and enacted at the end of time (Bornkamm, *TDNT,* vol. 4, p. 818). The Greek *mystērion* is found only here in the Gospel (and in the parallels). The mysteries of the kingdom go beyond a general understanding of the nature of the kingdom to the crucial fact that in Jesus the divine rule has become a historical reality. Bornkamm says that the mystery revealed to the disciples is "Jesus Himself as Messiah" (*TDNT,* vol. 4, p. 819). Those to whom this basic insight has been revealed will in turn grasp a great deal more, whereas those who do not understand that in Jesus the kingdom has come will forfeit what little they do understand (v. 12).

Jesus gives a direct answer to the disciples (v. 13). He speaks to the crowds in parables because, although they go through life with their eyes open, **they do not see**, and for all their hearing, **they do not hear or understand**. The parallel in Mark states that Jesus spoke to those on the outside in parables "so that" (*hina*) they might neither see nor understand (Mark 4:11–12). This "staggering assertion" (Beare, p. 292) is not present in Matthew. The Greek *hina* ("in order that") has become *hoti* ("because"). Jesus speaks in parables to those on the outside not to harden their hearts but because their hearts are already hardened (Schweizer, p. 299). At this point in his ministry Jesus deliberately adopted the parabolic method (cf. 13:34) in order to withhold from those who did not believe further truth about himself and the kingdom he was bringing. Since the knowledge of truth carries with it the responsibility of acceptance and appropriate action, the withholding of truth from those who were hardened against it should be interpreted as a desire not to increase judgment.

Many contemporary scholars think that the parables as spoken by Jesus were no more than simple illustrations. They were intended "to illustrate, clarify, and enforce truth and lead men to right decision as they faced his Kingdom teaching" (Filson, p. 160). The two explanations (vv. 18–23 and vv. 36–43) are held to be allegories added at a later time. This approach faces the serious difficulty of accounting for the parables' having to be explained to the disciples (vv. 18, 36) as well as accounting for the *logion* in verses 16–17 that points out how fortunate the disciples were in learning truth that former generations of righteous people

had longed to know. Parables were Jesus' method of teaching believers about the coming of the kingdom while at the same time
veiling the truth from those whose hearts had already hardened
against the message.

For those who neither see nor understand, everything
comes as parables (i.e., obscurely). They are the fulfillment of
Isaiah's prophecy about a people whose spiritual faculties have
grown dull. Isaiah 6:9–10 is cited almost word for word from
the LXX. This is the only fulfillment quotation that is ascribed
to Jesus himself. Because the heart of the nation has become cal-
lous, they refuse to turn to God and be healed. To his disciples
Jesus exclaims how fortunate they are, for they are privileged to
enter into truth that prophets and upright people have long desired to know; 1 Peter 1:10–12 also speaks of the Old Testament
expectation about the times of the Messiah (cf. also Heb. 10:1;
11:39f.; and Eph. 3:4f.).

13:18–23 / It is Matthew (rather than Mark or Luke) who
provides the title **the parable of the sower**. The parable itself deals
with the kinds of soil into which the seed falls rather than with
the action of the sower. An awkwardness is introduced by the
fact that the seed is not the message itself but **anyone** who **hears
the message**. The major difficulty, however, in the eyes of many
contemporary writers, is that the interpretation of the parable is
said to belong not to Jesus but to the allegorizing of the early
church. One view is that it represents the efforts of a Christian
evangelist to account for frequent failures in winning a steadfast
following. Natural hazards of agricultural life become human dis-
positions that impede reception of the kingdom message. It is
argued that people who had just been praised for their hearing
would not need an explanation of what they had heard. Gundry
counters with the observation (growing out of v. 12) that the explanation of parables comes as a gift to those who have, in order
that they may have more, rather than as a gift to those who do
not have (p. 259). Hill takes a somewhat mediating position by
noting that, although the interpretation of the parable belongs
to a later period, both parable and interpretation can bring us
"echoes of the authentic teaching of Jesus" (p. 228).

In a succinct excursus (pp. 299–302) on current interpretations of the parable, Beare mentions Bernhard Weiss (the first of

the great modern critics to recognize that the allegorical interpretation was a product of the early church), Jülicher (who firmly
rejected every trace of allegory in interpretation), Bultmann (who
holds that the original meaning of the parable is obscure), C. H.
Dodd (whose realized eschatology leads him to take the sowing
as the work of God with Israel in past centuries), Jeremias (who
would recover the original setting in the life of Jesus and explain
the parable of the sower as arising out of doubts stemming from
the failure of Jesus to win over many of his hearers), and Bon-
nard (for whom the essential question is what the parable meant
to the evangelist, as indicated by the setting in which he placed
it in his Gospel). This rather widespread disagreement on how
parables should be understood argues the fragile nature of critical conjecture. The interpretation that follows assumes that Jesus
provided for his followers two models of how parables should
be interpreted (vv. 18–23; 36–43). That the parables of Jesus are
capable of multiple application follows from the nature of the literary form. That the synoptic writers place the sayings of Jesus
in different contexts reflects the proverbial nature of Jesus' *logia*
and the freedom with which the Spirit uses the insights and perspectives of the Gospel writers to bring us the mind of God.

"To you (*hymeis* in v. 18 is emphatic), then, my disciples,"
said Jesus, "I will explain the parable of the sower." **The seed sown
along the path** represents the message of the kingdom that is not
understood and therefore quickly snatched away by the **evil one**.
To understand the message is to grasp the truth and make it one's
own. Seed sown **on rocky places** is the message received with
enthusiasm but given up when **persecution** arises. Unless truth
takes deep root in the human heart it will be recanted as soon
as it meets any opposition. Thin soil produces superficial commitment. When the message of the kingdom falls on thorny
ground, it produces no harvest, because worldly anxieties and
the lure of wealth (v. 22) choke it out. To be caught up in the wor-
ries of everyday living and to fall prey to the seductive appeal
of financial well-being is to guarantee a spiritual crop failure.

Seed that is sown on good ground is not only heard but
understood as well. It sinks in with all its theological and ethical
implications. **Good soil** yields a good return. These hearers bear
a rich harvest. Some yield as much as a **hundred . . . times** the
amount sown, others **sixty**, and still others **thirty**. Thus Jesus

speaks of four ways that the message of the kingdom is received. His opponents have already demonstrated that in their case the seed fell alongside the road and Satan took care of it. Others who heard him preach wanted to believe but refused to take the message seriously. Persecution proved their commitment was shallow. Still others looked like genuine disciples, but they got so deeply involved in pursuits of this world that there was neither time nor energy to let the message **produce a crop**. The disciples who had left all to follow Jesus were **good soil** in which the message would produce a rich and abundant harvest.

13:24–30 / At this point in the sequence Matthew inserts the parable of the weeds (Mark has here the parable of the seed growing secretly; Luke includes neither). Since Mark is widely held to be the first Gospel to be written and a basic source for the other two, some scholars take Matthew's parable of the weeds as a reshaping of Mark's parable in order to accommodate it to the interpretation to be given later (vv. 36–43). Gundry calls it a "prohibition against rigorism in church discipline" composed by Matthew, who conflates the otherwise omitted parable (Mark 4:26–29) and the parable of the sower (pp. 261–62). Schweizer holds that if the nucleus of the parable went back to Jesus it would represent a strong protest against the Pharisaic tendency (also characteristic of the Qumran community and the Zealots) to delimit a sect of devout believers (p. 304). Once again, it needs to be stressed that later applicability of a parable does not argue against its rightful place in the teaching of Jesus. Jesus had already encountered strong opposition. In Matthew 12:34 he called the Pharisees snakes. Would it be unreasonable for him now to tell a parable that points out that this same kind of opposition would continue until the day of judgment, at which time a final separation would be made?

What happens in the kingdom is like what happens when a farmer sows good seed but during the night when everyone is asleep an enemy comes and sows weeds in the same field. When the blades of wheat begin to appear, the weeds (which are similar in appearance) spring up as well. That the sower's workers slept does not mean that they are to blame for what happened: the point is that what the enemy did was done in secret.

When the servants ask, **Where then did the weeds come from?** the owner answers, "Some blackguard has done this to spite me" (Phillips). Shall we **pull them up?** they ask. No, because you might root up the wheat with them. **Let both grow together until the harvest**, then separate out the weeds first (bundle them ready to burn) and bring the grain into the barn.

The enemy, as we shall soon find out, is the devil. As in the parable of the sower, where seed sown alongside the path is gobbled up by the birds, Satan is the one who obstructs the growth of the kingdom. He is a "hostile man" (*echthros* in v. 39 is a qualifier) who stands over against the "man who sowed good seed" (v. 24). The "seed" he has secretly sown in God's field are all those who appear to be somewhat like Jesus' followers but whose basic allegiance will be made plain at the final harvest. The Old Testament commonly uses the figure of harvest for the last judgment (Jer. 51:33; Hos. 6:11; cf. Rev. 14:14–16). Quite often, after the grain had been cut with a sickle and removed, the remaining weeds and shorter stalks would be burned off. In Palestine, where wood was scarce, certain weeds would be cut and bundled together to be used as fuel. Grain was normally stored underground in large pottery jars or in pits lined with brick.

13:31–32 / Jesus illustrates the remarkable growth of the kingdom of heaven by comparing it to **a mustard seed**, which in time grows into a tree large enough to have birds nesting in its branches. The mustard seed was proverbial for its smallness. It was the smallest of the seeds commonly used in Palestine. Yet when it grew it became larger than any of the garden plants and became a veritable tree some eight to ten feet high. Its size attracted the wild birds, which would come and eat the little black seeds of the tree.

It is quite common for writers to interpret the birds as symbolic of the flocking of Gentiles into the kingdom. Though it is true that birds symbolize gentile nations in *1 Enoch* 90:30, 33, 37, it is highly unlikely that Jesus intended to convey that specific bit of theology in this parable. That birds are able to roost in the branches of the tree indicates its size. During the period of Jesus' earthly ministry the kingdom was small, like a tiny mustard seed. In time, it would grow into something immeasurably larger.

13:33 / Next Jesus compares the kingdom to leaven that a woman worked into a large batch of meal until it had completely risen. During the three Jewish festivals that required all the men to appear before the Lord, yeast was not permitted in any of the sacrifices (Exod. 34:25; 23:18). For the seven days of Passover, all yeast was to be removed from the house: the only bread to be eaten must be unleavened (Exod. 12:15–20). Against this background it is easy to see why leaven came to symbolize that which was unclean or evil (cf. Gal. 5:9; 1 Cor. 5:6–8). In this parable, however, the leaven does not carry that idea. Jesus is not saying that the kingdom is in certain respects evil! Lohmeyer explains that from the Jewish standpoint the tax collectors and sinners were unclean but would turn out to be those who initiate the redeemed community (pp. 220ff.).

The parable of the yeast is not unlike the parable of the mustard seed; in both, great results stem from small beginnings. Leaven was normally a small piece of dough kept from a previous baking and allowed to ferment. Three measures of flour would be about a bushel (all that a woman could handle at one time) and would produce enough bread to feed a large family. It may be that the parable of the yeast emphasizes the pervasive action of the kingdom in society.

13:34–35 / The parables in chapter 13 divide into two sections. Up to this point Jesus has spoken his parables to the crowds. From here on, he addresses the disciples. Verses 34–35 are a summary statement indicating that in fulfillment of Scripture Jesus spoke to the crowds only in parables. The passage quoted is Psalm 78:2. It is "prophetic" in the sense that the entire Old Testament points forward to the coming kingdom. Since the Psalm is ascribed to Asaph (who in 2 Chron. 29:30 is called a seer), some have accounted for the prophetic reference in that way. Codex Sinaiticus and several other manuscripts have "Isaiah the prophet" (which Metzger explains as a possible correction for Asaph, *TCGNT*, p. 33).

Jesus' use of parables is a fulfillment of the Old Testament prediction that he would speak to the crowds in enigmatic sayings (the Greek *parabolē* is the LXX translation of the Hebrew *māšāl*, which carries this idea). Since they refused to hear him, his message would fall on their ears as difficult and obscure. The truths that Jesus revealed to those who by faith had taken the first step toward understanding were secrets concealed since the beginning of time. Only in fulfillment, and then only to those who have the insight of faith, are the truths of God's sovereign

reign made clear. To outsiders they come as riddles and meaningless sayings.

13:36–43 / There is rather wide agreement among New Testament scholars that the interpretation of the parable as found in this section is Matthew's own composition (Gundry, p. 274; Beare, p. 311). Jeremias has identified thirty-seven linguistic indications of Matthean authorship (*The Parables of Jesus*, p. 82). The emphasis in the parable on allowing the wheat and the weeds to grow up together has shifted to one of final judgment. Hill suggests that we are dealing with a free adaptation of Jesus' teaching to the needs and conditions of the early church, but that in the application the authentic kernel is not lost (p. 235).

Note, however, that linguistic characteristics of the Gospel writer are to be expected in his presentation of the parable and its interpretation. The style of each of the evangelists is clearly evident in all their work. Further, the very nature of parabolic teaching allows for application to related situations. An adaptation of Jesus' words to a later situation should come as no surprise. What must be maintained is that in this further application the essential intent of the parable is not changed. For those who hold to a high view of Scripture the doctrine of inspiration guarantees this end.

Jesus now leaves the **crowd** and goes **into the house**, where his disciples question him about the meaning of the parable of the weeds. Their question indicates that the meaning of the parable is somewhat obscure. Although it can be said that the knowledge of the secrets of the kingdom of heaven has been given to them (13:11; cf. 13:16), they still need help to understand the full implications of Jesus' teaching.

The one who sowed the good seed is the Son of Man. The field is the world, seen as the place where both **the good seed** of the gospel and **the weeds** of the devil are sown. The parable is neither an account of final separation between real and professing Christians within the church nor a statement about the destiny of the human race. It assumes the universal proclamation of the gospel and therefore a final division between those who belong to the kingdom and those who have their origin in Satan's activity. The grouping of people into two radically different camps is characteristic of Jewish thought (cf. 1QS 2.4; 4.17).

It is somewhat strange that the good seed is identified with
those who accept it and the weeds with those who belong to the
evil one. Yet such freedom is characteristic of the parabolic
method. To be a "child of the kingdom" means to be obedient
to its authority. **The harvest is the end of the age** (cf. Joel 3:13;
Jer. 51:33; 2 *Bar.* 70:2; etc.), **and the harvesters are angels** (cf. *1
Enoch* 46:5; 63:1). Matthew emphasizes with this parable that a
period of final judgment awaits the return of Christ.

What it will be like at the end of the age is illustrated by
the gathering and burning of the weeds. Beginning with verse
41, the interpretation of the parable gives way to a description
of final judgment in the traditional terms of Jewish apocalyptic.
The Son of Man will send out his angels to uproot from his kingdom "everything that is spoiling it" (Phillips) and "all who violate His laws" (Weymouth). The same scene is portrayed later in
the Olivet Discourse (24:30–31). Some find it strange (Beare calls
it "grotesque," p. 313) that angels rather than demons inflict punishment, but in Revelation 14:18–20 angels are very much involved
in carrying out the vengeance of God on the wicked.

The **fiery furnace** (v. 42) into which evildoers are thrown
is a common feature of apocalyptic judgment (2 Esdras 7:36; Rev.
20:14). The **gnashing of teeth** is typically Matthean (*brygmos* occurs six times in Matthew and only once elsewhere in the New
Testament). In contrast to the fate of the wicked, the righteous
will **shine like the sun**. Matthew speaks both of the kingdom of
the Son of Man (v. 41) and of the kingdom of the Father (v. 43).
The former is the sovereignty given to the Son following his resurrection (cf. 28:18), and the latter is God's eternal reign which
appears to all following final judgment (cf. Paul's similar schema
in 1 Cor. 15:24–28). The message is important, so if you are able
to hear, pay attention.

13:44 / The next two parables (vv. 44–46) occur only in
Matthew. Both stress the same basic point that the kingdom of
heaven is of such supreme worth that everything must be sacrificed in order to attain it. The kingdom of heaven (the other
evangelists use "kingdom of God"; the terms are synonymous)
is like a man who happens onto a store of money (or valuables)
hidden in a field. In ancient times people often hid money and
articles of value in the ground (cf. the "one-talent man" in Matt.
25:25): without banks, and in view of frequent invasions by enemy

forces, this was a sensible thing to do. Many caches were lost or forgotten and are even today being dug up in Palestine.

The man in question appears to have been a farm laborer, undoubtedly poor. He was working (probably plowing) in a field that belonged to someone else when he came upon a treasure. Immediately **he hid it again** so no one else would know of it and, filled with joy, returned to sell all that he had in order to buy the field. Since we are dealing with a parable we should not get sidetracked into a discussion of the morality of the transaction. It is worthy of note, however, that according to rabbinic law, money that was found belonged to the finder. By purchasing the field, he would eliminate any basis for contesting ownership of his find. The kingdom of heaven is of supreme value. When we find it ("fully grasp its infinite worth"), we will joyfully let go of all competing claims on our lives and make it our one great possession.

13:45–46 / Although the parable of the **fine** pearl makes the same point as the preceding parable, the contrasts are of interest. Instead of a poor man who accidentally stumbles onto buried treasure, we have what appears to be a well-off traveling business man (*emporos* rather than *kapēlos* suggests this distinction). Along with gold, **pearls** were considered to be **of great value**. Produced by a living process in the sea, they were sought both in the Red Sea and in the Persian Gulf. The great harlot in Revelation 17 adorned herself with "gold, precious stones and pearls" (Rev. 17:4; cf. 18:16–17).

When the merchant found the "pearl of great price" (AV) he **sold everything he had** (*panta* is neuter, indicating he sold everything he owned, not simply the other pearls) and bought the one great pearl. The kingdom of heaven is like that pearl: it is of inestimable value and calls for us to let go of everything else in order to obtain it.

13:47–50 / The kingdom of heaven is now compared to the dragnet that gathers in a large catch of fish of various sorts. The fish are drawn onto the shore, where the good ones are separated into baskets and the bad ones are thrown away. In Jesus' day it was common to fish with a dragnet, a large square net that was made to hang upright in the water by means of weights. It was pulled into shore by ropes attached to the corners. By means of this seine net all sorts of fish would be gathered in. The worthless fish would be those forbidden by Jewish law (Lev. 11:10–11;) or perhaps simply those that were inedible. Legend (perhaps based on John 21:11) has it that there were 153 different kinds of fish. The Sea of Galilee is said to contain 54 different species.

Some writers think that verses 49–50 do not belong to the original parable. In verse 48 the fishermen sit down on the shore and separate the good fish from the bad. In verse 49 the separation is done by angels **at the end of the age**. It is often mentioned that though bad fish would be thrown back into the water or perhaps buried for fertilizer, they would not be burned (as in v. 50). Such "difficulties" result from a failure to realize that verses 49–50 are an eschatological interpretation of the parable itself. As fish are separated in the parable, so also will people be separated at the end of the age. That is the point of the parable. It was not intended to teach that "the appeal of the Gospel makes no discrimination of rank or class, wealth or poverty, trade or profession" (Beare, p. 316), although that, of course, is also true. The interpretation repeats the theme of verses 40–42.

13:51–52 / Jesus now asks his disciples whether they understand what he has just been teaching them in parables. Their answer is that they do. On that basis, then, he can say that every teacher of the law who understands the truths of the kingdom is like the master of the house who knows how to bring out from his treasury things new as well as old. The order **new** and **old** is probably significant. Stendahl (p. 786) notes that Matthew is anxious to relate Jesus' messianic manifestation and teaching (the new) to the promises of the Old Testament (the old). The **old** is all the teaching of the Old Testament that had to do with God's work in the world. The **new** is the messianic teaching of Jesus regarding the kingdom of heaven. The new does not replace the old, but it builds upon it.

Some are tempted to take the saying one step further and see in it an understanding of the role of the first-century New Testament teacher of the law. In this case the old would be the teachings of Jesus and the new would be their interpretation and application to fresh situations in the early church. But the **therefore** in verse 52, coming in response to the acknowledgment that the disciples had grasped what Jesus had taught, argues that Jesus himself is that teacher who brings out truths both old and new.

13:53–58 / The fourth major section of Matthew's Gospel begins at this point. It comprises a narrative that runs through the end of chapter 17 followed by instruction in chapter 18. The account of Jesus' rejection at Nazareth is placed earlier in Luke (4:16–30), where his sermon in the synagogue led to an attempt to take his life. In both Mark and Matthew, Jesus returns to his ancestral home, where his message is heard but not accepted.

When Jesus finished teaching the series of parables listed by Matthew in chapter 13, he **moved on from there** (Capernaum?) and returned **to his hometown**. The basic meaning of *patris* is fatherland (the place of one's *patēr*), but as Luke indicates, it refers to the town of Nazareth (Luke 4:16) rather than the country in which Jesus was born (see above on Matt. 2:3–6). There he began to teach (*edidasken* is imperfect) **the people in their synagogue**. It is sometimes noted that the Greek *autōn* (**their**) reflects the attitude of the church at the time of Matthew's writing. However, the account itself discloses an antagonistic setting that is more than adequate to account for referring to the synagogue as **their synagogue** rather than "the synagogue" (as the GNB has it).

Those who heard Jesus were impressed by his teaching and his power to do the miraculous. Yet they refused his message and undermined his role as prophet. Their question about where Jesus received **wisdom** and **miraculous powers** was not an honest inquiry. The Greek *touto* ("this fellow") in verse 54 is contemptuous. Isn't he simply **the carpenter's son**, and aren't we fully acquainted with his entire family? How could he have come by all of this? So they "began to find a cause of stumbling in him" (Rotherham).

Since in Palestine at the time of Jesus timber was scarce and houses were normally made of stone, the Greek word usually translated "carpenter" (*tektōn*) probably meant "stonemason." The mention of Jesus' mother, brothers, and sisters, without reference to his father, supports the conjecture that Joseph was an older man and probably had died by this time. Although his brothers did not believe in Jesus at this point (cf. 12:46–50; John 7:5), they later became prominent in the church. **James** was a leader in the Jerusalem congregation (Acts 15:13ff.) and wrote one of the books of the New Testament, as did Jude (**Judas**) as well. Jesus' brothers were children of Joseph and Mary born after Jesus (see commentary on 12:46).

The people of Nazareth were disturbed by Jesus' teaching and the impact of his presence. Moffatt says they were "repelled by him." Jesus responds with the proverbial saying, **Only in his hometown and in his own house is a prophet without honor** (v. 57). Familiarity breeds contempt. Even though they recognized that Jesus' words and works were extraordinary, they refused to believe (*apistia* in v. 58 reflects a basic unwillingness to believe). Because of their unbelief, Jesus performed only a few miracles there. That he was rejected by his own family is especially disturbing. It does, however, support the canonical accounts of his boyhood against the noncanonical infancy narratives that relate all manner of miraculous activity by the boy Jesus.

Additional Notes §13

Among the better books in English on the parable are those by Dodd, *The Parables of the Kingdom*; Crossan, *In Parables*; Hunter, *Interpreting the Parables*; Jeremias, *The Parables of Jesus*; Kistemaker, *The Parables of Jesus*; Linnemann, *Jesus of the Parables*; Stein, *An Introduction to the Parables of Jesus*; Via, *The Parables: Their Literary and Existential Dimension*.

13:11 / **Secrets**: The Gk. word *mystērion* appears in secular literature most often in the plural and in connection with the religious rites of Hellenistic mystery cults. What little is known of the rites (they were highly secretive) must be pieced together from scattered references. See R. E. Brown, "The Semitic Background of the New Testament *Mystērion*," *Biblica*, vol. 39, pp. 426–58; vol. 40, pp. 70–87; R. M. Grant, *Hellenistic Religions: The Age of Syncretism*.

13:19 / **Evil one**: Gk. *ho ponēros* is used for the one who is the absolute antithesis to God, that is, the devil. This distinctive New Testament usage reflects the moral understanding of *ponēros* as that which stands over against God, his law, the preaching of Jesus, and the message of the apostles (*TDNT*, vol. 6, p. 558).

13:25 / **Weeds** (Gk. *zizania*) are usually thought to be bearded darnel (*lolium temulentum*), which closely resembles wheat. Though it was often poisonous to humans because of parasitic growths, it was sold for chicken feed. It has been suggested that the Greek *zizanion* is connected with the Hebrew *zānāh* ("to commit fornication"), and this accounts for the Jews calling it "bastard wheat."

13:32 / The prophet Ezekiel spoke of Assyria as a tall cedar in Lebanon in whose boughs the birds of the air nested (Ezek. 31:1–9, cf. Daniel's reference to Belteshazzar as a tree whose top touched the sky, Dan. 4:20–22).

13:33 / **Yeast**: In the making of bread a piece of fermented dough (Gk. *zymē*, "yeast/leaven") from a previous batch was kneaded into the new loaf, causing it to rise. See R. S. Wallace, *Many Things in Parables*, pp. 22–25.

13:40 / **Fire**: Fire is regularly connected with eschatological judgment in Old Testament prophetic literature: Isa. 66:15f.; Ezek. 38:22; 39:6; Zeph. 1:18; etc.

13:44 / The parable is also found in the Coptic Gospel of Thomas (109), but in an altered form that tells of a son who sells an inherited field without realizing that his father had hidden a treasure in it.

13:45 / **Pearls**: The Greek *margaritēs* was a hard, rounded gem formed by certain oysters in response to an irritation caused by a foreign object within the shell. They were highly prized and, along with gold, served as symbols of wealth.

13:52 / **Storeroom**: Gk. *thēsauros*, "treasure box" or "storehouse [where important items were kept]." Cf. the English "thesaurus," a book containing a store of words.

13:55 / **Carpenter's son**: Albright-Mann note that *tektōn* covered a wide range of skilled craftsmen and conclude that Joseph, far from being a simple village carpenter, was probably a builder of some consequence who traveled widely throughout the area (pp. 172–73).

§14   Feeding of the Five Thousand
(Matt. 14:1–36)

Jesus was not the only prophet who was rejected by his own (cf. 13:53–58). John the Baptist had been treated the same way by Herod, ruler of Galilee and Perea. Matthew tells of Herod's concern that Jesus might be John the Baptist returned from the dead (v. 2). This in turn caused Jesus to withdraw from a public to a secluded area (v. 13). Verses 3–12 record the death of John the Baptist, which had taken place earlier but is brought into the narrative at this point by Matthew.

It is often pointed out that Matthew has shortened Mark's account and that this has led to inconsistencies. The main problem seems to be that in Mark it is Herodias who wants to kill John (Mark 6:19), whereas in Matthew, Herod is the one who wishes to put him to death (Matt. 14:5). Yet Herodias' antagonism is also seen in Matthew's account (the dancing daughter is prompted by her mother to ask for John's head on a platter, v. 8), and Herod's reluctance to carry out the execution is pictured by Matthew as well (v. 9). There is no question that both Herod and Herodias wanted to be rid of the prophet, although Herod is the one who is a bit reluctant. Green's opinion that Mark's version (adapted by Matthew) "rests on popular tradition, not to say bazaar gossip" and is therefore "no more reliable in its details than such sources generally are" (p. 139) is unnecessarily harsh.

14:1–5 / Matthew correctly identifies Herod as the **tetrarch** of Galilee. Before Herod the Great died, he divided his territory into three parts and willed them to his sons Archelaus (Judea and Samaria), Philip (Trachonitis and Iturea), and Antipas (Galilee and Perea). Herod Antipas ruled over Galilee from 4 B.C. until he was banished to Gaul in A.D. 39. Upon hearing about Jesus he was convinced that John the Baptist had **risen from the dead**. How else could he be performing such miracles? This supposition on the part of Herod reflects the contemporary belief in resurrection.

Earlier, Herod had arrested John and put him in chains in prison. Josephus identifies the place as the fortress of Machaerus on the east side of the Dead Sea and says that John was imprisoned because Herod "feared lest the great influence John had over the people might put it into his power and inclination to raise a rebellion" (*Ant*. 18.116-119). Matthew records that John was imprisoned because he had spoken out against the unlawful marriage of Herod to his brother Philip's wife. Herod Antipas was married to the daughter of the Nabatean king Aretas (cf. 2 Cor. 11:32), when he went to Rome and met and seduced Herodias, the wife of his half-brother, Herod Philip (not to be confused with Philip the tetrarch). He then divorced his first wife (which later led to defeat in war) and married Herodias. Whether or not his divorce was legal, his marriage to Herodias was not. According to Jewish law it was wrong for him to marry the wife of his brother while the brother was still alive (cf. Lev. 18:16; 20:21). Since Matthew does not actually say that Herod married Herodias (Mark does, 6:17), Gundry concludes that John was prohibiting the contemplation of marriage (p. 286). Certainly it is better to allow the two accounts to supplement one another than to invent a discrepancy. The evidence does not force us to conclude (as Gundry suggests) that Matthew "play[s] with the details in a way that transmutes a historical report into a semihistorical short story" in order to "shift the onus of guilt from Herodias to Herod" (p. 287).

John's rebuke of Herod was not an isolated remark, **for John had been saying to** (Gk. *elegen* in v. 4 is imperfect) Herod, **It is not lawful for you to have** Herodias (v. 5). The present participle *thelōn* (**wanted**) in verse 5 indicates Herod's continuing desire to get rid of John. It is best understood as a concessive participle and reads, "Though he wanted to put him to death, he feared public reaction."

14:6-12 / It was on the occasion of **Herod's birthday** celebration that John the Baptist was put to death. **The daughter of Herodias danced** before all the guests, and Herod was so delighted that he promised her anything she might want. Although it would have been unusual for a royal princess to perform an "immodest and provocative" dance (Filson, p. 169) in the presence of men, in view of Herodias' hatred of John and the drunkenness of the occasion, it is not difficult to believe that that is exactly what happened. The name of Herodias' daughter (Salome) is not supplied by the Gospel account but by Josephus. Salome was the daughter of Herodias by her first marriage to Herod Philip of Rome. She later married her granduncle, Philip the tetrarch.

It was at her mother's instigation that Salome requested **on a platter the head of John the Baptist**. Herod **was distressed**, but because he had made the promise in front of all **his dinner guests**, he ordered the execution. According to Jewish law it was illegal to put a person to death without a trial, but the pressure of the moment was too much for a weak person like Herod. The grisly act was carried out, and the head of the prophet was delivered **on a platter** to Salome, who then **carried it to her mother**. The Greek *korasion* ("little girl") in verse 11 may be somewhat ironic, in that it calls attention to the treachery of using a relatively innocent person in perpetrating such a cruel and violent deed. The disciples of John came and took the body for burial and then told Jesus about it.

14:13–17 / When Jesus heard everything that had taken place (cf. v. 12), he withdrew by boat to a secluded spot. Mark and Luke connect the retreat with the return of the Twelve, who needed a period of rest (Mark 6:30–31; Luke 9:10). The place was near the city of Bethsaida (Luke 9:10), on the northeast shore of the lake. This area was governed by the tetrarch Philip and would provide some immunity from Herod Antipas. Galilee at that time was a crowded land. Although its boundaries included only slightly more than a thousand square miles, Josephus tells us that it had more than two hundred towns with populations of fifteen thousand or more.

When the people heard of his departure, they left their villages and followed along the edge of the lake. Upon landing, Jesus looked at the **large crowd** and was deeply moved with **compassion**. He put aside for the moment his own need for privacy and **healed** those who were **sick**.

As evening came and the time for supper had already passed, the disciples came to Jesus with the request that the people be allowed to **go to the villages** and **buy themselves some food** (v. 15). To the disciples' surprise Jesus answered that there was no need for the crowd to leave. **You give them something to eat**, said Jesus. Their response, undoubtedly tinged with some skepticism, was, **We have here only five loaves of**

bread and two fish. Bread and fish were basic to the diet of the poor of that day.

14:18-21 / The bread was brought to Jesus, who then told the people to **sit down on the grass**. It is Mark who adds the colorful note that they sat in *prasiai* ("garden beds") of hundreds and fifties (Mark 6:40). He also indicates that the grass was "green," which suggests springtime (Mark 6:39). Jesus took the loaves and fish and looked **up to heaven** from whence all good gifts come. **He gave thanks** (*eulogēsen* in v. 19 does not mean that he "blessed" the bread in the sense of infusing into it some spiritual quality), **broke** the bread, and had the disciples distribute the pieces. Everyone had enough to eat, and when they picked up what was left over, there were **twelve basketfuls of broken pieces**. Matthew adds that there were **about five thousand men** (Gk. *andres*) who ate, not counting the **women and children**.

There is no question that Matthew depicts a miraculous multiplication of loaves. The account is found in all four Gospels (Mark 6:30-44; Luke 9:10-17; John 6:1-13). A somewhat similar feeding of four thousand is found in Matthew 15:32-39 and Mark 8:1-10 (Mark 8:19-20 indicates that we are dealing with two separate events). There are a number of interpreters, however, who are reluctant to take the miracle at face value. Beare, for instance, writes, "It is of course preposterous, if it be taken literally, as an account of an actual event" (p. 236). Barclay is a bit more gentle toward those who have no need to go beyond the simple story itself: he writes, "Let them remain for ever undisturbed in the sweet simplicity of their faith" (vol. 2, p. 102).

Those who resist taking the account as an actual miracle offer various explanations. Perhaps everyone had a lunch, but no one was willing to bring it out lest he or she would have to share it with others. When they were shamed into action, we see "the miracle of the birth of love in grudging hearts" (Barclay, vol. 2, p. 103). Beare rightly calls this particular approach (which was originally suggested by H. E. G. Paulus in 1828) "banal and inept" (p. 327). Others have taken it as a sort of midrash on the story of Elisha, who fed a hundred men with twenty loaves of barley bread and some heads of new grain (2 Kings 4:42-44). Albert Schweitzer sees the event as a token meal in which each person received a minute amount as a promise of the coming messianic banquet. Though the eucharistic interpretation is somewhat closer to John's presentation, it leaves unexplained the twelve baskets of scraps that remained. Unless a person feels compelled for some reason to disallow miracles in the life and ministry of Jesus, it is preferable to understand the account exactly as it is presented.

14:22–27 / As soon as the five thousand had been fed, Jesus "prevailed upon his disciples" (Knox) to cross over the lake ahead of him while he dismissed the crowds. The Greek *ēnankasen* is a strong word that means "to compel" (NIV, **made**). It suggests that the disciples would have liked to stay and share in the excitement of the crowd. In John's recounting of the story, we learn that "Jesus, knowing that they intended to come and make him king by force, withdrew again to a mountain by himself" (John 6:15). A strong popular reaction to the miracle would rouse national sentiment, and Jesus did not want to jeopardize his mission by encouraging a political uprising. Only here and in Gethsemane does Matthew speak of Jesus praying (cf. 26:36–44).

The Greek *to oros* ("the mountain," v. 23) refers to the hill country as distinct from the lowlands (especially the hills above the sea of Galilee, Abbott-Smith, p. 324). To the west of the lake these hills rise about 1200 feet above the surface of the water. When evening came Jesus was still there alone, and the boat with the disciples was a long way off shore (lit., "many furlongs," each furlong being just over two hundred yards) battling a strong head wind and at the mercy of a rough sea.

Sometime during the fourth watch of the night (3:00 to 6:00 a.m.; the Romans divided the period from 6:00 p.m. until 6:00 a.m. into four equal periods of time) Jesus went out to the disciples, walking on the sea. It is sometimes suggested that since the Greek for **on the lake** differs in verses 25 and 26 (in v. 25 the preposition *epi* is followed by the accusative case and in v. 26 by the genitive), we should interpret the first as "toward the sea" and the second as "by the sea" (cf. similar uses in Mark 16:2 and John 21:1). Taken in this way, Jesus, as he came toward the lake, saw the boat that had been driven to the northern shore by the heavy winds and then waded through the surf to be of help. Though such a reconstruction is grammatically possible, it needs to be remembered that the Greek preposition *epi* is notably imprecise.

When the disciples saw Jesus **walking on the lake** (Mark adds that he meant to pass them by, Mark 6:48), **they were ter-**

rified and cried out, **It's a ghost**. Jesus responded immediately, saying "It's all right!" (Phillips), "I AM" (*egō eimi*), the living God is present. Stendahl notes that the *"egō eimi* may have a numinous and divine ring" (p. 786), in which case it would be translated "I AM" rather than **It is I** (cf. Exod. 3:14; Isa. 43:10).

14:28–33 / The story of Peter's attempt to walk to his Master on the water is recorded only by Matthew (vv. 28–31). It is sometimes taken as an acted parable of Peter's career (i.e., in his pride he fell and had to be rescued and restored by Jesus). Christian elaborations on the theme would see the boat as the church, the water as the hostile world, and Jesus descending from the mountain as the ascended Lord coming to dispel the fears of the troubled church. Once again we are reminded that presuppositions control exegesis. Our understanding of the text is conditioned by allowing it to speak for itself. Filson reaches for middle ground, writing, "These miracle stories have grown in the telling, but they are nearer the truth than a gospel narrative stripped of miracles and high faith" (p. 174).

Peter asks the Lord that if it is really he, to command him to come to him across the water (note: *epi* with the accusative; cf. v. 25, where it was suggested by some that *epi* with the accusative meant "toward the sea"—hardly possible in vv. 28 and 29). In response to Jesus' word of command, **Peter got down out of the boat** (v. 29) and started **toward Jesus**. When he saw how strong the wind was, he lost his courage. **Beginning to sink**, he called out, **Lord, save me**. Jesus immediately reached out and caught him, saying, **You of little faith**, "What made you lose your nerve like that?" (Phillips). When both Peter and Jesus **climbed into the boat, the wind died down** (v. 32). Matthew records the worshiping response of the disciples, who exclaimed, **Truly you are the Son of God**. This profession of faith in Jesus anticipates Peter's great confession at Caesarea Philippi (Matt. 16:16). It is often pointed out that Mark ends his account noting that the disciples were astounded because they had not gained any insight from the feeding of the five thousand and their minds were closed (Mark 6:51–52). It is incorrect to compare this with Matthew's account of the disciples who responded by confessing that Jesus was the Son of God. Mark's words attach directly to the disciples' terrified response to seeing Jesus walking on the water. Matthew records the disciples' response to Christ's rescue of Peter (the account of which is not included in Mark's narrative).

14:34–36 / The boat with Jesus and the disciples came to shore at **Gennesaret** on the northwest shore of the lake, a small (four miles long and about two miles wide) and fertile plain lying between Capernaum and Magdala. Josephus described the beauty and lush vegetation of the area (*War* 3.516–521), and the rabbis spoke of it as "the Garden of God." Upon landing, Jesus was recognized by the local townspeople, who **brought all their sick to him and begged him to let the sick just touch the edge of his cloak, and all who touched him** were restored to health. The *kraspedon* (or "hem of a garment," especially the "tassel," Deut. 22:12) played an important part in the Pharisees' outward display of piety (cf. Matt. 23:5). The woman with an issue of blood believed that by touching the *kraspedon* of Jesus' garment she would receive his healing power (Matt. 9:20; Luke 8:44). That day in Gennesaret all who touched the fringe of Jesus' robe were made whole.

Additional Notes §14

14:1 / **Tetrarch**: Originally this title signified "ruler of a fourth part." This was appropriate in the case of Herod Antipas, because upon the death of Herod the Great, he and his brother Philip inherited one half of the territory ruled by their father (Josephus, *Ant.* 17.317–320).

14:3 / **Herod**: The family tree of Herod the Great is notably complex. Herodias was married to Herod Philip of Rome (Matt. 14:3; Mark 6:17; Luke 3:19), the son of Herod the Great and Mariamne II. Her daughter Salome (Matt. 14:6–11; Mark 6:22–28) married Philip the tetrarch (Luke 3:1), half-brother to Herod Antipas (younger son of Herod the Great by his Samaritan wife Malthace). For a full-length study, see Harold Hoehner, *Herod Antipas*; see also F. O. Busch, *The Five Herods*.

14:6 / **Daughter of Herodias**: In Mark 6:22 the UBS editorial committee decided "somewhat reluctantly" to follow the textual tradition *thygatros autou Hērōdiados* which makes the daughter herself called Herodias (Metzger, *TCGNT*, pp. 89–90). In v. 24, however, the dancing girl is the daughter of Herodias.

14:8 / **Platter**: Gk. *pinax*, "a board/plank," thus any one of several flat, wooden articles, such as a disc or a dish.

14:19 / **Gave thanks**: In Jewish families it was customary to pray both at the beginning and at the end of a meal. Such prayers expressed gratitude for God's goodness in providing for human needs (cf. Moore, *Judaism*, vol. 2, pp. 216–17).

14:20 / **Basketfuls**: The Gk. *kophinos* was probably a small wicker basket used for carrying food. By way of contrast, the *spyris* (used in connection with the feeding of the four thousand, Matt. 15:37) was a larger flexible hamper for carrying provisions. Paul was let down over the wall at Damascus in a *spyris* (Acts 9:25).

14:36 / **Healed**: The Gk. *diasōzō* is a compound (*dia*, "through," and *sōzō*, "to heal") and means "to heal completely."

§15 Defiled from Within (Matt. 15:1–39)

15:1–2 / Knowledge of Jesus and his ministry had by this time spread throughout Palestine. Scribes and Pharisees came all the way from Jerusalem to question him about his activities. The scribes were Jewish scholars who copied the sacred Scriptures of the Old Testament and consequently became the professional interpreters of Scripture. The Pharisees were a religious order, primarily laymen, who devoted themselves to strict adherence to the law. Most scribes were Pharisees, but not all Pharisees were scribes. The question used by the religionists from Jerusalem was more an accusation than an honest request for information. **Why do your disciples** keep breaking (*parabainousin* is present tense and suggests repeated action) **the tradition of the elders?** Specifically, why do **they eat** without the proper ceremonial cleansing?

The **tradition of the elders** was a body of oral literature that grew out of a desire to expound the written law and apply it to new circumstances. This growing body of oral tradition reaches back at least to Ezra in the fifth century B.C. but was not written until the second century A.D. The scribes and Pharisees considered it to be as binding as the written law itself, although the Sadducees rejected it, and the "people of the land" (the *'am-hā'āreṣ*) ignored it. The "washing" before eating had to do with ceremonial uncleanness, not personal hygiene. Leviticus 11–15 treats the subject of unclean foods. From the Jewish point of view, people became unclean by contact with any sort of ceremonially unclean object or person. To ensure purity, people would go through a rather elaborate ritual of purification **before they** ate. It involved pouring water on the hands with the fingers up so the uncleanness would flow off the wrists. It then was repeated with the fingers pointing downward. This was followed by rubbing each hand with the other fist.

15:3–9 / Rather than answer their question, Jesus, in rabbinic fashion, counters with another question. Why, in fact, do *you yourselves* (emphatic in Greek) keep on breaking (continuous present) God's commandment in the interest of your own tradition? Now for the example. **God said, "Honor your father and mother"** (Exod. 20:12), and **"anyone who curses** [them] **must be put to death"** (Exod. 21:17), but you say that if a person dedicates to God something his father or mother could use, he is then free of any obligation to be of help to them. In this way you have used your tradition to nullify the law of God.

Korban (a technical term for sacrifice found in Ezek. 20:28) was the practice of devoting things to God and thus making them unavailable to others who might have a legitimate claim on them (the word is used in Mark's narrative, 7:11). It was a solemn oath that strict scribes said could not be broken under any circumstances. Gundry writes, "Behind the declaration stands the purpose of retaining one's own use of the item" (p. 304). Though appearing to be terribly pious, such a practice was in direct violation of the fifth commandment.

Jesus cuts through all the religious pretense of his questioners with the stinging rebuke, **You hypocrites!** Isaiah described you rightly when he said you paid lip service to God but your hearts were a long way off (vv. 7–8). The Greek *hypokritēs* was a play-actor or pretender. The word became used for hair-splitting legalists who manipulated the law for their own advantage. Filson is correct when he observes that "wherever in the church tradition and forms gain ascendance over the Scripture, the Pharisee position has won control" (p. 177). The passage quoted by Jesus is from Isaiah's letter to the exiles and comes from the LXX translation (Isa. 29:13). Cold hearts and empty words make it impossible to worship God. When man-made rules are taught as the laws of God, all worship becomes useless. Barclay quotes William Temple, the renowned archbishop of Canterbury, as defining worship as quickening the conscience by the holiness of God, feeding the mind with the truth of God, purging the imagination by the beauty of God, opening the heart to the love of God, and devoting the will to the purpose of God (vol. 2, p. 117). Understood in this way, seldom is God actually worshiped. Twenty centuries after the Pharisees of Jesus' time, the words and rituals of much contemporary religion still echo the emptiness of human precepts.

15:10–11 / At the beginning of the chapter the Pharisees and scribes asked Jesus two related questions (v. 2). The more general question about why Jesus' disciples did not obey the oral tradition was countered in verses 3-9. (It was not really answered, because it was more an accusation than a question.) The second question had to do with the laws of ceremonial cleanness and is answered in verses 10-20 (note v. 20, which ties together the entire discussion). The major problem raised by the section is Jesus' apparent rejection of Old Testament laws of clean and unclean and why, if that was what he intended to do, there was so much difficulty in bringing Gentiles into the church (cf. Gal. 2:11ff.).

Jesus called the crowd to him and cautioned them to pay close attention to what he was about to say. Verse 15 calls the statement that follows a parable, that is, an enigmatic saying or riddle in the sense of the Hebrew *māšāl*. For the pious Jew who observed with care all the laws of ceremonial purity, the statement would have been radical. A person is defiled not by **what goes into** the **mouth** but by **what comes out**. This revolutionary concept would undermine the entire system of Jewish ritual practice. It threatened their basic idea of religion.

In the parallel account in Mark we find the added parenthetical remark, "In saying this, Jesus declared all foods 'clean' " (Mark 7:19). Beare represents those who feel that Jesus' statement annuls in principle the entire corpus of laws of ritual purity (p. 338). On the other hand, Tasker suggests that Jesus may have done no more than to emphasize that evil coming out of the mouth is far greater than any evil that could enter by eating food that was ceremonially unclean (p. 149). Gundry writes, "The cleansing of all foods does not countermand the law, but intensifies it by transmuting the dietary taboos into prohibitions against evil speech, just as the so-called antitheses in the Sermon on the Mount did not destroy the law, but fulfilled it" (p. 306). In either case, the point of the saying is clear: the ultimate source of defilement is the heart, not the diet.

15:12-14 / Verses 12-14 occur only in Matthew (although the statement about the blind leading the blind occurs in another context in Luke 6:39). The disciples' question (**Do you know that the Pharisees were offended when they heard this?**) would imply that the Pharisees understood Jesus' statement in verse 11, which seems strange in view of Peter's asking for an explanation in verse

15. No difficulty exists, however, if verses 12–14 are taken as an editorial insertion and if what offends the Pharisees is Jesus' rebuke of their casuistry in setting aside God's law by human tradition (vv. 3–9). Stahlin says that "the primary meaning is 'deep religious offense' at the preaching of Jesus" (*TDNT*, vol. 7, p. 350). The verb often has the force of "to lead into sin" (Matt. 13:21; 24:10) and in the present context implies that their "offense" included the sin of rejecting Jesus.

Jesus' response to the timidity of the disciples, who apparently did not wish to offend the religious rulers, was that plants not planted by his heavenly Father would be **pulled up by the roots**, so for the time being they may be left alone (cf. the parable of the wheat and the weeds, Matt. 13:24–30, 36–43). The image of Israel as a vineyard is common in the Old Testament (Isa. 5:1–7; 60:21; cf. 1QS 8.5). Not only has allegiance to oral tradition led them to dishonor the law of God, but it has placed them outside his favor as well. Schweizer writes, "Israel and its ruling class of Pharisees is not the vineyard planted by God but a wild thicket" (p. 327). They are **blind guides** leading the **blind**. The obvious result of that combination is for both to end up in a **pit**. Apparently rabbis considered it an honor to be given the title "leader of the blind" (cf. Rom. 2:19). They lead the blind, Jesus would agree, but how unfortunate that they also are blind. In the Old Testament falling into a pit was a metaphor for disaster (Isa. 24:18; Jer. 48:44).

15:15–20 / Peter now asks to have the parable (Gk. *parabolē*) explained to him and the other disciples. That which is not understood is the enigmatic saying in verse 11. Parables have a way of concealing their truth from outsiders but yielding it to those who will press for an explanation (cf. Mark 4:34). Jesus responds, "Are you, like them, still without understanding?" (the pronoun *hymeis* is emphatic, and the adverbial accusative *akmēn* places the stress at the beginning of the sentence). **Whatever enters the mouth** travels through **the stomach and then out of the body** into the drain (*aphedrōn*). It is what **comes out of** (not into) **the mouth** that defiles, because it originates in the **heart**. That is the real source of all that makes a person unclean. Matthew then lists seven evils (v. 19). After the first (**evil thoughts**), they follow in the order of the sixth through the ninth commandments (**murder, adultery,**

sexual immorality, theft, false testimony, slander). It is interesting that the listing of evils from the second half of the Decalogue follows the discussion of the violation of the fifth commandment in verses 4–6.

The final verse ties together the entire section from verse 1 on. A person is made unclean by what rises out of the heart, not by eating with unwashed hands. The question remains as to whether Matthew understands Jesus as thereby setting aside the entire pentateuchal system of dietary laws. Verse 19 would suggest that Matthew is transmuting dietary taboos into prohibitions in speech and conduct.

15:21–28 / Departing from Gennesaret (cf. 14:34), Jesus goes in a northwesterly direction to the area around the Phoenician cities of **Tyre and Sidon**. The journey of approximately fifty miles took him into gentile territory (although Jeremias cites evidence that the eastern Tyrian region was largely Jewish, *Jesus' Promise to the Nations*, pp. 31–32, n. 3; pp. 35–36). **A Canaanite woman** of that district came to him crying out on behalf of her demon-possessed daughter. During the time of the Judges the Canaanites were the major enemies of Israel. They were the heathen population of Palestine. Mark identifies her as "a Greek, a Syrophoenician by birth" (Phillips, Mark 7:26). Matthew's use of **Canaanite** emphasizes that the woman to whom Jesus talks is of a distinctly different ethnic background. "Crying at the top of her voice" (Phillips), she keeps calling out (Gk. *ekrazen* is imperfect) for mercy. Her daughter is harassed by a demon and is in a terrible state. By addressing Jesus as **Son of David** she shows an awareness of his messianic role.

Although the Canaanite woman keeps calling out for mercy, Jesus does not respond. The disciples come to him and urge that he **send her away** (without granting her request). They were annoyed because she was trailing along after them and continuing to cry out. The apparent insensitivity to suffering on the part of Jesus can be explained by the lesson in faith that follows in the next few verses. The disciples are without excuse. Jesus' delayed answer is that he has been sent **only to the lost sheep of Israel** (v. 24). The reference is to all those within Israel who wandered without spiritual direction, rather than to all Israel regarded as lost. Undaunted by his reluctance to help, the Canaanite woman

knelt before him (*proskyneō* may also mean "to worship") and
continued to call out for help.

Jesus continues to withhold help. He answers that it is not
appropriate to take bread that belongs to the children and **toss
it to their dogs**. Many modern commentators have taken severe
exception to these words. Beare says they exhibit "the worst kind
of chauvinism"—a "violent rebuff" that reveals "incredible inso-
lence" (p. 342). He decides that "the story is best understood as
a retrojection into the life of Jesus of the controversy over the
propriety of extending the Christian mission beyond Israel, with
echoes of the bitterness of the struggle within the early Church"
(p. 342).

Such a strong response is hardly necessary. We are dealing
with a proverbial statement by which Jesus is pointing out no
more than that his mission is directed to his own people. *Dog*
was a common Jewish term for Gentiles based on their making
no distinction between clean and unclean foods. It is not necessarily a derogatory term. It has been pointed out that the Greek
kynarion (diminutive of *kyōn*) referred to house dogs or little pup-
pies. Barclay reminds us that the tone in which something is said
and the look that accompanies it make all the difference: "We can
be quite sure that the smile on Jesus' face and the compassion
in his eyes robbed the words of all insult and bitterness" (vol.
2, p. 122).

The woman's retort is directly to the point. **Yes, Lord, . . .
but even the dogs eat the crumbs that fall from their masters'
table**. I am not asking for what belongs to others. I am simply
asking to be treated like the little house dogs that get to eat whatever falls on the floor. What remarkable faith, Jesus responds. You
will receive what you ask for. **From that very hour**, the demon-
possessed **daughter was healed**. The persistence of the woman
and her strong confidence in Jesus' ability to cure her daughter
result in a miraculous healing. "Indomitable persistence spring-
ing from an unconquerable hope," Barclay calls it (vol. 2, p. 124).

15:29-31 / In Matthew's account the scene shifts immediately from the vicinity of Tyre and Sidon (cf. 15:21) to the eastern
shores of the Sea of Galilee (the Markan parallel says "the region
of the Decapolis," 7:31). It is not certain how much time Jesus
spent in non-Jewish territory, although there may have been about

six months between the feeding of the five thousand in Matthew
14 (v. 19 says they sat "on the grass," thus indicating early spring)
and the feeding of the four thousand in Matthew 15 (v. 35 says
they sat "on the ground," *epi tēn gēn,* which suggests later in the
summer, when the grass would be scorched). A comparison of
Matthew and Mark indicates that the latter records the healing
of a deaf mute, while the former gives a summary of Jesus' healing ministry among the Gentiles. Though there were non-Jewish
settlements on both sides of the Sea of Galilee, they were clust-
ered far more heavily on the eastern side. Those who were healed
praised the God of Israel, a title most appropriate in the mouths
of Gentiles. Reference to the **lame, blind**, and **mute** stems from
Isaiah's prophecy in 35:5–6. The evangelist adds the **crippled** and
includes Isaiah's "deaf" in his inclusive **many others.**

15:32–39 / A great crowd had gathered, and as Jesus saw
them he was moved with compassion. They had been with him
for several days and no longer had food. Learning from his disciples that they had **seven loaves** of bread and **a few small fish,**
Jesus had the crowd seated, and they were fed. After they all had
eaten their fill, the leftovers were gathered, and there remained
seven basketfuls. Not counting the **women and children,** some
four thousand had been fed from the meager supply of the
disciples.

A question that is always asked concerns the relationship
between the two miraculous feedings as reported both by Matthew (14:13–21 and 15:32–39) and by Mark (6:30–44 and 8:1–10).
Luke records only one (9:10–17), and John 6 (vv. 1–15) seems to
combine the two. It has been suggested that Mark (followed by
Matthew) found two accounts of the same feeding in his sources
and copied them both. Lohmeyer (*JBL,* vol. 56, pp. 235ff.) supports the view that the duplication relates to the ethnic composition of the audience. The feeding of the five thousand is
addressed to a Jewish population (the twelve baskets of Matt.
14:20 represent the twelve tribes of Israel), and the feeding of the
four thousand relates to the Gentiles (the seven baskets of Matt.
15:37 symbolize the seven deacons of Acts 6:1ff.). Carrington (*The
Primitive Christian Calendar,* p. 16) says that the writer of the Gospel was following a lectionary that required the duplication. Beare
holds that we have here not simply a second account of a feeding but a more extensive cycle (p. 347).

It is more likely that we have not two accounts of a single event but two separate but similar events. It is unlikely that the Gospel writers, because of the limits of a scroll, would copy two accounts of the same incident. Though the two accounts have some points in common (desert location, lack of food except for a few loaves and fish, a large crowd), they also diverge at many important places. The number of people fed, loaves available, and baskets of fragments remaining are all different. The lessons Jesus teaches are different (utter dependence on God in the first and sympathy for the gentile world in the second). The most important point, however, is that Jesus himself separates the two feedings. In Matthew 16:9–10 he says, "Don't you remember the five loaves for the five thousand . . . or the seven loaves for the four thousand?" With evidence like that, it seems fruitless to pursue the possibility of duplicate accounts of the same event.

Additional Notes §15

15:5 / **A gift devoted to God**: Cf. Rengstorf's article *"korban,"* *TDNT*, vol. 3, pp. 860–66.

15:7 / **Hypocrites**: Albright-Mann translate "Shysters" and note that what is condemned is "the legalism which robs an otherwise legitimate gesture of all moral content" (p. 184).

15:19 / Mark's list contains thirteen evils (Mark 7:21–22).

15:21 / **Tyre and Sidon**: The Phoenician city of Tyre was originally situated on a rocky island some twenty-two miles south of Sidon. In 332 B.C. Alexander laid siege to the city by constructing a mole two hundred feet wide leading out to the island. The ancient city of Sidon owed its prominence to an excellent harbor formed by a series of small islands close to shore.

15:22 / **Came**: Gk. *exelthousa* does not mean that the woman came out of the gentile area. It is to be taken in a more general sense to mean that she came out to where Jesus was ministering. V. 21 indicated that Jesus went into the region (*eis ta merē*) of Tyre and Sidon.

15:27 / **Crumbs**: Gk. *psichia* were small bits of food, fragments of bread that fell when the hands or mouth were wiped.

15:37 / **Basketfuls**: It is often noted that the basket in the first incident was a *kophinos* (a stout wicker basket commonly associated with Jewish culture) and the basket in the second incident was a *spyris* (a hamper that could be large enough to carry a man; cf. Acts 9:25).

15:39 / **Magadan**: an unknown site, probably on the western shore. The parallel in Mark (8:10) has Dalmanutha, equally unknown.

§16 Peter's Messianic Declaration
(Matt. 16:1–28)

16:1–4 / Only here and in Matthew 3:7 do the **Pharisees** and the **Sadducees** come together in a common cause. In the earlier setting they went out to the Jordan to find out for themselves what John the Baptist was doing. Here they combine forces to tempt Jesus to show them some spectacular sign from heaven that will authenticate for them his divine mission. He answers them by pointing out that only an evil and adulterous generation seeks a sign. No sign (except the sign of Jonah) will be given.

Since elsewhere in the New Testament the Sadducees are not found outside of Judea, some have questioned whether or not they would stray so far from Jerusalem and the temple. One's response to such conjectures is determined by the larger question of textual reliability. It seems perfectly reasonable to accept the text as it stands and understand the two groups together as a sort of official representation of Judaism.

Most English translations note that verses 2b–3 are missing in a number of early manuscripts. Some scholars see the verses as a later addition from a source similar to Luke 12:54–56. Others argue the deletion of the verses on the basis that in parts of the world like Egypt, a red sky in the morning does not indicate stormy weather. The UBS Greek text encloses the passage within square brackets, indicating that including the section is the least unfavorable alternative.

The proverbial statement that Jesus employs simply says that a red sky in the evening promises good weather and a red sky in the morning indicates a coming storm. Jesus' concern is not to teach climatology, but to state in no uncertain terms that though his opponents are able to interpret the appearance of the sky, they are totally unable to read the signs of the times. In asking for spectacular proof from heaven, they show that they are spiritually unable to grasp what is taking place in the life and ministry of Jesus. They are hypocrites, because while pretending to pose a reason-

able request they are in fact **a wicked and adulterous generation**
(v. 4). Prophets of the Old Testament used the figure of adultery
to describe Israel in its infidelity to God (cf. Hos. 2:2ff., 9:1; Ezek.
16). Miracles were never intended to compel faith. To perform a
miracle for an "immoral generation" (Norlie) would be out of the
question. The only sign given was **the sign of Jonah**. Though
some have understood this to be Jesus himself, as a prophet like
Jonah, it is preferable to take the sign of Jonah as a reference to
the resurrection.

16:5–12 / Leaving behind the Pharisees and Sadducees,
Jesus and his disciples go **across the lake**. Jews traveling in predominantly gentile territory would take their own bread in order
to avoid eating food that was not ceremonially clean. On this occasion the disciples had forgotten to take bread. Jesus warns them
to be on their **guard against the yeast** (leaven) **of the Pharisees
and Sadducees**. Discussing this remark among themselves, they
conclude that Jesus must be talking about their failure to bring
an adequate supply of bread.

Jesus knows what they are thinking and rebukes them for
their lack of faith (v. 8). He reminds them of the abundance of
bread that they collected after the feeding of the five thousand
and again following the feeding of the four thousand. That he
was able to take care of their physical needs was abundantly clear.
This should indicate to them that the statement about guarding
against the leaven of the religious leaders had nothing to do with
literal bread. Then the disciples understood that he was warning
them **against the teaching of the Pharisees and Sadducees**.

In Old Testament ritual, leaven was regularly excluded
(Exod. 34:25; 23:18). Paul counsels the Corinthians to get rid of
the old leaven that they may be "a new batch without yeast"
(1 Cor. 5:7). Throughout the New Testament, except in Matthew
13:33, leaven symbolizes something evil. In the present context
Jesus is speaking of the teaching and influence of the Jewish religious orders. A parallel passage in Luke identifies the leaven
of the Pharisees as hypocrisy (Luke 12:1). The Pharisees were
bound up in a legalism that missed the entire point of God's intention (cf. Matt. 5:20). Fenton writes, "The band of disciples must
be on their guard against a self-conscious religiosity that demands
guarantees, when it is God's desire to break in unexpectedly
through the fixed notions of their system" (pp. 333–34). The Sad-

ducees were guilty of identifying the kingdom of God with material possessions and pinned their hopes on achieving it by political action (Barclay, vol. 2, p. 132). Rigid legalism and political opportunism are twin evils that permeate society and can never be used in the pursuit of righteousness.

16:13–14 / We come now to a critical juncture in the ministry of Jesus. He has withdrawn with his disciples to the northern **region of Caesarea Philippi.** There he questions them regarding people's understanding of who he is; then he directs the question to the disciples themselves. Peter, answering for the disciples, declares him to be "the Christ" (or Messiah), "the Son of the living God." It is upon this basic truth that Jesus will build his church. Now that the true identity of Jesus is clear, he will begin very shortly to teach his disciples that his role as Messiah leads first to death (16:21) and then to exaltation (16:21, 27–28; cf. 17:1–9).

The importance of this passage is clearly seen in the attention given to it by commentators. Many writers are convinced that the material goes back to the Aramaic-speaking community but contains a number of postresurrection additions. Schweizer, for instance, says that the sayings do not derive from either Jesus or Matthew, but "probably from the early community that identified itself with Peter" (p. 338). On the other hand, Gundry argues on the basis of structure, diction, theological motifs, Old Testament phraseology, and echoes of other Matthean passages that verses 17–19 were composed by the evangelist himself in order to portray Peter as a representative disciple who understood Jesus to be the Christ (pp. 330–36). When widely divergent interpretations are offered it is probably the part of wisdom to be on the lookout for tendentious handling of the data.

The town of **Caesarea Philippi** lay on the southwest slopes of Mount Hermon, about twenty-five miles north of the Sea of Galilee. From early times it had been a sacred place for the worship of a Canaanite ba'al. The Greeks turned it into a shrine of Pan, the goat-man god of fertility, naming it Paneas. It was rebuilt by Philip, the son of Herod the Great, and named Caesarea in honor of Augustus. In order to distinguish it from the coastal city of the same name (Caesarea Maritima) it was distinguished Caesarea Philippi (that is, "of Philip").

The question that Jesus poses to his disciples is, **Who do people say the Son of Man is?** As the parallel in verse 15 indicates,

Son of Man refers to Jesus himself and not someone yet to come. Throughout the Synoptic Gospels (fourteen times in Mark alone) it is Jesus' self-designation. The purpose in posing this question is not simply to learn what others are saying but to correct in the minds of the disciples a misconception of Jesus' role.

The disciples respond to Jesus' inquiry, saying that some believe him to be **John the Baptist**, while **others say Elijah** or **Jeremiah** or **one of the** other **prophets**. It is significant that all four answers reflect the popular view that Jesus is a spokesman for God. Those who heard him had no doubt that his was a message with supernatural authority. In Jewish apocalyptic, the reappearance of famous individuals prior to the arrival of the Messiah was common. The writer of 2 Esdras has the Lord say, "I will raise up the dead from their places . . . I will send you help, my servants Isaiah and Jeremiah" (2 Esdras 2:16, 18; cf. 2 Macc. 15:14f.). Through Malachi, God promises, "I will send you the prophet Elijah before that great and dreadful day of the Lord comes" (4:5). From Matthew 11:14 and 17:10–13 we learn that John the Baptist was interpreted as Elijah returned from the dead. Elijah was in many ways the greatest of the prophets, and Jeremiah was often listed first among the latter prophets in the Jewish Bible.

16:15–16 / But Jesus' primary concern was who his own disciples thought he was. **But what about you?** he asked them. **Who do you say I am?** This was the critical question. It was Simon Peter who answered, **You are the Christ, the Son of the living God.** *Christos* is the Greek transliteration of the Hebrew word for Messiah ("the anointed one"). Used with the article it refers to the central figure of Old Testament expectation. By his confession Peter is saying that Jesus is the One who comes in fulfillment of Israel's hopes and dreams. He is the **Son of the living God.** Some modern writers would agree with Beare's conclusion that this title is a "Christological confession cast in the language of the early church" (p. 352). Gundry, however, on the basis of Matthew's "they will call him Immanuel, which means, God with us" (Matt. 1:23) and the account of the virgin birth, argues that the title has the stronger connotation of essential deity (p. 330). Though in the Hellenistic world the idea of divine sonship was quite common (used extensively of kings and emperors), Peter's use of the title was deeply rooted in a Hebraic background. When Jesus ac-

cepts Peter's ascription, Son of God, he reveals his own consciousness of a unique and intimate relationship to his heavenly Father.

16:17–19 / You are indeed highly favored (**Blessed are you**,
Gk. *makarios*; cf. the opening expression in each of the beatitudes,
5:3–11), **Simon son of Jonah**, for the truth you have just spoken
came by revelation from God. There is no indication prior to this
time that the name Peter was ever used. As first used, it was a
nickname. Simeon was the Jewish name, which in Greek becomes
Simon. The Semitic *bar-yônā* (Gk. *Bariōna;* **son of Jonah**) has
caused some difficulty. In John 1:42 Simon is said to be the son
of John (*hyios Iōannou*). Cullmann suggests with some caution that
the patronymic may conceal an Aramaic designation for "terrorist"
(*Peter*, p. 23). Others conjecture a shortened form of Johanan
(equivalent of John). It is more likely that Simon is being designated a spiritual son of the prophet Jonah (cf. 12:39). The prophetic function is in the foreground. As with every true prophet,
the revelation has come directly from God and not through human channels ("flesh and blood," AV, is a rabbinic phrase used
to denote human beings in their weakness). Peter was not em-
boldened to declare Jesus to be the Messiah, son of the living God,
on the basis of human information. It came in response to direct
revelation from God himself.

It is important at this point to draw attention to the fact that
many critical scholars do not accept the response of Jesus in verses
17–19 as genuine. Beare is of the opinion that "this group of sayings does not commend itself as a genuine utterance of Jesus"
but "originated in some debate with the Palestinian community"
(pp. 353–54). The most common arguments supporting this con-
tention are (*a*) elsewhere in the Gospels Jesus does not speak of
founding a church (only here and in Matt. 18:17 is *ekklēsia* used);
(*b*) the rest of the New Testament provides no indication that Peter
enjoyed the administrative privileges recorded here; and (*c*) only
a few verses later (v. 22) Peter indicates that he really does not
understand Jesus.

Gundry, however, in an extended discussion (pp. 333–36),
argues persuasively that verses 17–19 are "an expansive composition [in the Greek language] by the evangelist himself" designed
"to portray Peter as a representative disciple" (pp. 330–31). That
contemporary scholars are so distinctly divided in their conclusions provides strong incentive to accept the traditional under-

standing that the verses in question do provide a reliable account of what Jesus actually said.

In response to Peter's **You are the Christ**, Jesus says, **And I tell you that you are Peter** [*petros*], **and on this rock** [*petra*] **I will build my church** (v. 18). This saying (along with the verse that follows) has become the foundation for the Roman Catholic position on the papacy and the church. The crucial question is the identity of the "rock" on which the church is to be founded. Jesus' statement involves a wordplay between *petros* (an isolated rock or stone) and *petra* (a rock ledge). Behind each word is the Aramaic *kepā'* (without distinction in gender), but if Gundry is right in his assertion that Matthew wrote the account in Greek, we are no longer "shackled by the need to suppose an Aramaic substratum" (p. 334). In either language the pun is present. Most modern scholars hold that Peter himself is the rock, in the sense that he is the first to identify fully and completely Jesus as Messiah. It is upon this foundation that the church is built. Christ's church (Gk. *ekklēsia*) is the new Israel, the New Testament counterpart to the Old Testament congregation of the elect (*qāhāl*). It consists of those who, like Peter (who was the first), acknowledge Jesus to be the Christ. Cullmann rejects all Protestant attempts to evade the Roman Catholic exegesis that Jesus is here appointing the impulsive and enthusiastic disciple Peter to be the foundation of his ecclesia (*TDNT*, vol. 6, p. 108). Yet the argument that had that been Jesus' intention it would have been simple to say, "And upon you I will build my church," is highly persuasive.

Some have taken the rock to be Peter's faith. Stendahl, however, holds that any distinction between Peter and his faith "presupposes a sophistication of a sort not to be expected in our text" (p. 788). Others have interpreted the rock as the truth about the messiahship of Jesus that was revealed to Peter. Acknowledging that it is impossible to separate Peter from his confession, this interpretation best answers the difficulties that are normally raised.

Against the church (that great company of those who confess the messiahship of Jesus) not even death itself ("the gates of hell," AV [or **Hades**]; cf. Isa. 38:10) will prevail. The image pictures the impotence of **Hades** (the place of departed spirits) to imprison in death those who belong to the messianic community. The promise of resurrection is deeply embedded in this promise regarding the church.

Peter is now told that he is to receive the **keys of the kingdom**. What he prohibits on earth will be prohibited in heaven, and what he permits on earth will be permitted in heaven (v. 19). The background is Isaiah 22, which prophesies the dismissal of Shebna the steward and his replacement with Eliakim the son of Hilkiah. Of the latter God says, "I will place on his shoulder the key to the house of David; what he opens no one can shut, and what he shuts no one can open" (Isa. 22:22; note v. 15). The keys that Peter is to receive represent the authority to determine what kind of conduct is worthy of those who live under the rule of God and what kind of conduct is not. To **bind** and to **loose** were technical terms used by rabbis indicating the authority to lay down binding rules or to declare exemption from them. This authority is not Peter's alone, for the same role is assigned to the other disciples in Matthew 18:18 (cf. John 20:23). Decisions made on earth by the leadership of the early church carry with them a divine sanction. Apostolic pronouncements will be ratified in the final judgment.

16:20 / Jesus gave strict orders to his disciples that they tell no one **that he was the Christ**. There was still much that they needed to learn about his messiahship, specifically that he must go to Jerusalem and be put to death (cf. v. 21). If his own disciples did not yet understand fully what messiahship entailed, how quickly would others of the Jewish faith rush to make him the fulfillment of their nationalistic hopes and dreams? Ill-informed action like this would make his role that much more difficult. Better to keep silent for now.

16:21–23 / **From that time on** marks a new stage in Jesus' revelation of himself to his disciples. They had acknowledged his messiahship, but now they must be prepared to follow a Messiah who would go to Jerusalem and suffer at the hands of the orthodox religious establishment. There he would be put to death, but after three days he would rise again. In verse 21 we have the first definite prediction of the passion (cf. 17:22–23 and 20:18–19 for the two other predictions in Matthew). When Jesus says that he must go to Jerusalem, he is saying that this course of action is determined by God's will expressed in Scripture. It is the divine intention that the Messiah be put to death. Opposition comes from the **elders** (respected community leaders), **chief priests**

(primarily Sadducees), and **teachers of the law** (or "Bible scholars" as Beck calls them). These three groups made up the Sanhedrin (the official court that governed Jewish religious and political life).

Peter takes Jesus aside and begins to reprove him (note the same Greek word, *epitimaō*, in 16:20), saying "may God in his mercy spare you this" (cf. *hileōs* in BAGD). Filson understands the expression to mean "God forgive you for saying so mistaken and shocking a thing" (p. 188). Jesus turns around (that is, turns his back on Peter) and says, "Out of my sight, you satan. You're a stumbling block in my path because your way of thinking comes from men not from God." It is instructive to compare Jesus' response to Peter with his words to the tempter in 4:10. In the earlier account, he says, "Go away, Satan" (*hypage satana*): here he says, **Get behind me, Satan** (*hypage opisō mou, satana*). To call Peter a "satan" is a strong rebuke, but those who oppose the will and plan of God are emissaries of Satan. Although Peter had just confessed Jesus as Messiah, he had yet much to learn about what that messiahship would entail.

16:24-26 / **Then** (that is, after Jesus had rebuked Peter so emphatically for playing into the hands of Satan) Jesus tells his disciples that if they wish to go his way (cf. *opisō mou* in vv. 23 and 24) they will have to renounce self, openly declare allegiance to a crucified Messiah, and accept the consequences. At this point Jesus is speaking to men who, though acknowledging the messiahship of Jesus, were not fully aware of the consequences. To **deny** means "to disclaim any connection with," "to repudiate." Jesus is not speaking of giving up certain benefits but of denying the self. Fenton writes, "The condition of discipleship is therefore the breaking of every link which ties a man to himself" (p. 273). It is obliterating self as the dominant principle of life in order to make God that principle (Barclay, vol. 2, p. 151). For a person to carry his or her cross means to accept the sentence of death on all personal ambitions and goals. The expression is figurative and derives from the practice of the condemned criminal carrying the cross bar of his instrument of execution through the streets of the city and enduring the insults of the crowds along the way. It is worthy of note that though the first two imperatives in this charge (**deny, take up**) are aorist (a Greek past tense indicating finality), the third (**follow**) is present. This would suggest defini-

tive action in the decision to enter into a life of discipleship and
the necessity of continuing faithfulness in following through on
a daily basis.

Verse 25 presents the supreme paradox of Christian discipleship. If a person tries to **save his life** (that is, abandon the way
of total self-sacrifice), he or she **will lose it**; if, however, he will
lose his life for Christ, he will find it. Jesus speaks of two kinds
of life—physical well-being and true (or essential) existence. The
immediate temptation is to look after one's physical well-being,
but when that becomes the dominant goal of existence, true life
is forfeited. It is only by losing life that true life can be gained.
Even if a person were to gain **the whole world** he or she would
still come out the loser if the conquest involved giving up "higher
life" (Williams). Nothing is as valuable as life in this ultimate
sense. "What could a man offer to buy back his soul once he had
lost it?" (Phillips). Though Jesus' statement is ultimately eschatological, there is a profound sense in which self-interest destroys
life here and now. Each decision of life is making us into a certain kind of person, and the opportunity to relive life is not open
to us. Life is lost (or gained) in living.

16:27–28 / If the path of self-denial seems too severe, it
will be of help to remember that **the Son of Man is going to come**
and he will **reward each person according to what he has done**
(cf. Ps. 62:12). Recompense is soon. In fact, there are some right
there who **will not taste death** without seeing **the Son of Man
coming in his kingdom**. The apparent meaning of these verses
is that the second advent will occur during the lifetime of the disciples. History has demonstrated that this interpretation is inadequate. Of the various suggestions offered, the two that seem most
plausible are that Jesus will shortly be transfigured before Peter,
James, and John (17:1–9) and that Jesus speaks of the intermediate kingdom of Christ in and through his church (Green, p. 154).
It is also possible that verse 27 refers to the Parousia (the eschatological return of Christ), and verse 28 speaks of the resurrection
as the open declaration of divine sonship (Rom. 1:4 says that he
was "declared with power to be the Son of God by his resurrection from the dead"). Both "comings" are part of the larger
theological plan but separated in point of time.

Additional Notes §16

16:1 / **Sign**: Gk. *sēmeion* is found seventy-seven times in the NT, predominantly in the Gospels (forty-eight times). It means **sign** either in the sense of a distinguishing mark or in reference to a miraculous deed (cf. *NIDNTT*, vol. 2, pp. 626–33).

16:6 / **Yeast**: see commentary on 13:33.

16:13ff. / For a history of the interpretation of this passage, see Cullmann, *Peter*, pp. 158–69.

16:18 / **Church**: Gk. *ekklēsia* was used in a secular sense in reference to any regularly summoned assembly or group. Applied to the early assemblies of believers, it became a regular designation for both a local gathering of Christians and the church universal as well.

16:21 / **On the third day**: Both Matthew (16:21) and Luke (9:22) have **on the third day**, whereas Mark (8:31) has "after three days." Vincent Taylor provides evidence that "in the LXX and in late Greek writers the two phrases were identical in meaning" (*Mark*, p. 378).

Jesus: Some manuscripts have "Jesus Christ," which occurs only in Matt. 1:1, 18; Mark 1:1; and John 1:17; 17:3, in the Gospels. In the verse under consideration it may have been added by a copyist influenced by the preceding account of Peter's confession.

16:23 / **Satan**: See commentary on 4:10 (also 12:26).

§17 The Transfiguration (Matt. 17:1-27)

17:1-3 / Following Peter's great messianic confession, Jesus begins to teach his disciples that his messiahship would involve rejection by the religious authorities and lead to death (16:21). To encourage his followers and to provide hope that victory lies beyond defeat, Jesus takes **Peter, James and John** to a **high mountain**, where he is **transfigured before them**. There is no particular reason why this account should be considered "a creation of mythopoetic imagination" that leaves us without "the slightest hope of recovering any element of historical fact that might conceivably lie behind it" (Beare, p. 361). We take it to be a reliable account of a supernatural transformation, the purpose of which is entirely appropriate to the ministry of Jesus the Messiah.

That Matthew locates the event **after six days** (following Caesarea Philippi) underscores the vivid impression that it left. Some view the time reference in a less historical manner and see the influence of Exodus 24:16, where after six days God called Moses into the cloud of glory that covered Mount Sinai. In biblical times divine revelation often took place on a mountaintop. Elijah was sent to the mountain to learn that the Lord was not in the wind, the earthquake, or the fire (1 Kings 19:11-12). The tradition that identifies Tabor as the Mount of Transfiguration is quite unlikely, because of its distance from Caesarea Philippi and because a castle and great fort dominated the summit at that time. Mount Hermon (fourteen miles from Caesarea Philippi and rising 9400 feet above sea level) is more likely. Luke tells us that Jesus went up the mountain in order to pray (Luke 9:28). **Peter, James and John** form an inner circle of the disciples and are found with Jesus at times of crucial importance (e.g., 26:37).

As the three disciples were watching, a change came over Jesus. **His face shone like the sun, and his clothes became as white as the light** (v. 2). Behm describes the transfiguration of Jesus as "the miracle of transformation from an earthly form into

a supraterrestrial" (*TDNT*, vol. 4, p. 758). The radiance of Moses'
face when he came down from Mount Sinai (Exod. 34:29ff.) anticipated in a partial way this transfiguration. Apart from this
scene, the Greek *metamorphoō* occurs in the New Testament only
in Romans 12:2 and 2 Corinthians 3:18.

The three disciples now see **Moses and Elijah, talking with
Jesus** (v. 3). Luke 9:31 tells us that they were talking about his
"departure" (his *exodos*, used regularly in the LXX for the departure
of God's people into the unknown en route to the land of promise). Moses and Elijah represent two of the great figures of the
Old Testament. Moses was the supreme lawgiver, and Elijah the
first of the great prophets. Gundry's argument that these two Old
Testament stalwarts do not represent the Law and the Prophets
is less than persuasive (p. 343). Their presence on this occasion
indicates that the path to the cross that Jesus is taking corresponds
with the intention of God as revealed in the Old Testament.

17:4-8 / Peter responds (Gk. *apokrinomai*, "to answer") to
the heavenly scene by offering to build three booths or shrines
for Jesus and his guests. What he intended were temporary **shel-
ters** such as those prepared for the Feast of Tabernacles (Sukkoth
was a major autumn festival). As he spoke a bright cloud en-
veloped them, and a voice from the cloud said, **This is my Son,
whom I love; with him I am well pleased. Listen to him!** In the
Old Testament the Shekinah was a cloud of glory that indicated
the presence of God (Exod. 24:15-18). Unlike a natural cloud, it
was luminous: it simultaneously revealed and concealed the
presence of God (Schweizer, p. 349).

The voice from the cloud is God's. The utterance is an exact repetition of what was spoken by the voice from heaven at
the baptism of Jesus (3:17). Peter has once again "blurted out"
(Taylor, *Mark* on 9:5) an idea that typifies the human approach.
It is critical that those who follow Jesus listen to him. He is the
beloved Son on whom God's favor rests. Pay attention to him.
Terrified at the sound of the voice, the disciples fall prostrate **to
the ground** (cf. Dan. 10:5-12). Jesus steps forward, touches them,
and encourages them to rise unafraid. When they look up, Moses
and Elijah are no longer there, and they see only Jesus. From the
transfiguration experience they would learn that even though the
Messiah would be put to death (16:21), glory and exaltation would
follow his resurrection.

17:9–13 / **As they were coming down the mountain** Jesus ordered his disciples not to tell anyone what they had seen until he had risen from the dead. To preclude the possibility of an uninformed messianic uprising it was necessary that news of what took place on the mountaintop not be spread abroad.

Jesus' disciples ask why the **teachers of the law say that Elijah must come** before the Christ. Malachi prophesied that God would send the prophet Elijah before the great and dreadful day of the Lord (Mal. 4:5). By claiming that the restoration of all things by Elijah had not taken place, the scribes could cast doubt on the messiahship of Jesus. Jesus answered that **Elijah has already come** but was mistreated in the same way that the Son of Man is "destined to undergo suffering at men's hands" (TCNT). Then they made the connection. **He was talking to them about John the Baptist**. John was the Elijah who came first in order to set things in order (cf. 11:14). The argument of the teachers of the law against his messiahship would not hold.

17:14–16 / On the following day (cf. Luke 9:37) as Jesus and the three disciples (Peter, James, and John; cf. 17:1) came down from the mountain, they encountered a scene of confusion not unlike that which greeted Moses on his descent from Mount Sinai (cf. Exod. 32). Mark tells of a great crowd and the scribes arguing with the disciples who had not been on the mountain with Jesus (Mark 9:14–16). A man with an epileptic son comes to Jesus and, falling on his knees, pleads with him for mercy. In calling him **Lord** the man is making a christological confession. If Jesus were simply another man (cf. GNB, "sir"), why would he seek healing from him?

In ancient days epileptic seizures were commonly connected with the changing phases of the moon. *Selēniazomai* means "to be moonstruck" (from *selēnē*, moon). All three Synoptic Gospels understand the boy's condition to be the result of a demon (Matt. 17:18; Mark 9:17, 25; Luke 9:39, 42). What we are dealing with is a case of epilepsy that, in this instance, was the result of demon control. Under the influence of an evil spirit, the boy would often "throw himself into the fire" (Knox) **or into the water**. The father had brought his son to the disciples, but they were unable to **heal him** (exorcize the demon, Mark 9:18; Luke 9:40).

17:17–21 / Jesus responds, **O unbelieving and perverse generation**. This phrase comes from the Song of Moses (Deut.

32:5) and is used by Paul in Philippians 2:15. It refers both to the disciples and to the crowd in general. The disciples were **perverse** (Gk. *diastrephō* means "to make crooked/pervert") in that they lacked the faith to believe that the power of God would work through them. Green suggests that their lack of faith must be attributed "to their involvement in a people hostile to Jesus and to what he stands for" (p. 156). The two rhetorical questions in verse 17 picture Jesus as visiting the world to establish his church. **How long shall I stay with you? How long shall I put up with you?**

Jesus orders the boy to be brought to him and, with a single command, orders the demon to depart (v. 18). Mark's account describes in detail the exorcism (Mark 9:20–27). **In private**, the disciples ask about their inability to perform the healing. It was **because you have so little faith**, answers Jesus. If they had **faith as small as a mustard seed** (understood as the smallest of all seeds), they would be able to move a mountain. Ancient people thought of mountains as pillars that supported the sky, and thus mountains were natural symbols of stability (Gundry, p. 353). To move a mountain was a proverbial expression for overcoming a great difficulty (cf. Isa. 54:10; 1 Cor. 13:2). With faith, nothing is impossible. Tasker writes, "The meaning of the verse is that strong faith can accomplish the apparently impossible, for the man of faith is drawing upon divine resources" (p. 168).

17:22–23 / When the disciples gather in Galilee (reading *systrephomenōn* rather than *anastrephomenōn*), Jesus speaks to them for the second time in specific terms of his coming death and resurrection (see also 16:21 and 20:18ff.). **The Son of Man is going to be betrayed into the hands of men. They will kill him, and on the third day he will be raised to life.** Upon hearing this the disciples were greatly distressed. They could understand Jesus being put to death, but apparently they were incapable of grasping the promise of resurrection. *Paradidōmi* (v. 22) in this context probably means no more than "to be handed over," although later it came to be part of the theological language of the Passion narrative.

17:24–27 / In New Testament times every male Jew twenty years of age or older was required to pay a half-shekel per year for the maintenance of the temple service (cf. Exod. 30:11–16).

This was equivalent to two day's pay for the average worker. When Jesus and his disciples arrived in Capernaum, those who collected the temple tax approached Peter to ask whether Jesus would be paying the required tax. The question, as stated in the Greek text, calls for an affirmative answer: "Your teacher, he pays the temple tax, does he not?" Peter answers, **Yes, he does.** Refusal to pay the tax would indicate a decision to withdraw from the religious community. Even the Essenes at Qumran, who had separated from Jerusalem in protest against the temple and its priesthood, paid the half-shekel tax.

Peter then "joined the rest indoors and was about to say something when Jesus spoke" (Rieu). **What do you think, Simon?** Do rulers of this world collect taxes **from their own sons or from others?** Peter answers correctly, **From others. Then the sons are exempt.** Duties (Gk. *telē*) were indirect and local, whereas taxes (Gk. *kēnsoi*; cf. English "census") were paid to the imperial treasury. The GNB understands **their own sons** as "citizens of the country" and **others** as "foreigners." It is much more probable that Jesus is comparing those who belong to the royal family and court with those who do not. Taxes are regularly imposed on citizens!

Jesus' point is clear. As those who belong to God's kingdom, they are under no obligation to pay the temple tax. Yet, there is another principle involved. In order that others may not be influenced to do something wrong (*skandalizō* means "to cause to stumble") Peter is told by Jesus to catch a **fish,** and in **its mouth** he will find the necessary tax money. Though there is no necessity for Jesus and his disciples to pay the temple tax (they belong to another kingdom), it is important that they do not set a bad example for others. To insist upon one's rights in a case like this would be to indulge in what Schweizer calls a "negative legalism," which holds that fundamental freedom must be demonstrated at all costs and is therefore no better than "positive legalism" (p. 357).

It has often been noted that this is the only miracle story in which the reader is left to infer that the miracle actually happened. It is therefore held by some to be a "bit of folk-tale" (Beare, p. 372). A somewhat similar tale is told of Polycrates, who throws his ring into the sea to satisfy the gods and when he is served fish for dinner gets it back. Others take it in a figurative sense.

What Jesus actually means is that Peter should return to fishing for a day and by selling the fish be able to pay the tax. The "miracle" is held to be contrary to the moral principle that God does not do for us what we can do for ourselves. It is also thought to violate Jesus' own decision not to use miraculous power for his own benefit. Although we may acknowledge the distinctiveness of this miracle, the recommended solutions are inadequate. To declare that a historical narrative is folklore has far-reaching implications for the reliability of the text. To suggest that the whole event is no more than an example of Jesus' sense of humor makes a farce of serious exegesis. Better to assume that Peter did exactly what Jesus told him to do and in fact found a four-drachma coin in the mouth of the first fish he caught.

Additional Notes §17

17:1 / **James**: Peter, James, and John are mentioned in Gal. 2:9, but that James is the Lord's brother, not the brother of John. It is interesting that three men (Aaron, Nadab, and Abihu) accompany Moses partway up Mount Sinai (Exod. 24).

17:2 / On the basis of v. 9, which speaks of the event as a *horama* ("vision"), some commentators hold that no physical change in Jesus' appearance needs to be inferred. The parallel in Mark 9:9 (*ha eidon*) strongly suggests that *horama* be taken in the ordinary sense of "what they had seen."

17:21 / This verse is omitted by a number of the best manuscripts (the original hand of Sinaiticus, Vaticanus, etc.) and was probably assimilated from the Markan parallel (9:29). If the passage was originally in Matthew, there is no apparent reason why it would have been omitted by a later copyist.

17:24 / **Temple tax**: The *didrachmon* (double drachma) was a Phoenician coin worth about one half-shekel. Since it was not in current coinage, two people often joined in paying a full shekel (the Greek equivalent being one stater, v. 27).

17:25 / Jesus' awareness of the thoughts of others is reflected in Matt. 12:15, 25, as well.

§18 Humility and Forgiveness (Matt. 18:1–35)

We come now to the fourth major discourse of Matthew. It ends with the usual formula in 19:1–2 (cf. 7:28; 11:1; 13:53; 26:1). Chapter 18 reads very much like an early church manual and deals with subjects such as humility (vv. 1–4), responsibility (vv. 5–7), self-renunciation (vv. 8–10), individual care (vv. 11–14), discipline (vv. 15–20), fellowship (vv. 19–20), and forgiveness (vv. 23–35; cf. Barclay, vol. 2, pp. 173–74).

18:1–5 / With the opening phrase, **at that time**, Matthew ties the teaching of chapter 18 to the preceding material. Mark locates the event in Capernaum (Mark 9:33) and, along with Luke, mentions the argument among the disciples about who was the greatest (Luke 9:46). Matthew does not mention the argument but simply puts the disciples' questions to Jesus, **Who is the greatest in the kingdom of heaven?** Jesus' teaching in Matthew 5:19 established that there would be distinctions in the kingdom of heaven ("least" and "great").

Jesus answered their question by summoning a child to stand before them. He then said that if they did not **change and become like little children** they would never **enter the kingdom of heaven**. The Greek *strephō* means "to turn around." As long as they were pursuing rank and status in heaven, they were heading in the wrong direction. Before they could even qualify for entrance into the kingdom, they would have to change completely their way of thinking.

The answer to the disciples' question is that **the greatest in the kingdom of heaven** is the sort of person (Gk. *hostis* should be taken qualitatively) who will humble himself and become like the little child who stood in their midst. Since children are not humble in the usual sense of the word, it is often discussed what quality Jesus had in mind. In the present context (a discussion of primacy and rank in the kingdom) it would seem that Jesus intended the comparison to point out the importance of lack of pretension or concern about status (Hill, p. 273). McNeile writes, "He will be the greatest who has the least idea that he is great" (p. 260).

The reference to children in verses 2–4 triggers an additional thought on the subject. **Whoever welcomes** a child like this **in my name** ("because of me") **welcomes me.** Contrary to current opinion about children (Jeremias notes that they were classed along with the deaf, dumb, and weak-minded: *New Testament Theology,* vol. 1, p. 227, n. 2), Jesus held them to be of infinite value. Since Jesus had taken his place with them, it follows that to receive one of them in his name was to receive Jesus himself.

18:6–9 / At this point Matthew moves from using the little child as an illustration of lack of concern about status to **little ones** as representing "average" members of the local congregation. The rest of chapter 18 deals with situations that arise in the church (causing others to sin, vv. 6ff.; bringing back those who have strayed, vv. 10ff.; reproving a brother, vv. 15ff.; reconciliation, vv. 21ff.; and forgiveness, vv. 23ff.).

Jesus' warning to those who lead others to lose their faith is severe. **It would be better for him to have a large millstone hung around his neck and to be drowned in the depths of the sea.** Beare notes that *skandalizomai* verges on the meaning "to lead into apostasy" and that the warning is probably aimed at "false teachers who lead simple Christians into error or unbelief" (p. 376). The admonition reminds us of Paul's caution in 1 Corinthians 8–10 about the improper use of Christian freedom. The millstone (Gk. *mylos*) to be tied around the offender's neck is called a donkey millstone (*mylos onikos*). The people of Jesus' day ground their corn between two circular stones. Larger stones required the power of donkeys to turn the mill. With a weight attached, a person would be carried immediately to the bottom of the sea.

It is a terrible thing that in the world there are influences that cause people to lose their faith. The temptations that lead astray will always be with us, but woe to the person through whom they come. Therefore **if your hand or your foot causes you to sin, cut it off** and get rid of it (v. 8). Far better to enter heaven crippled than to be cast into hell with hands and feet intact. Or **if your eye causes you to sin, gouge it out and throw it away.** Better to enter life one-eyed than **be thrown into the fire of hell** with both eyes wide open. Filson notes that "everlasting fire and fiery Gehenna both point to the everlasting consequences of moral collapse" (p. 200). Verses 8 and 9 also occur earlier in the Sermon on the Mount (cf. Matt 5:29–30). In that setting they were part of a warning against adultery. The words of Jesus are proverbial and therefore applicable in many situations. Vivid utterances like these were undoubtedly repeated by Jesus in many settings. It comes as no surprise that in the Gospels certain sayings are found in different contexts with various nuances of thought.

18:10–14 / Matthew continues with further instructions about **these little ones** (childlike believers). It is important that no one treats them with disdain because **their angels** are **in heaven** and have unrestricted access to the presence of God. The thought is that, since God is constantly informed by angelic beings of the welfare of his flock (both *dia pantos*, always, and *blepousi*, "continually see," emphasize constant awareness), for leaders in the local congregation to view those committed to their charge as unworthy of care would be to violate the divine intention. Teaching about angels was expanded greatly in Judaism following the period of the exile. The doctrine of ministering (guardian?) angels is clearly established here and in Hebrews 1:14.

Jesus tells a parable of a man with a **hundred sheep**, one of which has wandered away. He leaves the **ninety-nine** and sets out to find the one lost sheep. If he finds it his joy is greater over the one that has been found than over the ninety-nine that never strayed. The point of the parable is that God the Father does not want any of the childlike members of the congregation to wander from the truth and be lost. It is crucially important for leadership to recognize how important the "little ones" are to God.

Critics have sometimes asked why a shepherd would leave a large flock of sheep unattended in order to search for one who had wandered off. It is hardly necessary to envision a flock that belonged to the village and would therefore have several shepherds, thus allowing one of them to go after the lost sheep. The temptation to second-guess the details of a parable needs to be resisted. The essential point is the concern of the shepherd for every single sheep. God is like that: he is concerned about each believer. In this context, to **be lost** (v. 14) means to have got "out of right relation to God and in danger of eternal ruin unless sought out and restored" (Filson, p. 201).

18:15–17 / Matthew turns now to the question of appropriate action to be taken in case a Christian is guilty of sinning against another member of the community. Jesus taught that in such instances the aggrieved party should first take it up personally and in private with the one who acted wrongly. If that does not clear up the problem, the next step is to **take one or two others along**, not to prove the other's guilt but to help in reconciliation. If the person pays no attention to them, the matter should then be reported to the entire church. If this fails to bring about a satisfactory resolution, the person who has wronged should be excommunicated from the religious community.

The same three-step procedure is found in the Qumran legislation (1QS 5.25–6.1). Attempts at reconciliation should always begin one on one. More damage has been done by well-intentioned letters than by any other method. Taking witnesses along is based on the Mosaic legislation in Deuteronomy 19:15, although the purpose in the New Testament setting is not to establish a conviction but to help in settling a dispute. The Greek word for **church** (*ekklēsia*) occurs only here and in Matthew 16:18 in the Gospels. It refers to the local group of believers. Many writers have objected that Jesus would not have spoken derogatorily of the Gentiles and tax collectors, as he apparently does in verse 17. Beare is convinced that "there is not the least likelihood that Jesus himself ever spoke with such disparagement" (p. 380), and Barclay claims that it is "not possible that Jesus said this in its present form" (vol. 2, p. 187). There is no necessity, however, to read into the statement an attitude that need not be there. Pagans and tax collectors were widely considered by the Jewish population to be outside the circle of God's immediate blessing. It was simply another way of indicating what happens when a person is removed from the believing fellowship.

18:18–20 / Verses 18–20 are quite often included in the previous paragraph. Gundry says that Matthew composed verses 16–20 as an expansion of the saying in verse 15 (p. 370). They extend to the church the power of "binding and loosing" that was earlier given to Peter at Caesarea Philippi (Matt. 16:19). In the current context, prohibiting would refer to bringing judgment against the one who sinned against a fellow Christian and permitting would be pronouncing in favor of the accused. The final outcome would be excommunication or absolution. Whatever decision the church makes, it will be sanctioned **in heaven**.

Though verses 19 and 20 appear to be speaking of corporate prayer, the context suggests that the agreement reached with its heavenly sanction relates to the matter of church discipline mentioned in verse 17. The Greek text of verse 19 opens with the connective *palin* ("again"). That which two or three come to agree on (*symphōneō* means "to produce a sound together,"* cf. the English "symphony") has to do with the decision concerning an unrepentant member of the believing community. God will answer the united concern of praying people. In fact, wherever **two or three come together** earnestly desiring to know the will of God, he himself will be "right there with them" (Williams).

18:21–27 / Peter comes to Jesus asking him how many times he must forgive a **brother when he sins against** him. Rabbinic literature taught that "if a man sins once, twice, or three times, they forgive him: if he sins a fourth time, they do not forgive him" (m. *Yoma* 5.13). Going beyond the accepted limit, Peter asks, "Would seven times be enough?" (Phillips). **Not seven times**, replies Jesus, **but seventy-seven times**. Lamech's formula for revenge in Genesis 4:24 ("If Cain is avenged seven times, then Lamech seventy-seven times") is changed into a model of unlimited forgiveness.

To emphasize the need for unlimited forgiveness Jesus tells the parable of the unmerciful servant. It is recorded only in Matthew. There was a **king** who wished **to settle accounts** with his agents (the huge debt suggests that the *douloi* were those who gathered revenue for the king). One was brought in (from prison? *prosagō* means "to lead or bring to") whose debt "ran into millions" (NEB; **ten thousand talents**, NIV, roughly equal to ten million dollars). Since he was unable to settle such an enormous debt (more than the total annual revenue of a wealthy province), the king **ordered that he and his wife and his children and all that he had be sold** and the money be applied toward **the debt. The servant fell on his knees** and began to beg (*prosekynei* is inceptive imperfect) for an extension of time. Note the optimism of the servant: "Give me time, and I will pay you every cent of it" (Williams). Taking pity on the agent, the king canceled the entire debt (the Greek has *daneion*, "loan") and let him go free.

18:28–35 / Now comes the dark side of the story. This very same servant, as he left the king's presence with his huge debt canceled, met **one of his fellow servants who owed him** no more than a few dollars (NIV's **a hundred denarii** would amount to about twenty dollars). Seizing him by the throat, he demanded payment. Refusing his fellow servant's request for time to repay the debt, **he had the man thrown into prison**, thus depriving him of any chance to earn the necessary money. **When the other servants saw what had happened, they were greatly distressed.** Going to the king, they told him the entire story. The king called in the servant whose debt he had canceled and reproved him for his failure to extend to another the same mercy he had received. So angry was the king that he turned over the unforgiving servant (v. 32 calls him a "scoundrel," NEB) **to the jailers to be tortured, until he should pay** the debt in full. The Greek *basanistēs* ("jailer," v. 34) means "one who tortures." Though torture was forbidden by Jewish law, the practice was widespread in the ancient world. Debtors could be tortured in order to make them reveal unacknowledged sources of money.

Jesus concludes the parable with the stern warning that the heavenly Father will deal in similar fashion with anyone who will not from his or her heart forgive a fellow Christian. It expands the point made in 6:15 that those who do not forgive will not be forgiven. An unwillingness to extend mercy is proof that a person has never received mercy. God's forgiveness must of necessity create a forgiving spirit. The parable may be included here as a warning to the church to exercise the right of excommunication (vv. 16–20) with considerable caution. Though it may be necessary to exclude the nonrepentant from the believing community, personal forgiveness of the individual should never be withheld.

Additional Notes §18

18:6 / Josephus reports an uprising in Galilee in which the rebels seized the supporters of Herod and put them to death by drowning them in the sea (*Ant.* 14.448–450). It was a quick but crude method of execution.

18:9 / **Fire of hell**: Gk. *tēn geennan tou pyros* in v. 9 is the same as *to pyr to aiōnion* (**eternal fire**) of v. 8. *Geenna* is the Greek for the Hebrew "Valley of Hinnom," a ravine south of Jerusalem used as a refuse dump, in which smoldering fires burned unceasingly. In the days of the monarchy it was the place of idolatrous cult worship where children were sacrificed by fire to the pagan god Molech (cf. 2 Kings 23:10; Jer. 7:31).

18:11 / Verse 11 is not included in the better manuscripts and has undoubtedly been borrowed from Luke 19:10 to provide a connection with the parable that follows.

18:14 / In Luke the parable of the lost sheep is used to justify Jesus' practice of ministering to tax collectors and sinners (i.e., religious outcasts, cf. Luke 15:2ff.). In Matthew the parable serves to teach God's concern lest a single member of the flock, however insignificant, wander from the truth.

18:15 / Some manuscripts omit *eis se* (NIV **against you**). This could have been an interpolation based on *eis eme* (NIV **against me**) in v. 21. It is also possible that the phrase could have been omitted by a copyist in order to make the passage more broadly applicable. (Cf. Metzger, *TCGNT*, p. 45).

18:19 / *Pirke Aboth* provides an interesting parallel: "If two sit together and the words of the Law [are spoken] between them, the divine Presence rests between them" (3:2).

18:22 / **Seventy-seven times**: Gk. *hebdomēkontakis hepta* could be a shortened form of *hebdomēkontakis heptakis* (seventy times seven times) but is probably **seventy-seven times**. The identical phrase is found in Gen. 4:24, where the LXX translates a Hebrew text reading seventy-seven.

19:1–6 / When Jesus finished his discourse (as recorded in chap. 18), he left Galilee for the last time and went to the area of Judea that lay east of the Jordan. Great crowds followed him there and he healed them.

Some Pharisees came to him to test him (note the same use of *peirazō* in Matt. 22:18, 35) by asking him if the law allowed **a man to divorce his wife for any and every reason.** The Pharisees permitted divorce but differed on the appropriate terms. Deuteronomy 24:1 speaks of a man divorcing his wife "because he finds something indecent about her." The school of Shammai held this to be immorality on the part of the wife. The school of Hillel interpreted it to be anything at all that proved to be displeasing to the husband. Rabbi Akiba (early second century) went so far as to say that if a man met another woman more pleasing than his wife it was tantamount to finding "something indecent" in her and was an acceptable reason for divorce. God's declaration "I hate divorce" (Mal. 2:16) had conveniently been ignored by the more liberal school of thought.

Jesus responds with a counterquestion: **Haven't you read . . . that at the beginning the Creator "made them male and female"** (made them for marriage)? Therefore, when a man leaves father and mother to become one with his wife, no one is to separate what God has joined together. God's plan in creation was that man and woman should live together in monogamous marriage (Gen. 1:27). McNeile notes that "the first human male and female were intended solely for each other" (there was no one else to marry) and that this norm of an indissoluble union was intended for each succeeding pair (p. 273).

Genesis 2:24 sets forth the divine intention. Marriage brings man and woman together, not as two people who share certain things in common, but in order to create (it is significant that in v. 4 God is called *ho ktisas,* **the Creator**) something new. **The two will become one flesh** (v. 5). **They are no longer two, but one**

(v. 6). That is why it is wrong for man to separate **what God has joined together**. It is a reversal of the divine order.

19:7–10 / If divorce runs counter to the divine intention, then **why**, asked the Pharisees, **did Moses** give the law allowing **a man** to **give his wife a certificate of divorce and send her away?** Is Moses guilty of writing laws that run counter to the mind of God? Such an idea would be blasphemous in the religious culture of first-century Judaism. Jesus answers that Moses' injunction regarding divorce came as a result of their hardness of heart. Williams translates, "It was because of your moral perversity that Moses allowed you to divorce" (v. 8). But that was not what was intended in the beginning. Actually, the requirement of a written notice of divorce made the process more difficult. Prior to that time a marriage could be dissolved by the man simply declaring it to be so. A written notice would give time for anger to dissipate and common sense to regain control.

Jesus continues by pointing out that whoever **divorces** his wife for any cause other than marital infidelity and marries another is guilty of **adultery** (v. 9). In the parallel passage in 5:32 divorce is said to cause the woman who is put away to commit adultery. In the culture of that day a divorced woman would very easily find herself trapped into a life of prostitution. In the present passage it is the man who commits adultery by remarriage. The point is that in God's sight the man who divorces his wife for any cause other than her unfaithfulness is still married to her.

If that's the case between a man and his wife, respond the disciples, then it would be **better not to marry** at all. The difficulty of achieving a perfect marriage becomes an argument against marriage itself. Tasker writes that "this is the voice of the perfectionist, and the ascetic, who because the best is unlikely to be attained would avoid the second-best" (p. 183).

19:11–12 / Jesus' response to his disciples' conclusion about marriage is that not all men are able to accept (*chōreō*, "to make room," thus, in a mental sense, "to comprehend or accept," BAGD, p. 890) this saying (*ton logon touton*), but only those "who have the gift" (Moffatt). Commentators differ as to what this teaching refers to. Some take it as a response to the disciples' saying in the previous verse. For example, Knox translates, "That conclusion . . . cannot be taken in by everybody" (cf. Beare, p. 391;

Green, p. 169). The problem here, however, is that God is held as agreeing with the disciples' conclusion that it is better not to marry (v. 10). This runs counter to the divine intention in creation (Gen. 1:28).

It is better to take Jesus' statement in verse 11 as referring to his teaching on divorce and remarriage in verses 3–9. Not everyone is able to accept his strict position on the subject, but **only those to whom it** [the ability to accept] **has been given**. It is not a question of whether or not a person should refrain from marriage for the sake of evangelism or because the end of all things is not far off. The issue has to do with true disciples who have had to divorce their wives for immorality and "out of obedience to Christ's law concerning divorce they do not remarry" (Gundry, pp. 381–82). Those who cannot or do not accept the teaching are nondisciples and false disciples.

There are several reasons why men do not marry (or are unsuited for marriage). Some have been disabled from birth. Others were made that way by men (v. 12). It was not uncommon for servants in the royal harems to be castrated in order to protect the women. Also, in certain Mediterranean cults priests dedicated themselves to a mother goddess by self-emasculation (Beare, p. 391). Origen, one of the most influential thinkers of the early church, castrated himself, although in time he came to realize his error.

A third type of eunuch is the man who has renounced marriage **because of the kingdom of heaven**. This is voluntary celibacy, and, if one follows Gundry's argument, these are those who "live as eunuchs after they have had to divorce their wives for immorality" (p. 382). So Jesus concludes, **The one who can accept this** (teaching on divorce and remarriage) **should accept it**. It is the mark of a true disciple to live in obedience to God's best intention for human beings.

19:13–15 / When **little children were brought to Jesus** so that he might lay **his hands on them and pray**, the disciples rebuked those who brought them (Phillips says that they "frowned on the parents' action"). The disciples were annoyed that their journey to Jerusalem was being slowed down. Jesus, however, had different priorities. **Let the little children come to me, and do not hinder them, for the kingdom of heaven belongs** to the child-like. So first he gave them his blessing (i.e., **placed his hands on**

them) and then he continued on his way. Verse 14 has often been used in support of child baptism (cf. Cullmann, *Baptism in the New Testament*, pp. 71–80), but the argument lacks force (cf. Tasker, p. 185).

19:16–22 / The young man who comes to Jesus in this narrative is sometimes called the rich young ruler. That he is rich is clearly seen in all three Gospels. In Mark there is no indication of his age or rank. In Luke he is called a "ruler" (Luke 18:18), but his age is not mentioned. In Matthew he is twice designated **young man** (vv. 20, 22), but his rank is not indicated.

It is instructive to compare the young man's question to Jesus as recorded both in Matthew and in Mark. In Mark he addresses Jesus with the title "good teacher" and asks, "What must I do to inherit eternal life?" (Mark 10:17). Matthew has him address Jesus simply as **Teacher** and moves the adjective "good" to the question: **What good thing must I do to get eternal life?** This modification requires Jesus' response in Mark ("Why do you call me good?" 10:18) to become, **Why do you ask me about what is good?** in Matthew (v. 17).

Differences of this nature are not uncommon in the Synoptic Gospels. Some scholars go to great lengths to explain exactly how it all happened. The relationship between the first three Gospels, with their similarities and differences, is called the Synoptic Problem. It is sufficient to mention at this point that ancient literature need not be pressed into modern categories. The writers of the Gospels, to whatever extent they were aware of or copied from one another (or from some common source), produced their work without any sense of conflict or incongruity. The Gospels should be read with the same openness. The proverbial nature of Jesus' teaching and the fact that the disciples heard him teach over a period of some years would lead us to expect variations on the same essential truths.

The young man's question reveals a misunderstanding about spiritual matters: **What good thing must I do?** He felt that eternal life came as a reward for some great act. Jesus answers, as he so often does, with another question: **Why do you ask me** (emphasized in Greek) **about what is good?** As an informed Jew you already have God's revelation on the subject. If you want to enter life, **obey the commandments**. To the young man's query, "What sort of commandments?" (Williams; Gk. *poias*), Jesus responds by listing five of the Ten Commandments (numbers five through nine, according to Exod. 20:12–16) and adding Leviticus 19:18.

The young man responds that he has obeyed all the commandments listed by Jesus but still feels there is something else he needs to do (v. 20). His uneasiness reveals an instinctive human awareness that legalism falls short of God's intention. That he had not, in fact, fulfilled the requirement to love his neighbor as himself is brought out in the account as told in the *Gospel According to the Hebrews* (a second-century expansion of Matthew mentioned by several early Christian writers). In that account Jesus rebukes him for claiming to love his brother when many of them are "clothed in filth" and "dying of hunger."

When the young man heard from Jesus that in order to reach his goal (**to be perfect**; Gk. *teleios*) he would have to **sell** his **possessions and give** the money **to the poor** (v. 21), . . . **he went away sad** (v. 22). Unfortunately, he was very rich. Great wealth tends to break down fraternal relationships because it separates those who have from those who have not. The requirement to divest oneself of all possessions is not a universal requirement for entrance into heaven. It was, for this specific person, a test of his willingness to place God's priorities first in his own life. The monastic requirement of poverty grew out of a misunderstanding of this verse. The idea of two levels of moral obligation is not true to the intent of the passage.

19:23–26 / Turning to his disciples, Jesus summarizes the incident by noting how difficult it is for **a rich man to enter the kingdom of heaven**. In fact, **it is easier for a camel to go through the eye of a needle than for a rich** [person] **to enter the kingdom of God**. Obviously, Jesus is using hyperbole. The **camel** was the largest animal in Palestine and the **eye of a needle** was the smallest opening in a familiar object (Gundry, p. 390). The statement is proverbial and found in the Koran (*Sura* 7.38) as well as in the Talmud (cf. b. *Berak.* 55b, where "elephant" is used instead of "camel"). It is unnecessary to find ways in which "camel" can be understood as "rope" or a "piece of camel-hair" and the "eye of a needle" a reference to some low gateway in the wall of Jerusalem. What Jesus is saying is that the lure of possessions is so strong that a rich person is unable with his or her own strength to break its grip.

Because wealth in the Old Testament was generally regarded as a mark of God's favor (cf. Ps. 1:3), the disciples respond to Jesus' words about the difficulty of the rich entering heaven by asking, **Who then can be saved?** The answer is that although it is impossible from a human standpoint (to overcome the powerful attraction of money and place oneself in dependence upon God), with God's help anything is possible.

19:27–30 / Somewhat incongruously, Peter asks what reward there will be for the disciples who have given up everything in order to follow Jesus. The answer is that **at the renewal of all things, when the Son of Man** is enthroned, the twelve disciples will sit on **twelve thrones, judging the twelve tribes of Israel**. The Greek word translated **the renewal of all things** (*palingenesia*) occurs only here and in Titus 3:5 in the New Testament. It is a technical term developed by the Stoics, who expected a periodic renewal of the universe following its destruction by fire. In Jewish thought, regeneration referred to the renewal of Israel that would accompany the establishment of God's earthly kingdom. Christians linked the concept with the enthronement of the Son of Man.

The idea of judging (v. 28 has the participle *krinontes*) should be taken in the sense of ruling. The Hebrew judge was virtually the ruler of Israel. The symbolism of the twelve tribes is carried over into New Testament to represent the Christian church (cf. James 1:1). Everyone who has forsaken home and family will be rewarded **a hundred times** over **and will inherit eternal life. But many who are first** (those who have not made the sacrifice of family in order to follow Jesus) **will be last, and many who are last** (such as the disciples) **will be first**. That there are twelve followers is symbolic: it does not ensure a place in the New Age for Judas.

Additional Notes §19

19:1 / **Judea**: from the adjective *ioudaios* meaning "Jewish" and assuming Galilee and Samaria as well as districts east of the Jordan.

19:5 / Under extreme circumstances (e.g., if the man contracted a loathsome disease), a woman could force her husband to divorce her. Rabbinic law made divorce compulsory when there was adultery or sterility.

19:12 / According to Deut. 23:1, eunuchs were excluded from the assembly of the Lord. An animal with damaged testicles was not acceptable as a sacrifice (Lev. 22:24). Voluntary celibacy was uncommon in Jewish culture except in Essene Judaism (cf. 1QSa 1.25; 2.11).

19:18–19 / In Rom. 13:9 Paul lists three of the same commandments and adds the Leviticus passage ("Love your neighbor as yourself") as summing up all the commandments.

19:24 / **Camel**: Several inferior manuscripts read *kamilon* (a "ship's hawser" or "rope") rather than *kamēlon* ("camel"). In later Greek the *i* and the *e* were both pronounced *ee* (hence there was no way to distinguish orally, since both words were pronounced *kah-mee-lon*).

It is important to note the close tie between chapter 20 and the verse that precedes it. The saying about the first who will be last and the last who will be first (19:30) is repeated at the end of the first section of chapter 20 (v. 16). This Semitic device is called *inclusio*, and because the order is inverted it is also an example of *chiasmus* (for other examples compare 7:16 with 7:20, and 24:42 with 25:13). Chapter 20 also begins with the Greek conjunction *gar*, which emphasizes continuity.

20:1–7 / **The kingdom of heaven** is said to be **like a landowner who went out early in the morning to hire** laborers **to work in his vineyard.** In ancient times the working day extended from sunup until sundown (cf. Ps. 104:20–23); the grape harvest in Palestine ripened toward the end of September. Finding some workers, the owner agreed to pay them the usual day's wage for their labor and sent them into his vineyard. About three hours later (around nine in the morning) **he went out and saw others standing in the marketplace doing nothing.** Some commentators picture these men as sitting around idly gossiping, but with economic conditions as they were in Palestine at that time, this would be unlikely. The owner promised these men a fair wage (**whatever is right**), and they went to work for him.

At noon and at three in the afternoon the owner did the same thing. Then, about an hour before sundown, he returned to the marketplace and found yet another group still without work. "Why have you spent the entire day idle?" he asked. There may have been a bit of reproach in the question, and their answer ("no one hired us") could be a cover up for laziness.

20:8–16 / **When evening came, the owner** instructed his **foreman** to send for the workers and **pay them their wages,** beginning with **the last ones hired.** Jewish law held that a laborer should be paid on the evening of the same day he had worked, so that the poor would not go hungry (Deut. 24:14–15; cf. Lev.

19:13). The men who were hired last each received a full day's wage, which led those who had started earlier to expect that they would receive more. But that was not the case. They also received their denarius. As they left, they began **to grumble against the landowner.** Those that have worked only one hour have been treated exactly like those of us who have "sweated the whole day long in the blazing sun!" (NEB).

It is instructive to note that though the workers address the owner without any title of courtesy, he responds to them with **friend** (although *hetairos* probably implies a mild reproach; cf. 22:12; 26:50). The owner has not been unjust, because the first workers had agreed on an acceptable wage. If he chooses to pay the same amount to others that is certainly his right. After all, it is his money. The AV translation of verse 15b ("Is thine eye evil, because I am good?") is rendered well by the NIV with its **Or are you envious because I am generous?** (v. 15).

Jesus concludes the parable (as he began it) with the saying that **the last will be first, and the first will be last.** There has been a great deal of discussion among New Testament scholars regarding who is intended by the **first** and the **last.** In the context of Matthew's presentation the latecomers would be those who did not appear to have the same claim upon the goodness of God. They were the tax collectors and other religious outcasts. Gundry adopts a different approach, holding them to be Gentiles who had entered the church only recently, whereas those who came first would be their detractors among Jewish Christians (p. 399). Yet another approach is tied in with the observation that Peter's question in 19:27 reveals that he had not yet grasped that God rewards those who seek no reward. Following this suggestion opens the possibility that the parable is told to distinguish between two types of work: one that is based on a desire for reward and the other upon confidence that God will take care of those who leave everything to him. Note that to the second group he promises to pay "whatever is right" (v. 4), and there is no mention of pay to the others who start later. Once again the specific application of the verse is difficult because of the proverbial nature of the concluding statement. It is best to understand the parable and its application in the light of Jesus' own setting and ministry.

20:17–19 / As Jesus was going up to Jerusalem, he took the twelve disciples aside to tell them what would happen to him there. This is now the third prediction of his passion. Once again he speaks only to the Twelve. Three important points are made. First, he will be **betrayed to the chief priests and the teachers of the law**. *Paradidōmi* (**betrayed**) was a technical term for "release into custody." It refers primarily to the actions of Judas Iscariot (26:15ff.), although the passive tense may imply that God's purpose is being carried out.

Second, though it is the religious leaders who **condemn him to death**, it is the **Gentiles** (Romans) who will execute the sentence. They will make sport of him, scourge him, and he will be **crucified**. Matthew is the only synoptic author who indicates the specific nature of Jesus' death. He uses *stauroō* ("to crucify"), whereas the others have *apokteinō* ("to kill"). Crucifixion was not a Jewish form of punishment. It originated with the Phoenicians and was later passed on to other nations. It was commonly used with slaves, foreigners, and criminals of the lowest class.

It was difficult for the disciples to understand that Jesus the Messiah would be put to death. They still shared the Jewish view that Messiah would come in triumph (the parallel in Luke 18:34 says that "they did not grasp what was said"). It was even more difficult for them to understand that following his crucifixion he would be **raised to life** (v. 19). There is no real difference between Matthew's **on the third day** and Mark's "after three days" (ASV; Mark 10:34). Fenton notes that this entire section follows naturally after Jesus' statement in verse 16 that the last will be first. He is "last" in the humiliating events leading to his death but "first" in the resurrection and exaltation (p. 322).

20:20–22 / The **mother of Zebedee's sons** comes to Jesus with the request that her **two sons** (James and John) be given positions of honor in the kingdom. When Matthew 27:56 is compared with its parallel in Mark (15:40), we learn that her name is Salome. On the basis of John 19:25, it seems quite probable that she was the sister of Mary the mother of Jesus. This would make James and John cousins of Jesus and may explain why she imagined that they would receive special favor.

In Mark's account, it is James and John who approach Jesus with the request, whereas in Matthew it is their mother. For many critics this "artificial intervention of the mother" (Beare, p. 20) is held to be Matthew's device to protect the reputation of the disciples. Barclay says that Matthew "did not wish to show James and John

guilty of worldly ambition" (vol. 2, p. 229). However, the fact that
when the others hear about it they are "indignant with the two
brothers" (v. 24) shows that the mother was no more than a
spokeswoman. That the Gospel writers include an account that
puts two leading apostles in such an unflattering light strengthens
one's confidence in the historical reliability of the narrative. In-
cidentally, the account shows that there were women among the
followers of Jesus.

The request for positions of honor and authority (on either
side of the throne; cf. Josephus *Ant.* 6.235–238) assumes an earthly
kingdom and reveals a misunderstanding that lingered even into
the postresurrection period (cf. Acts 1:6). Jesus' response, which
is directed to the two disciples (*oidate* is plural), is that they **don't
know what** they **are asking.** Can they **drink the cup** of suffering
(cf. 26:39; Isa. 51:17) that he is about to drink? James and John
are certain that they can, but their desertion of Jesus in the garden (26:56) shows how unprepared they were for what would follow. Note that the AV's "and to be baptized with the baptism that
I am baptized with" is omitted. It is not in the best Greek manuscripts and can be explained as a copyist's addition based on the
parallel passage in Mark 10:38.

20:23 / Jesus' answer (**You will indeed drink from my
cup**) is thought by some to be a *vaticinium post eventum* (prophecy
after the event) and indicates that both James and John were
martyred by Herod the King about A.D. 44. The best tradition
holds that John lived to an old age in Ephesus and died a natural death in exile on the isle of Patmos (cf. Rev. 1:9; Irenaeus,
Adv. haer., 3.3.4; Eusebius, *Eccl. Hist.*, 3.31; 4.14; 5.8). They **will
indeed drink** from the cup of suffering, but positions of honor
are for those to whom they have already been assigned by the
Father. A strong element of predestination runs through Jewish
thought.

20:24–28 / When the other disciples heard what James
and John had done, **they were indignant**. It would appear that
they were prompted more by jealousy than by any sense of in-
appropriateness on the part of the two. Jesus speaks to *all* of them
in pointing out that, although pagan rulers lord it over their subjects, this is not the way it is to be among his followers. The secret of greatness is not the ability to tyrannize others but the

willingness to become their **servant**. Whoever would become first must become "the willing slave of all" (NEB).

The great example of servant leadership is Jesus himself. He is the **Son of Man,** who **did not come to be served, but to serve.** To sit at his right and at his left in the kingdom (v. 21) calls for a life of service as he also served. Jesus' final words in the paragraph are exceptionally important for the discussion about the substitutionary nature of Christ's redemptive death. The Son of Man has come to **give his life as a ransom for many.**

The Greek word for **ransom** is *lytron* and is not found apart from this setting in the New Testament. Its basic meaning is money paid to buy back prisoners of war. In the LXX it is often used in a cultic sense for the payment of a debt to a deity (*TDNT,* vol. 4, p. 340). It is also used in the LXX figuratively in the general sense of rescue without any question of a ransom being paid to someone (Beare, p. 409). This has lead some scholars to consider this verse of limited importance for the biblical doctrine of atonement. Barclay calls attention to what "the crude hands of theology" have done with this "lovely saying" and quotes Peter Lombard (as the extreme example), who writes that "the cross was a mousetrap to catch the devil, baited with the blood of Christ" (vol. 2, pp. 234–35). Others call attention to the fact that the saying is found in an ethical setting and should therefore not be pressed for its christological significance (Beare, p. 790). After all the caveats have been registered, Jesus still declares that he came to give his life as a means of redeeming humankind. The Greek text says that he gave his life *lytron anti pollōn* ("a ransom in the place of many"). It would be difficult to express the substitutionary nature of Jesus' death in clearer language. Büchsel concludes his article on the subject with the statement, "The understanding of Jesus' death as a ransom for us is a basic element in the Church's confession which it cannot surrender" (*TDNT,* vol. 4, p. 349).

20:29–34 / In both Matthew and Mark this healing takes place just before the triumphal entry into Jerusalem. Luke adds the story of Zacchaeus and the parable of the pounds, which took place as Jesus and the disciples went through Jericho. This may account for Matthew and Mark's placing the healing after Jericho while Luke places it "as they drew near to Jericho" (Luke 18:35). Matthew tells of two blind men; Mark and Luke speak of one.

Tasker suggests that two men may have received their sight, but the Petrine tradition, known only to Mark, concentrated on one who may have been known personally to Peter (p. 196). Matthew recorded a similar healing of two men in 9:27–31, which some have taken as a different narrative from the same source; but several differences exist, and the emphasis in each account is different (the men's faith in the first, and Jesus' compassion in the second). It is Mark who supplies the name of Bartimaeus and indicates that he was a beggar (Mark 10:46).

Those who made up the **large crowd** that followed Jesus out of Jericho were mostly pilgrims on their way to celebrate the Passover at Jerusalem. The size of the crowd reveals the mounting excitement about Jesus and what might happen at the sacred festival. When the **two blind men** heard that it was **Jesus** who was **going by,** they called out, "Have pity on us, Son of David!" Apart from this incident the title **Son of David** does not occur elsewhere in Mark or Luke (or ever outside the Gospels). For Matthew, it had messianic significance, and he uses it seven times. The *Psalms of Solomon* 17:23ff. picture the Son of David as a messianic king, and Isaiah 29:18 portrays restoration of sight as a sign of the messianic era. The healing of the blind at this particular point shows that the Son of David, even while on his way to Jerusalem to suffer and die, responds in compassion to the cry of those who need to be served.

When rebuked by the crowd, they **shouted all the louder . . . Jesus stopped,** and the blind men, in answer to his query, pleaded with him to open their eyes. Moved with compassion, Jesus **touched their eyes**; their sight was immediately restored, and they **followed him.** Tasker calls attention to an interesting textual variant in the Curetonian MS of the Old Syriac version, which adds *et videamus te* ("and that we may see thee") after "that our eyes may be opened" in verse 33 (p. 196). It calls attention to the central concern of the blind men: not simply to see but to see Jesus the Messiah.

Additional Notes §20

20:2 / **Denarius**: The *dēnarion* was a worker's average daily wage. Cf. Pliny 33.3; Tacitus *Ann.* 1.17.

20:15 / The "evil eye" (cf. AV) was a common expression in later Judaism that denoted a covetous eye filled with envy (cf. Mark 7:22: *TDNT*, vol. 6, p. 555).

20:17 / Some manuscripts read *mellōn de anabainein Iēsous* ("When Jesus was about to go up"; Montgomery), because topographically one did not go up until leaving Jericho (cf. v. 29).

20:19 / **Crucified**: Cf. the article in *HDB* rev., pp. 193–94.

20:22 / **Cup**: The cup is a familiar Jewish figure for judgment (Ps. 75:8) and suffering (Isa. 51:17). Ps. 116:13, however, speaks of a "cup of salvation."

20:30 / Manuscripts vary considerably in reporting the cry of the blind men. The editorial committee of the UBS decided to adopt the reading reflected in the RSV but enclosed *kyrie* within square brackets (*TCGNT*, pp. 53–54).

21:1–5 / Jesus and his disciples crossed the Jordan and traveled south through Perea in order to avoid Samaria. This brought them through Jericho and up to Jerusalem from the east. When they arrived at the village of **Bethphage**, Jesus sent two of his disciples ahead to secure a donkey and her colt. **Bethphage** was located on the Mount of Olives and considered the eastern boundary of Jerusalem (the name means "house of the country districts," Lat. *pagi*). **The Mount of Olives** is directly east from Jerusalem across the Kidron valley and held an important place in Jewish eschatology.

The two disciples are told that, if anyone says anything to them about untying the animals, they are to indicate that **the Lord needs them.** If the latter part of verse 3 (**and he will send them right away**) is part of the statement to the owner, it means that Jesus will return the animals soon. If it is addressed to the two disciples, it means that the owner will let the animals go. The title *kyrios* (**Lord**) suggests that the owner was a disciple of Jesus.

Matthew identifies this event as a fulfillment of a prophecy by Zechariah that Israel's king will come **gentle and riding on a donkey.** The first line of the quotation (which Matthew says was spoken through **the prophet,** singular) comes from Isaiah 62:11 and the rest from Zechariah 9:9. Schweizer says this is "consonant with rabbinic hermeneutics, in which a passage containing the same word as another serves to interpret the latter" (p. 405). Of interest is the omission from Zechariah of the descriptive phrase "righteous and having salvation." It appears that Matthew was interested mainly in emphasizing the humility of the Messiah.

It should be mentioned that in both Mark and Luke only the colt is mentioned (Mark 11:7; Luke 19:35). Matthew has two animals, a **donkey** and a **colt** (vv. 2, 5, 7). Since the colt was unbroken (cf. Mark 11:2), it seems reasonable that the mother would be brought along but not necessarily mentioned. Entering Jerusalem on a donkey would indicate a mission of goodwill (an aggressor would have ridden a war-horse; cf. *Pss. Sol.* 17.23–27).

21:6–11 / The disciples followed Jesus' orders and **brought the donkey**. When they had laid their outer garments (*himation* normally designates the cloak or outer covering) **on them** (the animals) Jesus sat **on them** (the garments). Gundry pictures the garments draped over both animals and Jesus sitting on the colt, which gives the impression of a kind of wide throne (p. 410). The large crowd that was following along with Jesus **spread their cloaks on the road**, as well as **branches** that they had cut from trees (cf. the festive scene in 2 Kings 9:13; also 1 Macc. 13:51). The crowds that led the way and those that followed behind were calling out (*ekrazon* is imperfect) **Hosanna to the Son of David!** **Hosanna** translates the Hebrew expression meaning "Save us" (Ps. 118:25), but by New Testament times it was simply a shout of joyous praise. **He who comes in the name of the Lord** may have been a messianic title. To come **in the name of the Lord** means to come as his emissary. **Hosanna in the highest** means something like, "Let even the angels in the heights of heaven sing praises."

When Jesus entered Jerusalem, the whole city "went wild with excitement" (NEB). They asked, **Who is this?** and **the crowds answered** that he was **Jesus, the prophet from Nazareth in Galilee**. Unless the multitude was intimidated by those in Jerusalem and decided to softpedal their messianic claims, it is best to understand **the prophet** as the eschatological prophet foretold by Moses (Deut. 18:15) rather than simply as a prophet well known in Galilee but not in Judea.

21:12–13 / The temple in Jerusalem consisted of an inner sanctuary (called the *naos*) surrounded by a series of courtyards. In descending order they were the Court of the Priests, Israelites, Women, and Gentiles. The entire temple area was designated as the *hieron*. It was in the outer court that the temple authorities arranged booths (called the Bazaars of Annas and belonging to the family of the high priest) to provide animals approved for sacrifice and to exchange foreign currency for coins acceptable for paying the half-shekel temple tax (cf. 17:24). Because most local coins were stamped with pagan symbols, they were not acceptable. Rabbinic tradition held that the temple tax should be paid with a high-quality silver Tyrian coin called the tetradrachma.

Jesus entered the temple area (Court of the Gentiles) **and drove out all who were buying and selling there.** He tipped over **the tables of the money changers** and the chairs of **those selling doves.** It is highly probable that the commercial transactions in the temple were very favorable to the priests. A certain amount was charged for the exchange of money, and animals were sold at a high price. For example, pigeons, which could be sacrificed by those too poor to buy a lamb, sold for several times as much inside the temple as they did outside (cf. Barclay, vol. 2, p. 245).

It is written, Jesus said, that **"my house will be called a house of prayer."** But they were making it **a "den of robbers."** (v. 13). The first statement comes from Isaiah 56:7, which says that God's house is to be "a house of prayer for all nations." Gentiles were allowed no closer to the sanctuary than the outer court. It was there that the commercialism was rampant—hardly a house of prayer for the non-Jew. The second statement is from Jeremiah 7:11. Beare comments on the setting in Jeremiah, which tells of worshipers who committed all sorts of evil deeds ("steal and murder, commit adultery and perjury," v. 9) yet came to stand before God in his house. To them God says, "Has this house, which bears my Name, become a den of robbers to you?" For Jeremiah "the 'bandits' were the people who came to worship, not the businessmen who operated the concessions" (Beare, p. 417).

Two problems should be mentioned. In Matthew, Jesus entered Jerusalem, went to the temple and drove out the money-changers. In Mark, Jesus went to the temple and after looking around, "went out to Bethany with the Twelve" (Mark 11:11), returning on the "following day" to cleanse the temple (Mark 11:12–19). If one accepts Mark as the first written Gospel, it would appear that Matthew has moved immediately to the climactic event and transferred the account of the cursing of the fig tree to the next day (21:18–19). It is important that we do not press onto Scripture canons of contemporary accuracy. Ancient literature speaks to essentials and enjoys a certain freedom in narrative.

The other problem has to do with the fact that though the Synoptic Gospels place the cleansing of the temple at the beginning of Jesus' final week, John tells of a similar cleansing at the beginning of Jesus' ministry (John 2:13ff.). It is quite possible that there were in fact two cleansings and that the initial cleansing was not a part of the tradition that the Synoptics were recording (cf. Tasker, *John*, p. 61).

21:14–17 / The reaction of the religious authorities to Jesus' cleansing of the temple is not recorded. Perhaps it would have been difficult for them to oppose so flagrant a violation of the sacred grounds. However, the **chief priests** (first mentioned here in Matthew) and the scribes were indignant when they saw Jesus healing the blind and the lame within the temple and heard the children shouting out praise to the Son of David. Oral law had excluded the blind and the lame from entering the temple to offer sacrifice. Some scholars hold that the appearance of children there seems unlikely. It is important to realize the festive nature of the Passover season and the exceptionally large number of pilgrims who would be in Jerusalem at a time like this. For children and the disabled to be in the temple precincts would be most natural. When the religious rulers ask whether Jesus hears **what these children are saying,** he says **Yes** and counters by asking if they know the Scripture that says, "Thou has made the lips of children, of infants at the breast, vocal with praise" (Knox). The quotation comes from the LXX text of Psalm 8:2. What more could be said? Jesus then leaves the crowd and goes out to Bethany to spend the night.

21:18–22 / The day after the cleansing of the temple Jesus returned to Jerusalem from Bethany. Seeing a lone **fig tree by the road, he went up to it but found nothing on it except leaves**. To the tree he said, **May you never bear fruit again!** The disciples were astonished to see the tree wither so quickly and asked in amazement how it had happened (v. 20). Jesus responded, saying that if they had faith and did not doubt they could not only do what he had done but could order a mountain to cast itself **into the sea** and it would obey. If they believed, they would receive anything they **ask for in prayer.**

The fig tree was a common and favorite tree throughout Palestine. Its thick summer foliage provided excellent shade (Jesus saw Nathanael while he was "still under the fig tree," John 1:48). In the spring it produced small immature figs called *taksh*, which were edible but not highly esteemed. The real harvest of the fig season came in August. When the fig tree, which had shed its leaves during winter, began to have leaves, one could expect some small green figs. They were the guarantee of a later harvest. The tree that Jesus approached was without *taksh.*

The close relationship between the cleansing of the temple and the withering of the fig tree suggests that the latter is to be taken as a prophetic action in which the Jewish nation is judged as having failed to produce the fruit expected of a people privileged by God. Earlier, John the Baptist had told the Pharisees and Sadducees that "every tree that does not produce good fruit will be cut down and thrown into the fire" (3:10).

Some have questioned the account on the basis that Jesus elsewhere uses his power only for unselfish and beneficent purposes. He is pictured here in a bit of a pique and "blasting a fig tree for not doing what it was not able to do" (Barclay, vol. 2, p. 252). Beare calls it "the only cursing miracle in the Gospels" (p. 419). Some have suggested that the entire episode is the result of the tradition behind Matthew and Mark taking the parable of the barren fig tree recorded in Luke 13:6-9 and turning it into an actual event. Apart from the problem of creating history out of a parable, the two accounts have nothing in common except a fig tree that had no figs.

Jesus' words to the tree should be taken more as a prediction than as a curse. History has demonstrated repeatedly that dead formalism leads to institutional decay. Jesus had come to Israel with the expectation of faith but found little or none (cf. John 1:11). Such a reception did not bode well for the future. The response of the disciples to the withering of the fig tree led naturally to instruction in prayer. To the person of faith, even the moving of mountains is possible. The important thing is to believe and not doubt. The one who believes receives whatever is asked for in prayer (cf. Matt. 7:7-11; 18:19; John 14:13-14).

21:23-27 / **The chief priests and the elders** came to Jesus as he was teaching in the temple (probably in one of the porticoes that lined the Court of the Gentiles) and asked by what sort (Gk. *poios*) of authority he was doing these things (e.g., riding into Jerusalem on a donkey, cleansing the temple, etc.), and **Who gave you this authority?** The **chief priests and elders** represented the Sanhedrin, whose authority would not be questioned in Israel. Jesus countered by asking them a question about the authority of John the Baptist. If they are willing to answer whether

John's baptism was sanctioned **from heaven** (or only **from men**), he will tell them about his authority. The practice of answering a question with a question is typical of rabbinic discussion.

The "spiritual hierarchy" was faced with a difficult dilemma. If they said **from heaven**, Jesus would ask them, **Then why didn't you believe him?** If they said **from men** they would be in trouble with the people, who considered John to be a prophet. So they said, **We don't know.** Forced to admit their incompetence as teachers, they were in no position to question the authority of Jesus. Jesus replies that since they are not able (or willing!) to answer his questions, neither will he answer theirs.

21:28–32 / The parable of the two sons is recorded only by Matthew. It is the first of three parables directed against the religious leaders of the day. Jesus calls on them to give him their judgment about which of the two sons did the will of his father. When the first (some take *prōtos* to be the older) was asked to **work . . . in the vineyard,** he refused, but later **changed his mind** (he was "smitten with regret," Rotherham) **and went.** The other son said he would go (notice the polite *egō kyrie,* **I will, sir**) but did not. Those to whom Jesus spoke answered correctly that it was the first son who did what his father wanted.

The second son represents the professedly religious Jews who rejected Jesus, while the first son represents the publicans and sinners who turned to him in faith. So Jesus concludes, **the tax collectors and the prostitutes are entering the kingdom of God ahead of you** (i.e., "instead of you"; another example of the last who will be first and the first who will be last, cf. 20:16). What a devastating shock to the religious sensitivities of those who were confident of their own spiritual superiority! John the Baptist had come showing the way of righteousness, and they would not believe him. However, the social outcasts believed and repented. But the religious leaders, even after they had seen this, did not change their minds and believe.

21:33–39 / The second parable directed against those who refused to accept the messianic implications of Jesus' ministry had to do with a landowner who leased his vineyard to tenants and left home. Preparations included putting a **wall** around the property to keep wild beasts out, hewing out a wine vat, and building a **watchtower** from which the entire operation could be overseen.

When the harvest time approached, the owner **sent his servants** to receive his share of the produce. Gospel accounts differ in the number of servants sent as well as the number of times they were sent. Matthew has **servants** (plural) in verses 34 and 36, whereas Mark 12:2, 4, and Luke 20:10, 11, have "a servant" or "another servant." A third trip is recorded by Mark and Luke on which "another" (Mark) or "still a third" (Luke) is sent. Differences of this sort are the "natural consequence of oral tradition" (Tasker, p. 205) and in no way affect the meaning of the parable. **The tenants seized his servants; they beat one, killed another, and stoned a third** (v. 35). All three forms of violence were common in Jesus' day. Stoning suggests execution on the basis of religious apostasy (cf. Lev. 20:2), although the only stoning of a prophet recorded in the Old Testament is that of Zechariah son of Jehoiada the priest (2 Chron. 24:20–21).

The owner then sent **other servants**, who were treated in **the same way** (v. 36). Some writers think that these may refer to the "latter prophets" and reflect the division in the Old Testament between the former and latter prophets. Any correspondence, however, is accidental. Finally the owner sends **his son** (called a beloved son in the synoptic parallels), with the hope that they will respect his son. However, the tenants reason that if they kill the son they will get his inheritance. So they seized the son, **threw him out of the vineyard and killed him**. Some question how property would fall to tenants if the son were killed. Gundry remarks, that since the son was an heir (*klēronomos*, v. 38), we may assume that the owner had died and the son was coming to claim the vineyard as his inheritance (p. 427). Green says that in Jewish law, three successive failures on the part of the owner to collect his share of the annual harvest gave tenants a case to claim it for their own (pp. 179–80). Though parables are taken from real-life settings, it is unwise to press every detail. The purpose of the parable may call for certain adjustments and would be understood as such by those who first heard the story.

21:40–41 / Jesus now questions his listeners as to what they think the owner will do to the tenants when he returns. They respond correctly, saying that he will put the scoundrels to death and lease out the vineyard to others who will give him his fair share of the crop when the time arrives.

Many scholars understand this parable as an allegory reflecting the Christology of the later church. The servants are the prophets, who were killed by Israel when they came on behalf of God. The son is Jesus, who had a rightful claim but received the same treatment from the nation. Now the **vineyard** (God's work in the world) is taken from the Jews and turned over to those who will respect its owner and pay him his due. Parables, however, need not in all cases be limited to a single truth and are now recognized as having some allegorical features. Such features appear regularly in Old Testament and rabbinical parables. Based on the parable's having no real doctrine of the atonement or clear mention of the resurrection, Filson concludes that it is "not what the Apostolic Age would have produced" (p. 228; see also Tasker, p. 204).

21:42–46 / Jesus quotes from Psalm 118 the passage about the stone rejected by the builders that became the capstone (vv. 22–23) and concludes that **the kingdom of God** is to be **taken away from** them and **given to a people who will produce its fruit**. That is the central point of the parable. By rejecting the message of the prophets and finally by rejecting the Son, Israel has demonstrated that it is incapable of producing the kind of conduct and life that are appropriate in God's kingdom. The kingdom is taken from Israel and given to the Gentiles. The passage from Psalm 118 was well known in the early church and is quoted in Acts 4:11 and 1 Peter 2:7 as well.

When the chief priests and the Pharisees realized that the parable was directed against them, they looked for a way to arrest Jesus. They were **afraid**, however, **of the crowd because the people held that he was a prophet.**

Additional Notes §21

21:7 / Codex Bezae and some others have *auton* ("it") rather than *autōn* (**them**) as the last word in v. 7, undoubtedly due to the incongruity of seeing Jesus mounted on two animals. Or, the plural could have been the natural result of a copyist confusing the sound of the letters omicron and omega.

21:8 / Some scholars hold that this entire scene belongs either to the Feast of Tabernacles, because of the heightened messianic expectation, or to Hanukkah (celebrating the rededication of the temple by Judas Maccabaeus in 165 B.C.), which would lead naturally to the cleansing of the temple.

21:9 / **Hosanna**: Nigel Turner mentions with favor the view that behind **Hosanna** may lie an Aramaic word for power. In that case, the Matthew passage would read, "Praise to the Son of David!" (*HDB* rev., p. 397).

21:12 / **Buying and selling**: Against those who picture the transactions in the temple as being exorbitant, I. Abrahams holds that everything was under strict control and, on the whole, quite fair (*Studies in Pharisaism and the Gospels*, vol. 1, pp. 82ff.).

21:14 / **Blind and the lame**: The "blind and lame" of 2 Sam. 5:8 are Jebusites able to defend Jerusalem because of its natural fortifications (cf. v. 6). The proverbial statement that "the 'blind and lame' will not enter the palace" (v. 8) may have nothing to do with physical handicaps. Any comparison of David, who demanded their slaughter, and the Son of David, who healed them, is tenuous.

21:25 / Matthew says that they argued *en heautois* and Mark (11:31) that they argued *pros heautous*. One seems to suggest inner reflection and the other outward discussion. There is no reason that both did not take place.

21:29–31 / The textual transmission of this parable is confused. The three principal forms are
1. First son says "No" but repents and goes. He is the one who does the father's will (Codex Sinaiticus and many others).
2. First son says "Yes" but does not go; second son says "No" but goes, and is the one doing the father's will (Codex Vaticanus).
3. Second son says "Yes" but does not go and is the one selected by the priests and elders as having done the father's will (Codex Bezae).
Of these, the last is nonsense (Jerome suggested that the priests gave an absurd reply to spoil the point of the parable), and the first two say the same thing in inverse order. The UBS follows the first order and is probably to be preferred (although the NEB follows the second). (See the full discussion in Metzger, *TCGNT*, pp. 55–56.)

21:33 / A simpler version of the parable is found in the *Gospel of Thomas* (65), but K. R. Snodgrass argues effectively against taking it as original (*NTS* 20, pp. 142–44).
Winepress: Winepresses normally consisted of two rock-hewn troughs, one higher than the other, with a connecting channel. Grapes were thoroughly trodden with bare feet in the upper trough and the juice filtered through the channel into the lower trough.

21:38–39 / **The heir . . . him**: In Mark 12:8 the tenants kill him and then throw him out of the vineyard. It has been suggested that this adds to the crime of murder the offense of refusing to bury the corpse (Beare, p. 429).

21:44 / V. 44 is considered by many scholars an early interpolation from Luke 20:18. However, in that case we would expect it to be brought in before v. 43 (to correspond with Luke). Manuscript evidence for its inclusion is exceptionally strong (Aleph, B, C, K, L, W, X, and others). Fenton observes, "If genuine it is a remarkable example of an agreement between Matthew and Luke against Mark" (p. 345), which raises the question of the appropriateness of textual theory (the priority of Mark) determining the text itself. The first line stems from Isa. 8:14–15 and the second goes back to Dan. 2:44. In both cases it is an extension of the role of the stone rejected by the builders but honored by God.

The parable of the wedding feast (vv. 1-14) is regularly considered to be an allegorical revision of an earlier more straightforward parable told by Jesus. Fenton lists as allegorical elements that strike the reader as strange and unnatural the killing of those who brought the invitation (v. 6), the destruction of the guests (v. 7), and the burning of a city while a meal is waiting to be served (v. 7). These are "no doubt additions, made by the Church or the Evangelist" (p. 347). Beare notes that there are three versions: Matthew's, which is a "fullblown allegory," Luke's ("a genuine parable"), and one in *The Gospel of Thomas* (pp. 432-34). Hill states that there can be no doubt that Matthew and Luke (14:16-24) present the same parable (p. 301), and Gundry holds that the "unrealistic features of the parable" are due to Matthew rather than to Jesus (p. 433). The issue is complicated by the fact that verses 11-14 seem to have been attached to this parable from another setting.

When one actually compares the accounts in Matthew and Luke, the differences are striking. Luke speaks of a "man" (rather than a king) who gives a "banquet" (not a marriage feast). Those invited give a series of excuses (in Matthew they make light of the invitation and go their separate ways), which causes the man to send out his servant (on two occasions) to compel the poor, maimed, blind, and lame of the city to come. The sending out of an army to kill those who refuse the invitation and the unit on the man without a wedding garment in Matthew have no parallel in Luke's story. In fact, there is no indication in Luke that Jesus intended the account to be taken as a parable.

Jesus undoubtedly told his parables in many different settings. One of the distinct advantages of the parable is that its major truth may be applied in various contexts. Whether or not the parable as recounted in Matthew comes intact from the lips of Jesus will be judged differently by various scholars, depending upon their view of the nature of Gospel literature. Interpretations of the parable will vary accordingly. Hill admits that there are "quite significant differences between the two texts" (p. 301) but explains them as evidence of the freedom with which oral tradition interpreted the parables of Jesus. It is better to take the two accounts as separate but related narratives told on different occasions in order to illustrate or strengthen basic truths. It would be highly unlikely for Jesus to have told each of his parables on one occasion only. The so-called strange and unnatural additions appear as such only to those who would rewrite Scripture to match twentieth-century expectations. Allowed the full expression of Near Eastern hyperbole, they cause no particular exegetical problem.

22:1–10 / Jesus again spoke to the Jewish people by means of a parable (*parabolais* is plural and refers to the three parables in 21:28–22:14). The kingdom of heaven is like what happens when a **king**, who has **prepared a wedding banquet for his son** and sent out **servants to those who had been invited**, learns that the guests have **refused to come.** He becomes angry, sends out his army to punish those who did not come, and invites to the wedding feast all manner of people from the streets. One man dressed improperly is evicted, and Jesus concludes, "Many are invited, but few are chosen" (v. 14).

The kingdom of heaven is compared to a marriage feast again in 25:10. The same word is used in Revelation 19:7 (*gamos*) of the "wedding of the Lamb." The figure of a marriage feast was widely used in ancient literature to portray the blessings of the life to come (e.g., Isa. 25:6ff.). This suggests that we are to interpret the parable in an eschatological setting. The **servants** who went out to those who had been invited represent God's messengers in the days of Jesus. **Those who had been invited,** who **refused to come,** are the Jewish people who rejected the invitation of Jesus. Instead of joining the marriage festivities, they ignored what was going on and went about their normal lives as if nothing important were happening. Even though the king's **oxen and fattened cattle** had **been butchered** (v. 4), one guest went "to his home in the country, another to his business" (Weymouth).

After sending his troops to kill those who spurned his invitation and to burn their city to the ground, the king sent his servants into the *diexodoi* (lit., "outlets") *tōn hodōn* (probably where the streets cut through the city walls and out into the country) in order to invite to the banquet everyone they found (v. 9), **both good and bad** (v. 10). No particular point is being made.

22:11–13 / Verses 11–13 seem to have been added as a supplement from another setting. Since Matthew's acknowledged style of composition is to gather into one place the teachings of Jesus on a specific topic, it would not be unusual for him to append to the first parable about a wedding feast additional teaching related to the same subject. Verses 1–10 stressed the Jewish resistance to the invitation of Jesus; verses 11–14 speak of one guest who came to the wedding feast improperly attired. Both deal with judgment, but the former deals with the judgment of the reluctant and the latter with the judgment of the impostor.

For the king to inspect his guests indicates God's intention to pass judgment on professing disciples. One man was **not wearing wedding clothes**. He is addressed by the king as **friend** (*hetairos*), a term used only by Matthew in the New Testament and always of those whose actions run counter to what the term normally implies (cf. 20:13; 26:50). Only if this paragraph belonged with the preceding would there be any reason to wonder why a king who brought in people off the street now questions why they are not properly dressed. Wedding garments speak of the "new life of good works which is to follow the preaching of the gospel" (Fenton, p. 350). In a similar context, Revelation 19:8 interprets the fine linen worn by the bride of the Lamb as "the righteous acts of the saints." The verses warn believers that without a changed life they will be rejected at the Last Judgment.

The improperly dressed man has no explanation (*phimoō* means "to put to silence," from *phimos*, a muzzle) for his presence at the feast. So the king commands his servants to bind him **hand and foot** and **throw him** out into "the darkness farthest out" (BAGD, p. 280), where **there will be weeping and gnashing of teeth**. Though the punishment seems severe, it is important to bear in mind that we are dealing with a culture quite different from ours and a literary style that must be interpreted as an expression of that culture.

22:14 / The two preceding paragraphs that make up this section describe the fate of those who reject God's invitation (vv. 1–10) and those who respond to it but fail to meet the conditions (vv. 11–13). Verse 14 concludes the entire unit: **Many are invited,**

but few are chosen. The invitation has gone out to all Israel, but only a few (those who accept and follow Jesus) are chosen. The **chosen** are those who demonstrate by works of righteousness the reality of their involvement in the kingdom. Stendahl says, "Man's behavior indicates whether he is elect or not" (p. 791) To be chosen does not mean to be thrust into the kingdom apart from our decision and regardless of our conduct.

22:15–17 / The Pharisees went to discuss how they could trap Jesus in an argument (*pagideuō*, only here in the New Testament, is a hunting term meaning "to snare or trap"). They decide to send some of their disciples, **along with the Herodians,** to pose a controversial question about paying taxes to the Roman Emperor. Nothing is known of the **Herodians** apart from their mention here. Supposedly they were Jewish supporters of Herod Antipas and favored collaboration with their Roman overlords. Naturally, they would be quite unpopular with the masses. That the Pharisees would join forces with a group so distinct in their goals and orientation shows the extent to which opponents of Jesus would go in their efforts to eliminate him.

They begin with flattery. **We know you are a man of integrity** and **teach the way of God** in all sincerity. You don't worry about what people think because you're not concerned to gain their favor (v. 16). So tell us, **Is it right to pay taxes to the Caesar or not?** The dilemma they pose to Jesus is crystal clear. If he opposed paying the tax, he would be in trouble with the civil authorities. The Herodians would charge him with attempting to incite rebellion. If he approved paying the tax, he would lose his popularity with the people. It would appear that there was no way he could answer the question and not come out the loser.

The tax referred to was a poll tax levied on every person from the time of puberty until the age of sixty-five. It was paid to the Imperial Exchequer in Roman currency. The tax was resented by the Jewish populace, because it reminded them that they were subject to a foreign power that had seized their land and now exacted from them payment that went into the emperor's coffers.

22:18–22 / Jesus, aware of his questioner's malicious intent, named them for what they were, **hypocrites.** He asked to be shown the coin used for paying the tax. Then he asked, **Whose**

portrait is this? And whose inscription? The denarius they brought was a Roman silver coin engraved with the head of the emperor and bearing religious claims offensive to the monotheistic faith of the conscientious Jew (the coins of Tiberius bore the inscription *divus et pontifex maximus*, "god and highest priest"). When his opponents answered that it was the face and name of the emperor that appeared on the coin, Jesus then said, **Give to Caesar what is Caesar's, and to God what is God's.** *Apodidōmi* ("give back") carries the idea of paying back to someone that which is his or her due. The tax collected by the emperor was not a gift but a payment for benefit received. In approving payment of the tax, Jesus indicated his disapproval of the extreme attitude held by the Zealots. The act would show that a person could pay tax to a foreign dignitary who was accorded divine status by some without compromising the first two commandments.

The other part of the answer is that they are to give back to God **what is God's.** Some have interpreted this to mean that life is clearly divided into two parts—the secular, with its appropriate obligations, and the sacred, with its duties to God. Such a division is actually quite impossible. Filson is correct in saying that "what Jesus means is that they have an obligation to the government over them, but they have a greater obligation to God; it covers all of life; in the present situation it includes the obligation to pay the tax to the power that God permits to rule the Jews" (p. 235). Jesus' answer "took them by surprise" (NEB), so they went away and left him alone. Their attempt to trap him had failed.

22:23–33 / On the same day that the Pharisees failed to trap Jesus with their question about paying taxes to the emperor, the Sadducees came to him posing a question that they thought would show the logical absurdity of the Pharisaic doctrine of resurrection. At the same time, it would force Jesus to commit himself in such a way that he would lose favor with one group or the other. The respective positions are summarized in Acts 23:8: "The Sadducees say that there is no resurrection, and that there are neither angels nor spirits, but the Pharisees acknowledge them all" (cf. Josephus *Ant.* 18.12–22). The Sadducees were the wealthy governing class and, in terms of doctrine, were traditionalists. They accepted as authoritative only the books of Moses.

The problem posed by the Sadducees relates to what is called levirate marriage (from the Latin, *levir*, "husband's brother"). Deuteronomy 25:5–10 taught that if a man dies without leaving a son, his brother (if they are living together) must marry the widow and raise children to the dead brother (cf. the case of Onan who is responsible to lie with Tamar and produce offspring for his brother Er; Gen. 38:7–8). The Sadducees asked what would happen if **seven brothers** all followed this instruction with the same wife and then died. **At the resurrection, whose wife will she be?** The line of argument is *reductio ad absurdum*: God would not order a practice that would lead to such an absurd situation. Therefore the idea of resurrection is invalid. The Sadducee's question is no question at all; it is an attempt to discredit Jesus as a logical teacher.

Jesus' response to the Sadducees is that they have wandered from the truth (*planaō* in the passive means "to go astray"), because they **do not know the Scriptures or the power of God** (v. 29). Taking these two issues in reverse order, Jesus points out that **at the resurrection . . . they will be like the angels** in that they will not marry. God's creative power will so transform the nature of existence that the normal conditions of life will no longer be in effect (cf. Paul's "We will all be changed," 1 Cor. 15:51ff.). Immortality will make procreation unnecessary. Any question about whose wife will a woman be who has married more than once fails to understand the true nature of eternal life. God is one who "calls into existence the things that do not exist" (Rom. 4:17, RSV).

As for the resurrection, the Sadducees had not grasped the fact that when God, speaking from the burning bush, identified himself to Moses as the God of Abraham, Isaac, and Jacob, he spoke not as **the God of the dead but of the living.** Jesus took the very Scriptures that the Sadducees accepted as binding and from them demonstrated the reality of the resurrection. This deduction rests upon the genitives being taken subjectively rather than objectively (i.e., "the God to whom Abraham belongs" not "the God whom Abraham worshipped"; see Tasker, p. 211). McNeile says that we must admit the possibility at this point that "Jesus condescended to a rabbinic style of argument" (p. 322). Whatever the case, the result was amazement on the part of the crowds who gathered to listen. Williams says, "They were dumbfounded at His teaching." They recognized the superiority of his logic to that of the Jewish leaders.

22:34–40 / **Hearing that Jesus had silenced** (cf. v. 12) **the Sadducees, the Pharisees got together** on a new approach (Rieu translates, "they put their heads together"). One of them, an expert in the law of Moses (*nomikos*, from *nomos*, "law") **tested him with** the **question**, "Which is the most important commandment?" Green notes that for rabbinic Judaism, all the precepts of the law were of equal significance, and therefore there could be no question of greater or less (p. 185). The issue, however, was regularly discussed by the rabbis.

Jesus' answer comes from Deuteronomy 6:4–5, which is the opening of the Shema, the fundamental creed of Judaism. The most important commandment is to love God with all one's **heart, soul**, and **mind**. Matthew's account substitutes **mind** for "strength" (Deut. 6:5); the parallels in Mark and Luke have both "mind" and "strength" (Mark 12:30; Luke 10:27). Elsewhere in the Old Testament we find simply "heart" and "soul" (Deut. 10:12; Josh. 22:5). The point is that God requires a love that involves the entire person. Barclay says it must be a love that dominates our emotions, directs our thoughts, and is the dynamic of all our actions (vol. 2, p. 278). Love of God is foremost (*prōtos* in v. 38 indicates rank) in that it is the supreme obligation. From it stems the ability and desire to love those who are created in the image of God (Gen. 1:26–27).

There is a second commandment that is like it: **Love your neighbor as yourself**. Jesus draws this from Leviticus 19:18. Jesus may have been the first to combine these two commandments in this way, although the ideas appear together in the *Testament of Dan* 5:3 and the *Testament of Issachar* 5:2 (which, however, may have been written later than the Gospels; the dates are disputed). In any case, Jesus has expanded the definition of neighbor from "fellow Israelite" (Lev. 19:18) to anyone in need (Luke 10:29–37) and even to one's enemies (Matt. 5:44). To love one's neighbor as oneself does not teach self-love, but requires that we extend to others the same kind of personal concern that we have for ourselves. On these two commandments, the law in its entirety and the teachings of the prophets depend (Gk. *kremannymi*, "To hang"; "as a door hangs on its hinges, so the whole OT hangs on these two commandments," BAGD, p. 450). All the other precepts and instructions in the Old Testament are ways in which these two fundamental principles find expression.

22:41–46 / Jesus, having answered three questions put to him by the Jewish leaders (payment of taxes, vv. 15–22; resurrection, vv. 23–33; most important commandment, vv. 34–40), now poses one of his own to the Pharisees. **Whose son** is the Messiah? **The son of David**, they answer. Then why did David, divinely inspired, call him **Lord**? If "David calls Christ his Master; how can he be also his son?" (Knox). No one was able to answer; nor did they dare to question him further. Opposition is forced underground, to appear in chapter 26 and achieve its purpose (Fenton, p. 360).

The Pharisees expected the Messiah to come as the Son of David to carry out a military mission related to Israel as a nation. Passages such as Isaiah 9:2–7 and 11:1ff. were understood as portraying national restoration and world prominence. But how could the Messiah be David's son (and therefore subject to David) if David addressed him as Lord? The implication is that the Messiah is to play a more exalted role than the Pharisees expected from David's earthly successor (cf. 22:6, 41). Stendahl notes that "the question is one of Haggadah, where two conflicting texts often were shown to be true" (p. 792). Jesus is at one and the same time a true son of David and also David's Lord.

Additional Notes §22

22:6 / **Mistreated**: Gk. *hybrizō* (cf. the English "hubris") means "to treat in an arrogant manner calculated to publicly humiliate."

22:7 / **Burned**: Critics who interpret the parable as the work of the evangelist or the church understand the burning of the city to be a reference to the destruction of Jerusalem in A.D. 70 under Titus (however, see Gundry for the view that it is a dramatic figure drawn from Isaiah's prediction of a past destruction, p. 437).

22:9 / **Street corners**: Hill thinks that "thoroughfares" probably refers to "the intersections of roads in the centre of a town, where the poor people would gather" (p. 302).

22:13 / For similar scenes, cf. Matt 8:12; 13:42; 24:51; 25:30.

22:15 / Beare calls attention to David Daube's essay, "Four Types of Question," in *The New Testament and Rabbinic Judaism*, pp. 158–69, in which the author notes the striking resemblance between this question sequence and the pattern of questions that belongs to the "Haggadah of the Seder," a Jewish family service held on the eve of the Passover (p. 437).

22:16 / **The Way of God** is a Jewish catechetical term that early on became the trademark of the primitive church: Acts 18:25–28; cf. Acts 9:2 (Stendahl, p. 791).

22:21 / This positive attitude toward government is reflected in Rom. 13:1–7 and 1 Pet. 2:13–17 as well. Qumran texts speak of a similarity between angels and the redeemed, 1QH 23.21ff.

22:34 / **Got together**: Cf. the LXX of Ps. 2:2 (*synēchthēsan epi to auto*). If Matthew's *synēchthēsan epi to auto* echoes the psalm, it emphasizes the hostile intent of the Pharisees.

22:36 / **Greatest**: *megalē* (lit., "great") is taken as a superlative, since in Semitic languages adjectives do not allow degrees of comparison. *Poia* (**which**) should perhaps be understood in the sense of "what kind of."

22:37 / *šᵉma'* is the Hebrew word "hear" with which the section begins. The complete statement includes Deut. 6:4–9, 11:13–21, and Num. 15:37–41.

22:42 / For discussion on the Messiah as the Son of David, see Str.-B., vol. 1, p. 525; Moore, *Judaism*, vol. 2, pp. 328ff.

§23 Hypocrisy Denounced (Matt. 23:1–39)

The last of Matthew's five major discourses begins with chapter 23 and runs through chapter 25 (see the standard closing formula at 26:1). It differs from the others somewhat in that there is a break and change of scene between chapters 23 and 24. The first section (chap. 23) is directed to a wider audience (cf. vv. 1, 13, 37); in the second (chaps. 24–25) Jesus speaks to his disciples in private. The material in chapter 23 has been compiled by Matthew on the basis of topical relevance. It was not a single speech given on a specific occasion. Tasker suggests that Matthew may have organized the material according to the pattern of Deuteronomy 32:1–40, in which Moses sang of Israel's ingratitude and idolatry and then of the goodness of God (p. 216).

Critics have questioned what they understand to be a "sustained note of fierceness" (Beare, p. 447) or "the extreme bitterness of this chapter" (Green, p. 187). Instead of being seen as reflecting the mind of the historical Jesus, the material is often held to reveal the antagonism that is said to have existed between the Jewish-Christian churches in the latter part of the first century and the Pharisaic Judaism that was rebuilding after the destruction of Jerusalem in A.D. 70. Without maintaining that all scribes and Pharisees would have automatically fallen under the condemnation of the chapter, there is still no plausible reason to suppose that the tendencies toward ostentatious and hypocritical religiosity that led to Jesus' death would not have received the scathing rebukes we find here. Accurate historical reconstruction demands that we not rewrite the past in the image of the present. Cultures are in a state of constant flux, and what may seem extreme today may well have been quite common in a former period.

23:1–12 / Jesus speaks to **the crowds** and **his disciples** about the **teachers of the law and the Pharisees.** They are said to **sit in Moses' seat,** that is, they are the authorized interpreters of Moses' law. **Moses' seat** is more than a metaphor; it was an actual stone seat on the synagogue platform close by the sacred scrolls (cf. Luke 4:20 and the fact that Jesus *sat* to teach). The **Pharisees** were a sect of strict legalists whose origin goes back to the second century B.C. The name means "the separated ones." Their energy was totally dedicated to keeping all the minute regulations of the law in both its written and (especially) oral forms. The "scribes" (v. 2, AV)—who were Pharisees for the most part— were the professional copiers and **teachers of the law**. They were held to be the authoritative exponents not only of the writings of Moses but also of the oral tradition, which, on the basis that it went back to Moses through a long succession of teachers, was considered equally binding.

Since the scribes and Pharisees were the authoritative exponents of the law of Moses, Jesus counsels his listeners to follow their instructions, but not their example, because **they do not practice what they preach**. In view of verses 13–28, we should qualify the first part of the charge in verse 3. We must suppose that the intention of Jesus was that the interpretation of the scribes be followed only in the major and undisputed areas of the written law. The scribes are criticized for piling up "back-breaking burdens" (Phillips) and not lifting a finger to help. Contrary to what Jesus said of his own teaching ("my yoke is easy and my burden is light," 11:30), the scribes and Pharisees were intent on increasing religious obligations. The burden of Pharisaic legislation had become impossible for people in the various trades who had to work for a living. The Pharisees were a religious sect that had all but separated themselves from the normal pursuits of life and were able to spend all their time and energy observing the minutiae of the law. They did nothing (they didn't **lift a finger**, v. 4) to help those who were unable to devote that amount of attention to keeping the law.

The Pharisees lived for adulation. Jesus said that "they make broad their phylacteries, and enlarge the borders of their garments" (v. 5, AV). Much has been written about these practices. The Greek *phylaktērion* was an amulet or protective charm. It has become associated with the Jewish custom of wearing "tephillin" (small leather boxes containing portions of Scripture) on the forehead and left upper arm (cf. Exod. 13:9, 16; Deut. 6:8; 11:18). The terms were taken figuratively until after the time of the Babylonian exile. By New Testament times they were being carried out literally. "Broadening" phylacteries has been explained as widening the straps or making them of metal foil (unlikely) or as referring to the amount of time they are worn (the tephillin were normally put on for morning and evening prayer only). The **tassels** that, according to Deuteronomy 22:12, were to be attached to the four corners of their **garments**, came to be used of the four tassels on the corners of the rectangular prayer shawl. Both practices belong to what Jesus called "acts of righteousness" that should not be paraded before others (6:1ff.). The Pharisees loved to sit in the most important places at banquets and in the front seats of the synagogue, where they would face the congregation. They enjoyed being **greeted in the marketplaces** (custom called for those less knowledgeable in the law to salute their superior) **and to have** people **call them** "**Rabbi**" (v. 7; **rabbi** transliterates the Hebrew *rab* ("great") with the suffix "my" (hence, "my great one").

Verses 8–11 appear to be addressed to Jesus' disciples only. He cautions them that *they* (the Greek is emphatic) are not to claim the title **Rabbi**, because for them there is only one "great one" and they are all brothers of equal rank. No one on earth is to be called **father** because they have but **one Father and he is in heaven**. What Jesus is speaking against is the tendency to develop ecclesiastical hierarchies that elevate certain persons above others. The only hierarchy that the church is to know is Jesus as Teacher and God as Father. In a similar vein, verse 10 warns against taking the title **teacher** (Gk. *kathēgētēs*, from a verb meaning "to go before, guide"), because they have but one **Teacher, the Christ** (*ho Christos*). The one who would be "greater" (note play on "Rabbi," v. 8) must be **servant**. Phillips translates verse 11, "The only 'superior' among you is the one who serves the others." Those who exalt themselves will be humbled, and those who take a lowly role will be honored. The desire of the scribes and Pharisees to attract attention to themselves will lead to their undoing.

23:13–22 / We now come to some of the most severe words ever uttered by Jesus. His deep concern about religious hypocrisy is expressed in a series of six woes (v. 14 is missing in the better manuscripts). They are not so much curses as they are expressions of sorrow and warnings of punishment. What

A. T. Robertson calls a "thunderbolt of wrath" (*WPNT*, vol. 1, p. 181), Beare declares to be a "masterpiece of vituperation" (p. 452). Once again it is plain to see that interpretation is affected less by the data than by one's basic orientation. Beare is led to say that "there is very little in this chapter that can be regarded as language ever used by Jesus, or at all in accordance with his spirit" (p. 461). But a Jesus who is not allowed by his critics to say anything contrary to their tastes will be a Jesus quite different from what we should expect to find in history. A. M. Hunter lists as examples of the "astonishing variety of portraits of Jesus which our learned men have given us: Renan's 'Amiable Carpenter,' Tolstoy's 'Spiritual Anarchist,' Schweitzer's 'Imminent Cataclysmist,' Klausner's 'Unorthodox Rabbi,' and Otto's 'Charismatic Evangelist' " (*The Work and Words of Jesus*, p. 14).

The Old Testament pattern for a series of woes is found in Isaiah 5:8–23. **Woe to you, teachers of the law and Pharisees!** (v. 13). They slammed the door of the kingdom in the face of others, while at the same time they did not enter in themselves. Although they posed as religious leaders, they prevented others from entering the kingdom.

A second woe had to do with the effect of Pharisaic activity on converts to Judaism (v. 15). Jesus said they scoured the land and sea to make a single convert, and when they succeeded, they made him "twice as ripe for destruction" (Phillips) as they themselves. Although Judaism has never been noted for its zeal to proselytize (cf. Hare, *Theme of Jewish Persecution in Matthew*, pp. 9ff.), there were those who went beyond becoming "God-fearers" (cf. Acts 10:2, 22; 13:16, 26; 17:4, 17) and were circumcised so as to be full-fledged proselytes to Judaism. The denunciation has nothing to do with the effort expended to obtain a convert but with what then happened to such a person. The scribes and Pharisees turned a convert into a "child of hell" (AV) who was twice as worthy of suffering the punishment of gehenna as they. The reference is to the typical zeal of the convert.

Verses 16–22 treat the practice of manipulating oaths so as to achieve personal and selfish ends. Apparently it was held that when a person swore by the **temple** (v. 16), by the **altar** (v. 18), or by **heaven** (v. 22), the oath was not binding. On the other hand, vows made by the **gold** in the temple (v. 16) or by the **gift** on the altar (v. 18) were held to be obligatory. To swear by God guaranteed truthfulness, but the Jews of that day were reluctant to use his name. So they identified things related to God (heaven, altar, etc.) and then, by a process of equivocation, limited these to their strictly literal connotations (Green, p. 191). In this way what appeared to be the lesser turned out to be greater and therefore binding.

Their conclusions lacked common sense. They were **blind fools**. The temple **makes the gold sacred** (v. 17) and the altar **makes the gift sacred** (v. 19). To swear by the altar is to swear by the gifts on it, and to swear by the temple (or by heaven) is to swear by God who lives there. All vows carry the responsibility of fulfillment.

23:23-24 / The fourth woe relates to the Pharisees' practice of scrupulously tithing even the vegetables and spices of the garden but failing in the weightier demands of justice, mercy, and integrity. "These last," said Jesus "you ought to have put in practice, without neglecting the first" (TCNT). According to Deuteronomy 14:22, the Israelites were to "set aside a tenth of all that [their] fields produce each year." **Mint** (*hēdyosmon*) was a garden plant, as was **dill** (*anēthon*), and was used for seasoning. **Cummin** (*kyminon*, of Phoenician origin) produced tiny fruits (or "seeds") that were tithed despite their slight value (BAGD, p. 457). Jesus does not oppose their practice of tithing garden spices, but criticizes them for having neglected the essential qualities of justice and fidelity (cf. Mic. 6:2). Their hypocrisy lay in their desire to appear conscientious about even the minute details of religious law while ignoring those central issues that were infinitely more important. They are blind leaders who filter their wine in order to avoid drinking a ceremonially unclean **gnat** (cf. Lev. 11:41; perhaps the larva of a gnat) yet gulp down a **camel** (v. 24). There may be a wordplay in Aramaic between "gnat" and "camel" (the words sound very much alike). In any case, it is a typical example of Jesus' use of hyperbole (cf. 7:3 and 19:24 as well).

23:25-28 / In the fifth and sixth woes (vv. 25-28), Jesus denounces the scribes and Pharisees for appearing clean on the outside but inside being filled with all manner of evil. They are careful to **clean the outside of** their **cup and dish**, while on the inside they are full of "violent behavior and uncontrolled desire" (BAGD). The comparison moves from the cup and plate to the

Jewish leaders themselves. The advice is to cleanse **the inside of the cup** first and **then the outside also will be clean**. The same point is made on another occasion, when Jesus teaches that "nothing outside a man can make him 'unclean' by going into him. Rather, it is what comes out of a man that makes him 'unclean' " (Mark 7:15).

The scribes and Pharisees are like **whitewashed tombs** that **look beautiful on the outside but on the inside are full of dead men's bones** (v. 27). The law taught that "anyone who touches a human bone or a grave, will be unclean for seven days" (Num. 19:16). Some think that the allusion is to the practice of whitewashing tombs to keep people from accidentally touching them on their way to Passover and thus becoming unable to take part in the festival because of ceremonial defilement. It is more likely that Jesus is comparing the condition of the Pharisees to tombs that are made attractive by ornamental plastering but inside are filled with all manner of corruption. They may look righteous to others, but in fact are filled with hypocrisy and wickedness. It is the dramatic difference between appearance and reality that makes them hypocrites.

23:29–36 / By building tombs for the prophets and decorating monuments for the righteous of the past, the scribes and Pharisees were providing evidence against themselves. They claimed that had they been there they would not have taken part in the murdering of prophets. Thus they admit that they are the descendants of those who killed the righteous. "Go on then," said Jesus, and "finish off what your fathers began" (NEB). **The descendants** (Gk. *hyioi*, "sons") **of those who murdered the prophets** (v. 31) are those who have inherited their evil nature. To admit the relationship is to accept the guilt. The charge **to fill up then** what their ancestors started (v. 32) reflects the Jewish view that the judgment of God comes only after people have sunk to the depths of sinfulness.

Jesus' most scathing denunciation is found in verse 33: **You snakes!** (Gk. *opheis*); **You brood of vipers!** (Gk. *gennēmata echidnōn*, probably poisonous). The epithet recalls the deceit of Satan, who appeared in the garden as a serpent (Gen. 3:1ff.; cf. Rev. 12:9). How can they hope to escape the judgment of hell? **Prophets and wise men and teachers** (leaders of the early church) will be sent to them, but they, like their forefathers, will perse-

cute and kill the messengers of God. As a result, the guilt for
all the innocent blood shed on earth will fall on them. The acts
of violence reach from the murder of **righteous Abel** (the first recorded homicide, Gen. 4:8) to the murder of **Zechariah son of
Berekiah** (the last recorded homicide, Zech. 1:1). The punishment for **all this will come upon** the **generation** alive at the time
of Jesus. That Jerusalem fell in A.D. 70 is partial fulfillment of this
prophecy.

 23:37-39 / The apparent severity of the preceding verses
is moderated by the poignant lament of Jesus in the final verses
of the chapter. Jerusalem's inhabitants can rightly be described
as those who **kill the prophets and stone those sent to you** (cf.
Acts 23:27). Stoning was the method of execution for idolatry
(Deut. 17:5) and sorcery (Lev. 20:27). Again and again, Jesus
wanted to enfold the nation in his arms **as a hen gathers her
chicks under her wings**, but they would not let him. The phrase
how often indicates that, although it is not recorded in the Synoptic Gospels, Jesus taught in Jerusalem on repeated occasions,
undoubtedly during religious festivals. This serves as a reminder
of how sketchy our information really is. John was right: if everything Jesus did had been written down, not even the whole world
would have room for the books that would be written (John 21:25).
The imagery of a bird protecting its young is common in the Old
Testament (Isa. 31:5; Ps. 36:7). Jerusalem, however, repeatedly resisted God's love. Jerusalem was invited to the messianic banquet but refused to come (cf. 22:3, 5-6).
 To refuse God's overtures is not without consequences.
Their **house** (the temple as symbolic of the entire commonwealth)
is left forsaken and **desolate**. Goodspeed has, "Now I leave you
to yourselves." Jesus came and was turned away: now they have
no one but themselves—the ultimate punishment. From that point
on, they will never see him again until they say, **Blessed is he
who comes in the name of the Lord** (v. 39). Some think that this
contains at least a slight hint of the eventual conversion of Israel
(cf. Rom. 11:26). In any case, it would be contingent upon Israel's
recognition of the messiahship of Jesus. This is always true in-
dividually and may happen corporately.

Additional Notes §23

23:10 / **"Teacher"**: Some have suggested that *kathēgētēs* should be taken as equivalent to the Hebrew *môreh*, a technical term for the Teacher of Righteousness in Qumran literature. In modern Greek the word is used for the title "professor."

23:13 / **Teachers of the law and Pharisees**: Gundry suggests that the constant pairing of scribes and Pharisees suggests that Matthew may be writing only about scribes who belong to the Pharisaical sect (p. 454). This would reduce the size of the group coming under such severe condemnation and allow for there being among the Pharisees those less worthy of public denunciation.

23:24 / A rabbinic saying in the Talmud reads, "He that kills a flea on the Sabbath is as guilty as if he killed a camel" (b. *Shab.* 12a). Any relationship to the saying of Jesus would probably be accidental.

23:34 / Jesus' words at this point are said, by Luke, to come from "the Wisdom of God" (Luke 11:49). Some have suggested that Jesus is here quoting from a noncanonical book, but no such book is known that contains these words. Morris says that he may be saying, in effect, "This is in accordance with God's wisdom" (*The Gospel According to Luke*, p. 206).

23:35 / The notion that innocent blood cries out until it is avenged is seen in Gen. 4:10; Isa. 26:21; Rev. 6:10.

Zechariah: Because there is no indication in the Old Testament that Zechariah son of Berekiah was martyred, some think that Matthew refers to Zechariah son of Jehoiada, who, according to 2 Chron. 24:21, was stoned to death in the courtyard of the temple. Others suggest Zechariah son of Baris (or Bariscaeus), who was murdered in the temple by Zealots shortly before the fall of Jerusalem (Josephus, *War* 4.334ff.). This identification takes the words from Jesus and assigns them to the later church. Gundry holds that Matthew conflated the first two "for the literary-theological purpose of correlating the betrayal of Jesus' innocent blood with the shedding of the righteous blood of OT martyrs" (p. 471). Since Chronicles is placed last in the Hebrew Bible, identification with the Zechariah whose murder is recorded in that book would furnish a first and last relationship that seems to be the point. J. S. Wright says that "the naming of Abel and Zechariah in this verse would be the equivalent of our phrase 'from Genesis to Revelation' " (*IBD*, p. 1677).

§24 Eschatological Discourse (Matt. 24:1-51)

24:1-2 / In Matthew's Gospel the first two verses of chapter 24 are closely related to the last two verses of chapter 23. Jesus had said, "Your house is left to you desolate" (23:38) and now adds that **not one stone** of the temple **will be left on another** (24:2). Mark's intervening account of the widow's gift (Mark 12:41-44) is omitted. As Jesus was walking away from the **temple** (*hieron*, the entire complex), his disciples called attention to the buildings. In 20-19 B.C. Herod the Great obtained permission from his subjects and began to rebuild the temple of Zerubbabel. An architectural masterpiece, it was fully completed only a few years before its destruction by Titus in A.D. 70.

Jesus responded with the prediction that the buildings would be brought to ruin. Not a single stone would be left intact. Critics who think that the bulk of Matthew comes from the early church rather than from Jesus himself are hard pressed to explain why there is no mention at this point of the burning of the temple. A *vaticinium ex eventu* (prophecy after the event) would not have omitted such a specific item.

The remainder of chapter 24 is notably difficult. The essential problem is that Matthew seems to move back and forth between an impending crisis (the fall of Jerusalem) and the end of the age, when Jesus would return in judgment. If Jesus held that these two events were contemporaneous, then history has proven him wrong. On the other hand, if we accept the theory of the "Little Apocalypse" (that an apocalyptic pamphlet circulated during difficult days was wrongly attributed to Jesus), we can no longer hold to the dominical origin of the teaching. One helpful insight notes that verses 15-35 answer the disciples' question, "When will this happen?" (v. 3a), and the remaining verses of the chapter respond in a general way to the second question, "What will be the sign of your coming and of the end of the age? (v. 3b., cf. Tasker, pp. 223-31; esp. p. 228, note on v. 3).

It is helpful to remember that apocalyptic literature is a genre that does not share our Western concern for orderly continuity. If we allow Matthew the freedom to enlarge on a specific discourse delivered by Jesus by adding related material from other settings, we are not at all surprised to find the chapter as fluid as it appears. It is not uncommon for prophetic material to move between type and antitype without calling attention to exactly what is happening. Predictions of the future were of necessity couched in language taken from the prophet's own setting. The coming destruction of Jerusalem was an anticipation of the end of the age. The same essential principles are in play. To speak of the end of history in terms taken from the impending crisis was quite natural. A parallel situation in Revelation pictures the final conflict in terms of hostility brought to bear on the church through the powers of the Roman Empire in consort with the religious leaders of the Asian church. The Olivet Discourse (as it is often called) is best understood if we do not press it unduly at points where we may be uncertain about an exact temporal fulfillment. Matthew moves freely between the coming destruction of Jerusalem and the final consummation. Whether or not he understood them to be one and the same is a question that leads away from any helpful understanding of the essential point being made. The discussion that follows is offered from this perspective.

24:3–14 / Jesus' statement about the temple's destruction undoubtedly surprised the disciples. They approached him as he **was sitting on the Mount of Olives** (a setting connected with apocalyptic expectations; cf. Zech. 14:4) and asked two questions: **When will this happen?** and, "How can we tell when You're coming back and the world will come to an end?" (Beck). In the Greek text a single article governs both parts of the second question, indicating that they are to be considered as a single unit. The expected "sign" of Jesus' coming will also herald the consummation. The word *parousia* (**coming**) occurs in the Gospels only in this chapter (vv. 3, 27, 37, 39) but is common throughout the rest of the New Testament. It is widely used in nonbiblical texts for the arrival of a person of high status.

Jesus warns his disciples against being led astray by pretenders who will come claiming to be the Messiah (v. 5). However, when they hear of wars, famines, and earthquakes (signs of the approaching end in Jewish apocalyptic), they are not to be alarmed. These are but the "birth-pangs of the new age" (NEB). Theudas and Judas the Galilean (Acts 5:36–7), as well as "the Egyptian who started a revolt" (Acts 21:38), fall into the category of nationalistic messiahs. The followers of Jesus are to beware of those who come claiming to speak with the authority of Christ.

By and large the *Pax Romana* (scarcely known before Augustus) had put an end to the many conflicts that raged during the Hellenistic period. Apocalyptic writing envisioned a return to the chaos of earlier periods. **Famines** accompany conflict. **Earthquakes** are frequently mentioned in Revelation in connection with the end of history (Rev. 6:12; 8:5; 11:13, 19; 16:18). All these things, however, are but **the beginning of birth pains** (v. 8; Gk. *ōdin* is used for the "terrors and torments that precede the coming of the Messianic Age," Str-B., vol. 1, p. 950).

When all these things begin to happen, the faithful will be tortured (**handed over** *eis thlipsin*, v. 9) and **put to death** by a pagan society that despises those who honor the name of Christ (cf. Dan. 12:1). At the same time many will deny their faith and vent their hatred by turning on one another. False prophets will arise to confuse the issue even further (cf. Acts 20:29–30). With the spread of wickedness, **the love of most** (*tōn pollōn* in v. 12 probably means "of the majority") **will grow cold**. But those who stand firm to the end will be saved. The **gospel of the kingdom** is to be proclaimed throughout the entire inhabited earth (*oikoumenē*), so that all nations may hear the truth, and "only after that will the end come" (Knox). Only when the church has completed its worldwide mission of evangelization will the Parousia no longer be delayed.

24:15 / Jesus predicts that a time of extreme trouble will be heralded by the appearance of the "abomination of desolation" (AV) **standing in the holy place**. The background for this **"abomination that causes desolation"** (RSV calls it "the desolating sacrilege," and TCNT translates "the Foul Desecration") is Daniel's prophecy of the "seventy 'sevens' " (Dan. 9:27; 11:31; 12:11). The reference is to the pagan altar to the Olympian Zeus that Antiochus IV Epiphanes (ruler of the Seleucid Empire) erected in the temple court in Jerusalem (1 Macc. 1:54). Among the many things he did in his attempt to defame Judaism was a directive to "sacrifice swine and unclean animals" (1 Macc. 1:47) in the temple (cf. 2 Macc. 6:1–11).

A comparison of the synoptic accounts reveals interesting differences. Mark (13:14) uses a masculine participle for "standing" (*hestēkota*), although it modifies the neuter word "abomination" (*bdelygma*). This would indicate that he understood the critical phrase as referring to a person. Some have thought that Mark may have been alluding to the abortive attempt of Caligula (Gaius Caesar, A.D. 12–41) to have his statue set up in the Holy of Holies. The cryptic "let the reader understand" (Mark 13:14) is used in support of this conjecture. Matthew changes the masculine participle to neuter (*hestos*) and, instead of Mark's "where it ought not to be," substitutes **in the holy place**. Luke says that the desolation is near when they see Jerusalem surrounded by armies (Luke 21:20). This would seem to indicate (but not demand) that Luke understood the section in terms of the fall of Jerusalem in A.D. 70.

Tasker holds that the clue for understanding the passage is found in Luke. He concludes that "the 'abominable sign' would most naturally refer to the ensign carried by the Roman soldiers, to which the image of the emperor was attached" (p. 229). However, because of the verses that follow (specifically the mention in v. 21 of the suffering of this period that will never again be equaled), it is unwise to limit the interpretation to a specific time in history past. A more satisfactory answer to the identification of the "abomination of desolation" is to find its origin in that critical period that gave rise to the Maccabean revolution, and then to understand that it has surfaced in history whenever the purposes of God have been violently assaulted by the forces of evil and will assume a personal embodiment in the Antichrist of the last days (cf. 2 Thess. 2:1–12; Rev. 13, 17). It is generally agreed that the counsel to **let the reader understand** (v. 15b) is offered by the Gospel writer. It is like the word in Revelation 13 regard· ing the number of the beast: "This calls for wisdom: let him who has understanding reckon the number" (v. 18).

24:16–22 / When the "appalling Horror" (Moffatt) appears, then it is time to take flight. Those **in Judea** are to take refuge in the mountains. Those resting on rooftop terraces should not attempt to save anything below. If a person is working **in the field**, he must not go back to pick up his coat (Gk. *himation* here would be an outer **cloak** laid aside in order to work). It will be especially difficult for **pregnant women and nursing mothers**. It is hoped the flight will not take place in the rainy season, when the wadis flood and the roads get mired in mud, or on the **Sabbath** (because travel is severely limited on that day). The distress of that time will be greater than the world has ever known—or will ever know. In fact, if God had not decided to cut short that time of tribulation, no human being would be able to survive. However, for the sake of his own chosen people, the time will be shortened.

The siege and collapse of Jerusalem was a time of enormous suffering. Josephus tells us that over a million inhabitants died, mostly of famine. One particularly grisly account tells of a mother who killed, roasted, and ate her baby (*War* 6.201–213). The fall of Jerusalem becomes a type of the great and final tribulation that, if God should not intervene, would bring an end to the human race. Verse 22 reflects the Jewish understanding that the events of history are predetermined by God, but that he is free to alter them according to his best judgment.

24:23–28 / The central point in verses 23–28 is that believers are not to be deceived by false prophets who claim to have special information about the whereabouts of the **Christ**. The **coming of the Son of Man** (Messiah) will be "as instantaneous and as universal as a flash of lightning" (Tasker, p. 225). Paul speaks of the deceptiveness of the Antichrist (2 Thess. 2:9–11), as does John in the Apocalypse (Rev. 13:13–15). Little wonder, since the first contact of Satan with the primal pair was one of subtlety and deceit. The miracle-working power of false prophets reminds us of the ability of the Egyptian magicians to match the early plagues of Moses (Exod. 7:22; 8:7). The followers of Jesus will not have to depend upon "prophetic voices" to tell them of the arrival of the Parousia! When Christ comes there will be no more doubt about it than there would be about whether or not **lightning** had just flashed **from the east is visible . . . in the west**.

Verse 28 appears to be a proverb added at this point to emphasize the "unmistakable visibility of the Son of Man's coming" (Gundry, p. 487). Only if we were to limit this section to the fall of Jerusalem would it be reasonable to suggest that the "eagles" are the Roman army (the symbol appeared on the Roman standards) who swoop down on the "corpse" (Jerusalem in its final days). Though *aetos* normally means "eagle," here it should be taken as "vulture" (eagles are predatory but do not flock together around a carcass). Schweizer makes the interesting comment that the end of the age was attested even then by the false messiahs and prophets who were converging like vultures (p. 455).

24:29–31 / Immediately after the **distress of those days** (vv. 4–28, esp. 9–11 and 15–22), there will appear great cosmic disturbances. The language is apocalyptic and draws from Isaiah 13:10 ("The stars of heaven . . . will not show their light"), Isaiah 34:4 ("All the starry host will fall"), and Haggai 2:6 ("I will once more shake the heavens"). Similar language is used in Revelation when the sixth seal is opened (Rev. 6:12–14). Tasker finds in verses 29–31 a cryptic description of the Roman conquest of Jerusalem and the subsequent spread of the Christian faith (pp. 226–26). It is better to take the passage as setting the stage (by means of the rhetoric of apocalyptic) for the return of the Son of Man. The "heavenly bodies" (v. 29) are sometimes identified as astral divinities, but it is better to take the phrase in a more literal way.

At that time the sign of the Son of Man will appear in the sky (v. 30). Context would suggest that the **sign** should be understood as a star or comet. However, the genitive could be construed as an appositive, in which case the sign would *be* the Son of Man. Some refer back to the messianic passage in Isaiah 11, where the sign (*sēmeion*, v. 12) is a banner or ensign. Schweizer writes, "Matthew is merely trying to say that the standard of the Messiah will be raised and the trumpet blown when he comes to establish God's Kingdom" (p. 456). Whatever the exact meaning of **sign**, the point being made is that the coming of the Son of Man will be clearly visible to all people everywhere.

When the heavenly sign appears, then "all the tribes of the earth" (AV) will beat their breasts as a sign of mourning (v. 30; *koptō* in the middle voice means "to strike"). Zechariah 12:10ff. pictures the clans of Israel mourning when they look on the one they have pierced (cf. John 19:37 and Rev. 1:7). When the Son of Man returns, the mourning will be universal. All the nations of the earth will realize how irrevocably wrong they have been about the person and messianic claims of Jesus. Not only will all see his return but they will hear the **loud trumpet call** that announces his arrival. The trumpet was used in ancient Israel to gather God's people for religious purposes and to signal activities on the battlefield. In speaking of a time yet future when the Israelites will be gathered, Isaiah says that "in that day a great trumpet will sound" (Isa. 27:13). At the sound of the eschatological trumpet (cf. 1 Cor. 15:52; 1 Thess. 4:16), the angels will be sent to the **four winds** (cf. 13:41, 49) to gather God's elect (for Old Testament parallels, cf. Zech. 2:6 and Deut. 30:4). The scene depicted is clearly that of the return of Christ at the end of history as we know it.

24:32–35 / The **fig tree** has a lesson to teach. When its tender shoots appear and begin to open into leaves, then **you know that summer is near.** In the same way, when you see all the things just described, know that the end **is near, right at the door.** The fig tree shed its leaves in winter and budded late in spring. Since harvest in Palestine took place in the summer, the budding of the fig tree would indicate that the end (symbolized by harvest) was at hand. **All these things**, says Jesus, will happen before **this generation . . . will pass away** (v. 34). This remarkable statement is more certain than the universe itself. **Heaven and earth will pass away** but the words of Jesus will stand forever.

The problem is obvious: the generation alive at that time has long since passed away, but the eschatological events described in the passage have not taken place. There have been many suggestions as to how this apparently insoluble problem may be resolved.

First, if the entire discourse is understood as relating to the fall of Jerusalem (Tasker, pp. 223–31) the problem disappears. This answer can be held only by overlooking the rather obvious meaning of a number of verses in the discourse.

Second, Jesus was simply wrong at this point. Doesn't he, in fact, indicate his limited knowledge in verse 36? Put rather boldly, Beare says, "It must be recognized that the entire apocalyptic framework of early Christian preaching is shattered beyond any hope of rescue" (p. 473). But if the limitation of knowledge mentioned in verse 36 is to be taken as referring to the *general* time of his return rather than the "actual day and time" (Phillips), why would Jesus contradict himself with the analogy of the budding fig tree?

Third, perhaps the Greek *genea* (**generation**) means the Jewish race, or the human race in general, or perhaps the generation alive when the series of final events begins (the establishment of the nation of Israel in 1948?). Green holds that it is a promise that the church will survive to the end (p. 202).

Fourth, if *genētai* (**happened**) is taken as an ingressive aorist, the sentence would indicate that before the generation alive at that time had died, all the things described in connection with the end *will have started to take place*.

Fifth, Hill suggests that we are probably dealing with a "shortening of historical perspective," which is common in prophecy (p. 323). C. H. Dodd is quoted as saying that "when the profound realities underlying a situation are depicted in the dramatic form of historical prediction, the certainty and inevitability of the spiritual processes involved are expressed in terms of the immediate imminence of the event" (*Parables*, p. 71). Although this seems reasonable in a somewhat abstract way, it fails to correspond to the certainty Jesus claims for his statement (v. 35).

Sixth, biblical prophecy is capable of multiple fulfillment. In the immediate context, the "abomination of desolation" (v. 15) builds on the defilement of the temple by Antiochus Epiphanes, is repeated when the sacred temple in Jerusalem is destroyed by the Roman army in A.D. 70, and has yet a more complete fulfillment when the eschatological Antichrist exalts himself by taking his seat in the "temple of God" proclaiming himself to be God (2 Thess. 2:3–4). In a similar way, the events of the immediate period leading up to the destruction of Jerusalem portend a greater and more universal catastrophe when Christ returns in judgment at the end of time. Gundry is right in his observation that double fulfillment (I would say "multiple fulfillment") involves an ambiguity that needs to be accepted as fact rather than objected to on literary grounds (p. 491).

24:36–44 / The discourse began with two questions: the first asked when the temple would be destroyed, and the second, what would be the sign of Jesus' coming (24:3). The answer to the first is that it will take place in the lifetime of the present generation. The answer to the second is that the events connected with Jesus' return (vv. 5–29) are like the budding of a fig tree that indicates the arrival of summer. The exact time, however, (**that day or hour**), is known by no one (**not even the angels in heaven, nor the Son**), **but only** by **the Father** (v. 36). This "pillar passage" (Schmiedel) has long intrigued scholars. It is a candid admission by Jesus of limited knowledge. The omission of *oude ho hyios* (**nor**

the Son) in a number of manuscripts is undoubtedly the result of theological difficulties caused by the phrase (cf. Metzger, *TCGNT*, p. 62). Even without the phrase, the difficulty remains, because it is "the Father *only*" who knows the exact time when the Son will return. As the omnipotence of the Son did not come into play in the temptation scene (4:1–11), now his omniscience is veiled in a specific area. Were this not the case, the incarnation would be something less than a full and genuine entrance into the condition of humanity (cf. Heb. 4:15).

The case of those alive at the time of Noah and living as if a crisis did not exist illustrates what will happen to those who fail to watch for the unexpected return of the Son. Vigilance is in order because **no one knows** the exact time of the Parousia. Those alive **in the days of Noah** are not pictured as especially wicked. Absorbed in the daily round of living, they were taken unawares by the flood. **So it will be at the coming of the Son of Man**. A great separation will take place. The man working **in the field** (v. 40) and the woman **grinding** meal (v. 41) will be **taken** away in judgment (not to safety; cf. parallel in v. 39 with those "taken away" by the flood: Knox says the flood "drowned them all"). The followers of Jesus are to be on the watch because they **do not know on what day** their **Lord will come** (v. 42). You can be sure that the head of a house would stay awake if he knew when the thief would arrive and tunnel through (Gk. *dioryssō*) the wall in order to rob him. In the same way, believers **must be ready** because the Son of Man will return at an hour when he is least expected.

24:45–51 / **Who then is the faithful and wise servant?** The paragraph that follows is directed to those appointed to positions of leadership in the church (those responsible to "manage [the] household staff" and "issue . . . rations at the proper time," NEB). The **wise** (or sensible) **servant** is the one who, when the master returns, will be found to be faithfully carrying out his or her responsibilities. The master will reward such a servant by placing him over the entire estate. The **servant** who **is wicked** is the one who is led to believe that the master will be away for a long time and therefore seizes the opportunity to bully fellow servants and spend time carousing with drunkards. Beare notes that "the danger of arrogance developing in religious leaders is not a mediaeval or modern phenomenon" (p. 478). When the master does return unexpectedly, this wicked servant will be **cut . . . to pieces** and assigned his fate with the **hypocrites, where there will be weeping and gnashing of teeth** (cf. 22:13). Dismemberment was a severe punishment but not unknown in the ancient world (cf. Heb. 11:37). Some have suggested that in this context *dichotomeō* ("to cut in two") should be taken metaphorically to mean excommunication (i.e., to separate from the community). Others have suggested that it is perhaps a mistranslation of the Aramaic word that means either "give him blows" or "assign him his portion" (cf. Fenton, p. 395). The final sentence in verse 51 (**there will be weeping and gnashing of teeth**), however, indicates physical death and what awaits the sinner after that.

Additional Notes §24

24:2 / Green argues in a curious fashion that since *tauta panta* (**all these things**) is neuter plural and does not specifically refer to buildings (as it does in Mark), it follows that the reference is "to the content of the discourse so far" (p. 198). Such a reconstruction makes difficult any attempt to understand in context the remainder of verse 2.

24:4 / Hill finds Jesus' reply to the disciples' questions summed up in three verses: vv. 4, 27, and 36 (p. 317). Although the point they make is important to the discourse, it is questionable that Jesus' major intention in the chapter is to calm apocalyptic enthusiasm.

24:13 / **To the end**: Hill understands *eis telos* in the sense of "without breaking down" rather than "to the End" (p. 321). Schweizer maintains that the "holding out" is to be understood in reference to false teachers rather than in the midst of persecution (p. 451).

24:15 / **"The abomination that causes desolation"**: For a rather complete survey of the various ways in which this figure has been interpreted, see G. R. Beasley-Murray, *A Commentary on Mark Thirteen*, pp. 59–72. Beare says that "the desolating sacrilege—*to bdelygma tēs erēmōseōs* is a more or less literal rendering (LXX) of a Hebrew phrase of Daniel, *shiqūts shomēm*. The Hebrew phrase is itself a contemptuous play on the proper Semitic form *ba'al shamēm* (Aramaic; Hebrew *ba'al shamayīm*), 'the Ba'al [i.e., Lord] of the heavens' " (p. 467).

24:30 / **Sign**: Filson asks whether the sign could perhaps be the "brilliant light of his coming" (p. 256). Patristic exegesis understood the sign in the form of a cross.

24:31 / **Trumpet**: The Greek *salpinx* may refer either to the instrument itself or the sound it produces (BAGD, p. 741).

24:36 / **Nor the Son**: The idea that this phrase was added to the text in order to explain why Jesus miscalculated the time of the end begs the question.

24:43 / The illustration of a thief coming unexpectedly occurs in 1 Thess. 5:2; 2 Pet. 3:10; Rev. 3:3 and 16:15.

Chapter 24 closed with a parable warning what will happen to servants who are unfaithful while the master is away. The same general theme continues throughout chapter 25. Like the foolish young women of verses 1–13, they will be excluded from the marriage feast; like the worthless servant who buries his talent, they will be thrown outside into the darkness (vv. 14–30); and like the "goats" who do not respond to the needy, they will suffer the fate of the devil and his angels (vv. 31–46). The clear-cut distinction between the two groups reminds us of the parable with which Jesus closed his Sermon on the Mount (7:24–27, the wise man who built on rock and the foolish man who built on sand). Both the first and the last of the five discourses in Matthew end with the same emphasis.

25:1–5 / Many writers find a number of allegorical features in this parable and judge, therefore, that if it had its origin with Jesus it has under gone considerable modification. But if one's concept of parable allows it to illustrate more than one truth, the problem of allegorization is no longer so threatening. The very nature of proverb and parable indicates that they allow (perhaps encourage) multiple application. A parable whose immediate application could have been a judgment against the scribes and Pharisees (like the foolish maidens who were unprepared for the coming of Christ, the bridegroom) could also serve in a predictive way as a warning to the later church that the second coming of Christ should find them prepared. The question of whether the marriage customs reflected in the parable are consistent with first-century Palestinian practice cannot be proven or disproven from extrabiblical sources (although Jeremias is certain that they reflect the realities of life at that time, *Parables*, pp. 172–75).

Jesus compares the kingdom of heaven to what happened to ten bridesmaids who were waiting for the bridegroom to appear and take his bride in procession to the wedding banquet.

In ancient Palestine a marriage normally had three stages: engagement, betrothal (which was legal and binding), and the marriage itself. The setting of the parable is that of bridesmaids waiting at the bride's house ready to light torches for the procession back to the groom's house, where the ceremony will take place. The five who are called **foolish** took their torches (*lampas* here is probably a torch rather than a lamp or lantern) but no extra **oil**. The **wise** took containers for the additional oil that would be needed for the procession and the dancing that would follow. That there were **five** foolish and **five** wise does not mean that half the world will find salvation. The numbers simply provide two categories. Wisdom consists in being prepared: foolishness is the lack of preparation for unexpected circumstances that may arise. Because the groom was **a long time in coming**, the bridesmaids grew drowsy and fell asleep.

25:6–13 / At midnight a cry rang out announcing the imminent arrival of the groom. The ten girls awoke and **trimmed their lamps** (*kosmeō* means "to put in order" and could refer to the preparation of torches as well as the trimming of a wick). The foolish were short on oil. Not only did they fail to bring additional oil, but their torches, when lit, burned with a low flame (they were **going out**, v. 8). When asked by the foolish for more oil, the wise refused, on grounds that there would not be enough for all. The decision was not selfish but based on common sense (if *all* the torches went out, the procession would be a disaster). The foolish girls went to the store to purchase oil (on a festive night in a rural village, everyone would be up and about for such a celebration, Schweizer, p. 467), but while they were away the groom came and led the entourage off to the banquet hall. Central to the parable is the point that, once the wedding party was inside, **the door was shut** (v. 10).

When the foolish five returned and found the door closed, they pleaded to be admitted. The bridegroom's answer was **I tell you the truth, I don't know you**. This phrase is said to be a formula used by rabbis to prevent certain disciples from approaching (Green, p. 205). The failure of the foolish to prepare for the bridegroom's arrival led to their total exclusion from the marriage festivities.

The conclusion that Jesus draws is, **Therefore keep watch, because you do not know the day or the hour**. In context, **keep**

watch means to be thoroughly prepared and ready for the Parousia. The remaining verses in the chapter suggest that readiness involves using the opportunities provided and responding to the needs of the disadvantaged. Though the parable primarily teaches the necessity of being ready for the return of Christ, it also contains a number of related truths of practical importance: religious merit cannot be transferred (v. 9); the door to eternal life, once shut, will not be reopened (vv. 10–11); the end will arrive unexpectedly (v. 13). As with every good parable, the message is applicable in any number of related circumstances.

25:14–18 / Jesus provides another parable to emphasize the importance of using the interval before his return in a wise manner. Just before a man was to leave on a trip, he called his servants together and placed them in charge of his money. To one he gave **five talents of money** (over five thousand dollars, cf. NIV text note), to another **two talents**, and to the third **one talent**. The three servants received different amounts based upon the particular ability of each. This parable has led to the use of the word *talent* in English in the sense of a natural or supernatural gift.

The servant entrusted with **five talents** doubled the amount by wise investment. So also did the servant who received **two talents**. The third servant, however, dug a hole and buried his master's money (not at all an uncommon way of protecting valuables in the ancient world). Schweizer reports that, according to rabbinic law, burying property was conceived of as the safest possible course of action (p. 471) and therefore would absolve the servant from any liability.

25:19–30 / After an extended period of time, the master returns to settle accounts. The first servant reports his earnings and is commended as a **good and faithful servant** (v. 21). As a reward for managing faithfully a small amount, he will be "put in charge of something big" (NEB). In addition he is invited to **come and share** his **master's happiness**. The second servant (who has done equally well with the two talents) receives the same commendation and reward as the first. But it is another story with the servant who failed to invest his allocation of money. He attempts to defend himself by impugning the character of the master. "You're a 'tight-fisted' man" (v. 24, Norlie) who insists

on a return even where you haven't invested, so I did the only
reasonable thing and kept what you gave me in a safe place.
The master, however, doesn't let him get away with the
attempt to make laziness a virtue. You are a **wicked, lazy servant**. Verse 26b is a question: So you knew that I reap where I
haven't sown, did you? Then you should have deposited my
money in the bank so I could have collected not only the principal but the interest as well. The master orders the talent to be
taken from the lazy servant and given to the one with the most.
Verse 29 states the general principle that those who have, receive
more, and those who do not, forfeit what little they do have. In
context it means that faithfulness is rewarded by expanded opportunities, whereas the lack of fidelity leads to impoverishment.
The law of spiritual atrophy is that when gifts are not exercised
they are withdrawn. The "good-for-nothing slave" (Goodspeed)
is flung out into **the darkness** (described in v. 41 as "eternal fire"),
where he can "weep and wail over his stupidity" (Phillips). The
warning is appropriate for Christians who rest upon their religious profession without any apparent desire to live out its implications. The point of the parable is crystal clear. The servants
of Christ, as they await his Parousia, have been entrusted with
the responsibility of utilizing the gifts they have been given by
the Master. To fail in this critical obligation is to be excluded from
the kingdom when Christ returns.

25:31–46 / Shortly after the transfiguration, Jesus prophesied that, when the Son of Man returns in the glory of his Father
and accompanied by angels, he will "repay every man for what
he has done" (Matt. 16:27). Matthew closes Jesus' fifth major discourse with a description of this apocalyptic event as a separation of **sheep** and **goats** (v. 33) on the basis of their response to
the needs of **these brothers of mine** (v. 40). Final judgment allows
no shades of gray. Each person will either enter into **eternal life**
or be sent away into **eternal punishment** (v. 46).

The **Son of Man** is pictured as a **King** seated on his **throne
in heavenly glory** and surrounded by an angelic court. Before him
are gathered **all the nations** of the world. **As a shepherd**, who
in the evening **separates the sheep** (who like the open air) **from
the goats** (who need the warmth of shelter), the king **will put
the sheep on his right and the goats on his left** (cf. Ezek. 34:17,
20, 22). The masculine *autous* ("them") in 32b following the neu-

ter *ethnē* (**nations**) in 32a indicates that the separation will be between individual people rather than between nations. The scene
does not depict a trial but the passing of a sentence on those
whose judgment has already taken place. The righteous are invited to take possession of the kingdom ready for them **since the
creation of the world** (v. 34). Their blessedness stems from their
response to the needs of the deprived (the hungry, thirsty, homeless, poor, sick, and imprisoned). The righteous are unaware that
in ministering to the dispossessed they have been ministering to
the King.

Scholars are divided on exactly who is intended by the
phrase **these brothers of mine** (v. 40). If they represent anyone
in need, then the section seems to teach that future judgment
rests on broad humanitarian principles. On the other hand, if the
reference is to the disciples of Jesus (cf. 12:49; 28:10)—and by extension all who follow Christ (note 12:50)—the application is nar-
rowed to the treatment afforded those who minister in his name.
Green writes that the contrast is between "heathen who serve
Christ without knowing him and Christians who know him without serving him, in the persons of their suffering fellow Christians" (pp. 206–7). Although the New Testament clearly teaches
that deeds of kindness in and of themselves do not secure salvation, it also teaches that when faith is real it must of necessity
express itself in a life of concern for others. The warning is directed against **goats**, who, as they mingle daily with **sheep**, might
be led to think that they can get by as sheep.

Those who have been placed on Jesus' left are **cursed** (v.
41). They are sent from the presence of the King to the **eternal
fire** that was **prepared for the devil and his angels** (cf. Rev. 19:20;
20:10, 14, 15; 21:8). Unlike the righteous, they did not minister
to Christ when he was hungry, thirsty, homeless, poor, sick, and
in prison. In a tone of "injured innocence" (Tasker), they asked
when it was that they saw him in such straits and would not help.
The answer is that when they refused help to the least important
of Christ's followers they refused help to Christ. Their judgment
rests not on acts of wickedness but on their failure to respond
compassionately when faced with human despair. Their destiny
is **eternal punishment**, whereas that of the upright is **eternal life**.
Although *aiōnios* (**eternal**) is primarily a qualitative word, its temporal aspect should not be overlooked. Verse 46 offers little sup-

port for those who would like to think of eternal life as endless and eternal punishment as restricted in some way. That the adjective modifies both nouns in the same context indicates that we understand it in the same way.

Additional Notes §25

25:1 / Some manuscripts add the words *kai tēs nymphēs* ("and the bride"). Some argue that they were original and were omitted because they would be incompatible with the idea of Christ (the bridegroom) coming to take his bride (the church). It is more likely that they were added by a scribe in order to bring the parable into line with the customary practice of holding the wedding in the home of the groom's parents, not noticing that mention of the bride would upset the allegorical interpretation of the story (cf. Metzger, *TCGNT*, pp. 62–63).

25:3 / **Lamps**: Torches used to light the way for wedding ceremonies would be sticks wrapped with rags and soaked in olive oil. Since they would burn out in about fifteen minutes, it was necessary to take along extra oil in a separate container.

25:13 / The idea of the Messiah as bridegroom grew out of such Old Testament passages as Hos. 2:19 and Isa. 62:5.

25:14 / In ancient days servants were often entrusted with responsible activities such as the management of capital.

25:15 / **Talents**: Gk. *talanton*. The **talent** was originally a measure of weight and later a unit of monetary reckoning. Its value was related to the metal involved (gold, silver, or copper) as well as the time and place.

25:31–46 / T. W. Manson supports the authenticity of this unit, noting that it contains "features of such startling originality that it is difficult to credit them to anyone but the Master himself" (*Sayings*, p. 249).

The Passion narrative is the account of the suffering and death of Jesus. It normally includes all the events beginning with the garden scene in Gethsemane and finishing with the burial. The centrality of the cross in early Christian preaching is reflected in the major emphasis given to it in each of the four Gospels. Matthew 26 records the events of Wednesday and Thursday of the final week of Jesus' life.

26:1–5 / When Jesus finished **saying all these things** (probably the content of chaps. 23–25) he told his disciples that in two days it would be time to celebrate the Passover and that at that time the Son of Man would be **handed over to be crucified.** *Paradidōmi* ("to hand over") was a technical term in court meaning "to hand over into the custody of" (cf. BAGD, p. 614). Reference to the Passover as **two days away** suggests that it was Wednesday of Holy Week.

The **chief priests** and **elders** (Mark and Luke say "teachers of the law") got together at the palace of **the high priest . . . Caiaphas,** and **plotted** how they might capture Jesus in some subtle way **and kill him.** In an earlier period the office of the high priest was hereditary and lasted for the entire life of the incumbent. During the Roman period high priests came and went at the whim of their secular masters. Caiaphas held office from A.D. 18 to 36 (Josephus *Ant.* 18.29–35). Acts 4:6 refers to Annas as high priest (cf. Luke 3:2), although he had been officially deposed in A.D. 15. This indicates the significant influence that Annas continued to exercise among the priestly hierarchy in Jerusalem.

To do away with Jesus during a religious festival posed a special problem. It could incite a riot on the part of the many worshipers, who had flocked to Jerusalem for the Passover and would be in sympathy with Jesus. *Mē en tē heortē* (**not during the Feast**) probably means "apart from the festal crowd" rather than "not during the time of the feast" (See Jeremias, *The Eucharistic Words of Jesus,* p. 48).

26:6–13 / During the Passover season Jesus apparently spent his evenings in the town of Bethany, located on the southeast slope of the Mount of Olives on the Jericho road less than two miles from Jerusalem. On this occasion he was staying with **Simon the Leper** (obviously cured earlier but still designated by the epithet). A parallel account in John places the scene in the home of Mary, Martha, and Lazarus (John 12:1–8). It may be that Simon was the father of Lazarus and his sisters. **A woman came to** Jesus **with an alabaster jar of very expensive** ointment (*myron* was a fragrant oil or perfume) and poured it on Jesus' head while he was at table. The disciples were indignant and questioned the act as unnecessarily wasteful. Rather self-righteously, they noted that the ointment could have been sold at a good price and **the money given to the poor.**

Jesus, who was aware of what they had said (probably among themselves), declared that what the woman had done was **a beautiful thing** (v. 10). What the disciples saw as waste Jesus interpreted as a preparatory anointing for burial. The broken vase (cf. Mark 14:3) portrayed his body, soon to be broken, and the poured-out ointment anticipated the burial that would follow. The disciples failed to see this deeper meaning in the generous act of the woman and reacted accordingly. The pouring of the oil on Jesus' head could also be taken as the anointing that declared him as king (see, e.g., 2 Kings 9:6). Wherever **this gospel** (the story of Jesus' redemptive death) is told throughout the world, the part played by the woman, and its deeper meaning, would be included in her honor.

26:14–16 / **Judas Iscariot**, one of the twelve disciples, went to the chief priests and asked how much they were willing to pay if he would deliver Jesus into their hands. The motive behind Judas' treachery is not completely clear. Perhaps he felt that since Jesus had "failed" to take command as a militant messiah it was time for Judas to separate himself from the movement and get what he could out of what appeared to be a lost opportunity. He may have acted out of greed (cf. John 12:6), except that **thirty silver coins** (the amount assessed for a bull having gored a slave, Exod. 21:32) is a paltry sum for such an act (cf. Zech 11:12). The suggestion least damaging to Judas is that he was simply trying to force Jesus' hand and never intended that the scheme would bring about his death. Whatever the motive, the act stands in dramatic contrast to the generous outpouring of the ointment in the previous pericope. The chief priests carefully weighed out (*estēsan* means "placed [on the scales]") the required amount and gave it to Judas. From that point on Judas kept looking (*ezētei* is imperfect) for an opportunity to betray Jesus.

26:17–25 / On the first day of the **Feast of Unleavened Bread** Jesus' disciples asked him where he wanted them to prepare for the **Passover** meal. According to Exodus 12 (the institution of the Passover), a lamb was to be slaughtered on the fourteenth day of the first month (Nisan) at twilight (vv. 2, 6) and eaten on the same night (v. 8). This was followed by a seven-day feast in which no leavened bread was to be eaten (vv. 15–20). Apparently the Jews, over a period of time, began to remove the leaven a day early, and this gave rise to the improper designation of Nisan 14 as the first day of the Feast of Unleavened Bread. A famous controversy centers around the fact that the Synoptics present the Last Supper as a Passover meal whereas John (18:28; 19:14, 31, 42) places the crucifixion on the day before Passover. Some writers hold that the apparently contradictory passages may be harmonized; others think that John adjusted his material to emphasize the theological point that Jesus was the Lamb of God slain for the sins of mankind.

The disciples are told to **go into the city to a certain man** and tell him that **the Teacher** has said that his **appointed time is near** and that he will **celebrate the Passover with** his **disciples at** the man's **house**. The **appointed time** (v. 18; Gk. *kairos*) that has drawn near is the time of the redemptive death of the Son of Man. All history pointed to that crucial moment when the kingdom of God was to be established by the sacrifice of the Son. The disciples did as they were instructed and prepared the Passover meal. In addition to the lamb, it would be necessary to secure saltwater, bitter herbs, *harosheth* (a broth of mashed nuts and fruit), and wine.

When evening came Jesus was reclining (*anekeito*, imperfect) with his disciples at table. In earlier days the Passover was eaten standing up (cf. Exod. 12:11), but by New Testament times it was served like other meals on low tables around which those who took part reclined on cushions. During the meal Jesus made the startling announcement that one of them would betray him. The disciples were "sick at heart" (v. 22, Rieu) and began to say one after the other, **Surely not I, Lord?** The form of the question in Greek indicates that a negative response is expected, although the possibility that it could be affirmative cannot be ruled out entirely (i.e., "*I* am not the one, Lord, am I?").

The betrayer is one who has dipped his hand into the bowl with Jesus. In Eastern cultures, the sharing of a meal established a bond of intimate fellowship. To betray that relationship would be treachery of the worst sort. The **bowl** (Gk. *tryblion*) was a deep dish containing the broth into which the guests dipped pieces of bread or meat. The seriousness of the betrayal is seen in Jesus' statement that although the **Son of Man will go** as foretold in Scripture, **woe to that man who betrays** him! **It would be better for him if he had not been born.** Divine predestination does not alleviate human responsibility. Judas, who was to betray him, asked the same question as the others (cf. vv. 22, 25) but refers to Jesus as **Rabbi** rather than "Lord." The change of address is significant (cf. 23:8) and reveals an attitude that corresponds to what we are learning about Judas the man. Jesus answered *sy eipas* (lit., "you have said it"), which the NEB translates, "the words are yours."

26:26–30 / While they were still at table **Jesus took bread, gave thanks** (he did not "bless the bread") **and broke it,** and handed it **to his disciples saying, "Take and eat; this is my body."** This departure from the normal Passover pattern took place just before the final cup. Hill notes that in Aramaic there would be no connecting verb in the phrase **this is my body,** although it would be implied, and adds that "to insert *is* suggests a relationship of identity which there is no reason to assume, whereas the rendering 'represents' may convey only a purely figurative suggestion" (p. 339).

Then he took the cup and, after giving **thanks,** passed it to his disciples, directing them to drink it. It is the **blood** of Christ, **poured out** for all (**many** is a Semitism for "everybody") **for the forgiveness of sins.** The pouring out of blood portrays violent death (cf. 23:35; Rev. 16:6). The **blood of the covenant** recalls Exodus 24:8 (rather than Jer. 31:31), in which the sprinkling of the blood was a sign that the people were included within the covenant relationship. Jesus then tells his disciples that he will not drink again of the wine until the day he drinks it new with them in his Father's kingdom (v. 29). He looks beyond the scene in which his obedience will take him to the cross and pictures a joyous banquet in the fully realized kingdom in which once again he will share the intimacy of table fellowship with his disciples. Then, after they had sung **a hymn** (following the order of the Passover it would be the second half of the Hallel, Pss. 115–118), **they went out to the Mount of Olives.**

26:31–35 / On the way to the Mount of Olives (east of Jerusalem across the Kidron valley), Jesus tells his disciples that that very night they will desert him (*skandalizomai*, "find a cause of stumbling," Rotherham). Their failure is described by the prophet Zechariah, who wrote, "Strike the shepherd, and the sheep will be scattered" (Zech. 13:7). Both Matthew and Mark change the imperative (of the MT and LXX) "strike" to the first person future (**I will strike**), which marks God as the one who takes the action. However, after Jesus has **risen** he will **go ahead of** them **into Galilee.** *Proagō* ("to go before") may be taken in the sense of time (i.e., he will return to Galilee before they do; cf. 28:16) or, in this instance, may be a continuation of the shepherd image and mean that, when they are together again in Galilee, he will take his place at the head of the flock (Palestinian shepherds lead their sheep) and guide them (see the promise in 28:20).

Peter vehemently declares that he will never desert Jesus. Even though the others are "scandalized," he will remain true (v. 33). Not so, responds Jesus. This very night, before cockcrow (no article before "cock"), you will deny me **three times.** In New Testament times the night was divided into four watches, the third being designated as the "cockcrow" (midnight until three a.m.). Some think that the reference is to the trumpet call that marked the end of the third watch, although as dawn was approaching it could well mark the time when roosters began to crow. The point is that even before morning dawned Peter would deny Jesus three times. The compound *aparneomai* means "to deny completely."

26:36–39 / Crossing the Kidron (the deep ravine to the east of Jerusalem) Jesus goes to a garden (cf. John 18:1) called **Gethsemane.** The name is from the Aramaic and means "oil press," indicating the location is an olive orchard. Well-to-do citizens of Jerusalem maintained groves on the west slope of the Mount of Olives. In Matthew's account it was there that Jesus would within a few hours be separated from his disciples until they would meet again in Galilee following the resurrection (Matt. 28:16ff.). How typical of human weakness to be unavailable when needed most! The scene in the garden has profound implications for our understanding of Jesus' perfect humanity. Leaving the eight disciples (Judas had left the group by then) at a spot perhaps near the entrance of the garden, Jesus took **Peter and the two sons of Zebedee** a bit farther to be near him while he prayed (see 17:1–8 for the same group).

A great sense of grief and dismay laid hold of Jesus. To the three disciples he acknowledged that his heart was at the point of breaking with sorrow. The GNB aptly translates, "The sorrow in my heart is so great that it almost crushes me" (v. 38). The words reflect Psalms 42:5–6 and 43:5. To the three, Jesus says, "Wait here and stay awake with me" (Rieu). He then went a bit farther and fell prostrate in prayer. To "fall on one's face" is a biblical expression indicating an earnest attitude of serious prayer (see Gen. 17:3; Num. 14:5). Luke adds that he was "in anguish" and that "his sweat was like drops of blood falling to the ground" (Luke 22:44). To God, his **Father**, he asks that if possible, the **cup** be taken from him. In the Old Testament the cup is a metaphor for punishment and suffering (Ps. 75:8; Isa. 51:17). The agony of Jesus in Gethsemane was not the anticipation of the pain and cruelty of the crucifixion but the awful truth that he was the Lamb about to be sacrificed for the sins of the world. It would appear that even in this crucial moment Satan was tempting him to draw back from the cross. His complete and final commitment to the redemptive plan of God is seen in the words, "Not my will but yours be done" (Norlie).

26:40–46 / Returning to the three disciples, Jesus finds them **sleeping**. Although addressing his question to Peter, he speaks to all three (*ischysate* is second person plural: the NIV amplifies the Greek text to read **you men**). Didn't any of you have the strength to stay awake with me for just one hour? As able-bodied fishermen they had toiled all night without sleeping, but here they were unable to resist the comfortable heaviness of approaching slumber. The answer to the question of how sleeping disciples would know what Jesus had said in his prayer is that they undoubtedly were listening for a time before they dozed off. They were close enough to hear. This adds to their culpability.

While Jesus was in the agony of prayer they went to sleep. Jesus warns them to **watch and pray** (present imperatives emphasizing continuing action) that they may be spared the coming trial (of fidelity). Their failure in the approaching crisis stemmed from their halfhearted commitment to prayer. Even at a time like this, when Jesus needed the support and human sympathy of his closest companions, he could offer an explanation for their thoughtless conduct: **the spirit is willing, but the body is weak** (v. 41). Human nature cannot always measure up to the noble aspirations of the spirit. In the most central conflict of human existence Jesus exhibited the victory of the spirit over the flesh while the disciples displayed the victory of the flesh over the spirit (Fenton, p. 421).

Jesus returned a second time to his place of prayer. Mark reports that he "prayed the same thing" (Mark 14:39), but Matthew's wording suggests a growing acceptance of the cross as God's determined will (cf. v. 42 with v. 39). **May your will be done** carries out the essential commitment that Jesus taught his disciples in the Lord's Prayer (Matt. 6:10). Returning, he finds the disciples sleeping once again. "This time he went away without disturbing them" (v. 44, Knox). After a third session alone in prayer, he comes to the disciples and asks in pained surprise, **Are you still sleeping?** The crucial **hour** is at hand, and the Son of Man is about to be delivered into the **hands of sinners.** Jesus has to rouse the disciples in order to tell them that the betrayer is approaching (note the same verb [*ēngiken*] in both v. 45 and v. 46: not only the critical hour but the traitor as well "has drawn near").

26:47-56 / **While Jesus was still speaking, Judas** arrived accompanied by a **large crowd armed with swords and clubs.** The mob (which included both Roman soldiers and temple guards; see John 18:3) was **sent from the chief priests and the elders** (Luke 22:52 indicates that some of the religious leaders went along as well). Judas (who by the time of the writing of the Gospel had become known as **the betrayer**) had told the crowd that he would identify Jesus for them by greeting him with a **kiss.** Going directly to Jesus, he said, "Hail, Rabbi!" and **kissed him.** *Kataphileō* (a compound of the verb "to love/to kiss" and the intensive pronoun) suggests an elaborate show of affection. It is used in Luke 15:20 of the father's embrace of the prodigal son and in Acts

20:37 of the affection of the Ephesian elders for Paul. According to rabbinic tradition, it was wrong for a disciple to greet his master first. Not only was the kiss a way of letting the mob know whom they should seize, but it was also a "studied insult" (Albright-Mann, p. 329). Earlier, Jesus had told his disciples that they should not be called Rabbi (23:8). In Matthew's Gospel only Judas uses the title for Jesus, here and in 26:25.

There is a question as to whether Jesus' response in verse 50 should be taken as a command or as a question. The Greek is elliptical (*eph' ho parei*), which requires that we supply words intended but not provided. If it is taken as a question ("Why are you here?" RSV) it should be understood as a method of bringing out into the open what was already quite obvious. Most modern translations take it as a command (**Do what you came for**, NIV; "Be quick about it," GNB).

When Jesus was seized by the crowd, one of the disciples drew **his sword** and cut off the ear of **the servant of the high priest**. John's Gospel identifies the disciple as "Simon Peter" and the servant as "Malchus" (John 18:10). Jesus orders Peter to put his sword back in its place and adds that **all who draw the sword will die by the sword**. This appears to be a proverb (cf. Gen. 9:6 and Rev. 13:10) and therefore must be interpreted with careful attention to the context. It is not a general rule that forbids defensive action at any time whatsoever.

Jesus did not need the help of a few relatively harmless disciples, because he had at his disposal (had he chosen to take the route of personal defense) a vast army of angels. **Twelve legions** would be in excess of 72,000 (a Roman legion numbered 6,000 infantry plus 120 cavalry). However, if he called upon God for angels to defend him against the mob, the Scriptures that said that everything must take place as it did would then go unfulfilled.

The covert and cowardly nature of the actions of Judas and his mob is brought out by Jesus' query as to why they came out at night as they did to seize him as if he were **leading a rebellion** (the Greek *lēstēs* in this context means "revolutionary" or "insurrectionist"). After all, he sat daily with them **in the temple courts** (note that *ekathezomēn* in v. 55 is imperfect), and they **did not arrest** him there. But all this is happening in fulfillment of prophetic Scripture. The boldness of Jesus, in spite of his being in the hands of the mob, was more than his disciples could endure. In the moment of trial they **deserted him and fled**. Abandoned by his closest friends, he had to suffer the remaining hours of his earthly life without human support.

26:57–61 / Jesus was led off under arrest to the house of **Caiaphas, the high priest**. The trial of Jesus involved three separate steps. First, there was the preliminary gathering at night in which a charge was developed against Jesus (26:57–68). The following morning, a second meeting was held, at which time the religious leaders "met in conference to plan the death of Jesus" (27:1, NEB). The so called "civil" trial before Pilate (27:11–26) was the final step in the proceedings. Because the Gospel accounts of the trial are at odds with Pharisaic jurisprudence as reported in the Mishnah, some commentators have held that they are therefore unreliable. This judgment reflects a failure to realize that Sadducean practice in New Testament times may not have corresponded to later Pharisaic rules for procedure (cf. Marshall, *NIDNTT*, vol. 1, p. 364). This same attitude toward the reliability of the biblical text surfaces in the opinion that Matthew was influenced by theological considerations that led him to minimize the Roman government's involvement in the death of Jesus and emphasize the culpability of the Jewish leaders.

When Jesus arrived at the house of Caiaphas, the group had already gathered. **Peter**, who had been following along **at a distance**, entered the courtyard and **sat down with the guards** "to see the end of it all" (NEB). At this point he had not fully understood the promise of the resurrection (see v. 32). Filson says the scene suggests "hopeless despair and dogged loyalty" (p. 283). Although it was night, the **whole Sanhedrin** had met in an attempt to secure evidence that could lead to Jesus' death. The imperfect tense in verse 59 (*ezētoun*, "were looking") suggests that they were sifting through evidence already provided by various witnesses. The word **false** may be an early scribal insertion: the council would not be looking for *false* evidence, but for evidence that would effectively bring about the death of Jesus. Such action was inconsistent with the legitimate role of the Sanhedrin, which was to maintain custom and ensure justice. This 71-member council, chaired by the high priest, was made up of leading priestly officials, leaders of the lay aristocracy, and a number of scribes.

Although many accusers presented their allegations against Jesus, nothing was found that would warrant the death sentence.

On the basis of Deuteronomy 17:6 a person could not be put to death except on the testimony of two or three witnesses. **Finally two** stepped forward to report that Jesus had claimed to be able to destroy the temple and rebuild it in three days. But Jesus had never said that *he* would destroy the temple, only that the temple would be destroyed (Matt. 24:1–2). Furthermore, the "temple" of which Jesus spoke in John 2:19 was "his body" (note John 2:21).

26:62–68 / The high priest asked Jesus if he had any answer to the accusation made against him, but Jesus remained silent. This impressive refusal to speak on his own behalf moved the high priest to put Jesus **under oath** and demand that he acknowledge whether or not he was **the Christ, the Son of God.** It was against all the procedures of Jewish law to require a person to incriminate himself. The answer, "You have said so" (v. 64, RSV; Gk. *sy eipas*), has been variously interpreted. The parallel in Mark (a straightforward "I am," 14:62) suggests that we not look for subtle innuendos. Gundry says that the response of Jesus "stoutly affirms that the questioner himself knows the affirmative answer as obvious" (p. 545). Jesus is saying to Caiaphas that his assumption that Jesus may be the Messiah is correct. What's more, from that time on, he will **see the Son of Man sitting at the right hand of the Mighty One** (lit., "the Power," a Jewish periphrasis for "God") **and coming on the clouds of heaven**. Though Green holds that "the two images are parallel and express the same truth" (namely, the immediate glorification of the Son of Man, p. 217), a reference to the Parousia is quite clear. The first clause is from Psalm 110:1 and the second from Daniel 7:13. Gundry distinguishes between a "mental seeing" of the glorified Christ and a "literal seeing" of his coming on the clouds of heaven (p. 545). This majestic statement of Jesus forms the "Christological climax" (Green, p. 216) of the Gospel. A new era of human history has begun, and God's redemptive purpose in Christ is being fulfilled.

According to the Mishnah (*Sanhedrin* 6.5) a judge is to tear his garments if he hears blasphemy. The high priest would not consider Jesus' messianic claim to be blasphemous but would understand his statements about sitting on God's right hand and returning in clouds of heaven as tantamount to an assertion of deity. So he exclaims **blasphemy!** (v. 65). Witnesses are no longer necessary. The claim of deity can be made to imply political power and thus be presented as a threat to Roman rule. Turning to the council, the high priest asks, "What is your verdict?"

The obvious response is that he deserves to die (the penalty for blasphemy according to Lev. 24:16). Then they **spit in his face and struck him with their fists** (*kolaphizō* is derived from *kolaphos*, "knuckles/closed fist"). Although Matthew does not specifically identify those who abused Jesus in such a degrading manner, the context would lead us to understand that it was the members of the Sanhedrin who are intended by the pronoun **they** in verse 67. In the Marcan parallel, however, it was the guards who "took him and beat him" (Mark 14:65; Luke 22:63 says that it was "the men who were guarding Jesus" [in the courtyard, 22:55ff.] who mocked and beat him). To spit in a man's face was a gesture of contempt. Matthew assumes Mark's reference to Jesus being blindfolded (Mark 14:65) when he tells of the cruel game of blind man's buff, in which Jesus was slapped in the face and asked to prophesy who it was who hit him. For the religious authorities to lower themselves to such abuse reveals the depth of their hatred for the one whose life and testimony laid bare their hypocrisy.

26:69–75 / Earlier in the chapter, we learned that Peter followed (although at a distance) the mob that arrested Jesus and sat down with the guards in the courtyard to see how it would all turn out (v. 58). The houses of the well-to-do in first-century Palestine were built around open courtyards. Mark's reference to Peter being "below" in the courtyard (Mark 14:66) indicates a prominent building of more than one story. One of the servant girls of the high priest challenged Peter with the allegation that he *also* (as well as others) had been **with Jesus of Galilee**. Peter openly **denied** that he knew what she was talking about. Leaving the fire (John 18:18), Peter moved to **the gateway** (probably a covered enclosure that would be less well lighted and provide easier access to the street). There he is accosted by **another girl** (Mark 14:69 seems to say it was the same maid), who informs the bystanders that "this fellow certainly was with Jesus the Nazarene!" (Montgomery). Again Peter denies the charge, this time **with an oath** (v. 72).

A bit later (Luke 22:59 says "about an hour later"), the men who were standing there came to Peter and said **Surely you are one of them, for your accent gives you away**. The more Peter denied, the more he gave himself away. Galileans spoke Aramaic with an accent that was considered uncouth by those who lived in Jerusalem. Barclay says their accent was so ugly that they were not allowed to pronounce the benediction at synagogue services (vol. 2, p. 346). Recognizing that he was now inescapably cornered, Peter **began to call down curses on himself**, and swore for a third time that he did not know **the man** (an expression of contempt). **Immediately a rooster crowed**, and Peter remembered Jesus' prediction (26:34) that before a cock crows (no definite article before *alektora*) Peter would deny him three times (one denial for each failure to remain awake and pray; cf. 26:36–46). The drama of the scene is heightened by Luke's mention that at that very moment "the Lord turned and looked straight at Peter" (Luke 22:61). Apparently this happened just as Jesus was being led down from the chambers where he had been declared guilty and humiliated by the Sanhedrin.

Peter leaves the courtyard with an unbearable heaviness of heart. Going out, he **wept bitterly**. His remorse was unlike that of Judas, who went out and hanged himself (Matt. 27:5). Paul speaks of a "godly sorrow" that "leads to salvation and leaves no regret" as contrasted with a "worldly sorrow [that] brings death" (2 Cor. 7:10). Whatever else may be said of Peter, he was not a coward. Apart from John (who was known by the high priest and allowed to enter the courtyard; cf. John 18:15), all the disciples except Peter fled into hiding. At this moment, however, he was anything but the "rock" (cf. 16:18) on which Christ would build his church. Yet godly sorrow brought him to repentance, and repentance to restored fellowship and usefulness.

Additional Notes §26

26:6ff. / In Luke a related account occurs earlier in Jesus' ministry (chap. 7), Simon is designated a Pharisee (v. 36; no mention of leprosy), and the woman (apparently of questionable repute) anoints the *feet* of Jesus (v. 38). Although Beare says that the story is "obviously misplaced in Mark and Matthew" (p. 505), the differences between the accounts are great enough to suggest separate occasions.

26:14 / **Iscariot:** Gk. *Iskariōtēs*, a surname of Judas, is often taken geographically as a reference to his place of origin; i.e., from Kerioth, a town in southern Israel (see the textual variants in John 6:71, esp. *apo Karyōtou*, "man of Kerioth"). Others take it as a transliteration of the Latin *sicarius* ("assassin") and link him with the Zealot movement. Hill (p. 335) lists two additional possibilities: a corruption of the Greek *Ierichōtēs* (which would make him an inhabitant of Jericho), and a transposition of the Aramaic *šaqqārā'* ("deceiver").

26:17 / If the Last Supper was not an actual Passover meal, it may have been a preparatory meal at which a lamb was not eaten. There is some evidence for a "Diaspora Passover," which was eaten on the evening of Nisan 14. For the possibility that Jesus was arrested on Tuesday evening, see the summary of Jaubert's thesis in Lane, pp. 498–99, n. 33. The problem of the chronology of the passion is surveyed at length in Jeremias, *The Eucharistic Words of Jesus.*

26:36 / **Gethsemane**: Modern Gethsemane (at the foot of the Mount of Olives) has several olive trees that are hundreds of years old but could hardly date from the time of Christ. The two traditional sites (side by side) are without doubt in the general vicinity of the original garden, but no exact location can be proven. Jerome connects *Gesamani* with the "fertile valley" of Isa. 28:1.

26:45 / **Sleeping and resting**: If *katheudete* and *anapauesthe* are taken as imperatives, it introduces into the text a note of irony ("Go ahead and sleep. Take your rest"). Knox, translating from the Vulgate, takes *iam* (Gk. *loipon*) in the sense of "hereafter"; thus, "Sleep and take your rest hereafter [later]." The NEB understands this sentence as a question but inserts a bit of subtle sarcasm: "Still sleeping? Still taking your ease?"

26:53 / **Angels**: In the Qumran War Scroll angels are represented as joining with the righteous in the battle for deliverance (1QM 7.6).

26:57 / Irregularities in the trial of Jesus include the fact that he was tried at night, during the Passover season, without a day's delay before the verdict, not in the Hall of Hewn Stone, and without examining the two witnesses separately. For further information, see Josef Blinzler, *The Trial of Jesus*; David R. Catchpole, *The Trial of Jesus*; A. N. Sherwin-White, *Roman Society and Roman Law in the New Testament*; and S. Zeitlin, *Who Crucified Jesus?*

26:63 / **Remained silent**: The silence of Jesus recalls such passages as Isa. 53:7 ("As a sheep before her shearers is silent, so he did not open his mouth") and Ps. 38:12–14. The imperfect *esiōpa* indicates that Jesus remained silent during the entire period of accusation.

That the terminology **Christ, the Son of God** belongs to the church rather than to Jewish leaders (so Stendahl, p. 796) does not prevent Caiaphas from phrasing his question in language appropriate to the messianic claims of Jesus.

26:64 / **It is as you say**: Catchpole says that "the phrase is affirmative in content, and reluctant in formulation" ("The Answer of Jesus to Caiaphas [Matthew 26:64]," *NTS*, vol. 17, pp. 213–26).

26:74 / **A rooster crowed**: The changing of the Roman guard in the Castle of Antonio at three a.m. was signaled by a trumpet call known in Latin as the *gallicinium* ("cockcrow"). Matthew's reference could have been to this accustomed signal or to the crowing of a rooster.

§27 The Trial and Death of Jesus (Matt. 27:1–66)

27:1-2 / At daybreak the chief priests and elders met in full council to plan the death of Jesus. The morning session also served to legalize the clandestine meeting that had taken place the previous night. Since their concerns about Jesus' religious claims would carry little weight with Roman authorities, it was necessary to develop a charge that would appear revolutionary from a political standpoint. Luke cites a threefold charge of seditious teaching, opposition to taxation, and claim of kingship (23:2). Having formulated their plans, they marched him off in chains to **Pilate, the governor.** Pilate was the fifth procurator of Judea (which also included Samaria and Idumea), serving the emperor in that capacity from A.D. 26 until 36. He was a cruel and corrupt official, who was not at all sensitive to Jewish mores (a flaw that put him in trouble with the Jewish populace from the very first).

27:3-10 / Matthew interrupts the narrative to report the end of **Judas, who had betrayed him.** The exact sequence of events is uncertain. Some have questioned how the chief priests and elders could be in the temple (vv. 3-5) and accusing Jesus before Pilate (v. 12) at the same time. It was not Matthew's purpose, however, to provide a strict chronological account of all the events that took place in the last few hours of Jesus' life.

When Judas learned that **Jesus was condemned,** he regretted what he had done. *Metamelomai* is a milder word than *metanoeō* ("to repent") and probably means in this context "to regret/change one's mind." Returning to the chief priests, he attempted to return the **thirty silver coins,** but they would have none of it. That he had **betrayed innocent blood** (v. 4) was of no concern to them. Judas hurled (*rhiptō* is a strong verb) **the money into the temple** (*naos* need not refer exclusively to the inner sanctuary, Josephus, *War,* 6.293; cf. BAGD, p. 533, 1.a), and **went away**

and hanged himself. Schweizer suggests that throwing money into the temple may have been a Jewish custom for canceling an agreement (p. 505).

Acts 1:18 records that Judas died by falling headlong so that his body burst and his intestines spilled out. In a desire to harmonize the two passages, some have suggested that the fall and subsequent disembowelment could have happened quite naturally if the hanging had taken place over the edge of a cliff and the hastily secured knot had eventually slipped. The apparent differences between the two accounts were of no great concern to the writers of the Gospels. The suggestion that Matthew may have been influenced by the account of the death of Ahithophel (so Green, p. 219), who hanged himself when his advice was not taken (2 Sam. 17:23), is no more than conjecture.

Gathering up the coins, the chief priests agreed that they could not be placed in the temple treasury, because they were **blood money**. So **they decided to use the money to buy the potter's field as a burial place for foreigners**. This explains why the place has been called "Blood Acre" ever since. Matthew understands this as a fulfillment of a prophecy by **Jeremiah**, although it is primarily taken from Zechariah 11:12–13. Assigning a composite quotation to the more prominent individual appears to have been a regular practice (cf. Mark 1:2 where a quotation from Malachi and Isaiah is said to come from "Isaiah the prophet"). In Jeremiah 18:2–3 the prophet is told to go down to the potter's house, and in 32:8 he is told to buy a field at Anathoth. In Zechariah 11 the prophet is paid thirty pieces of silver, which he throws into the house of the Lord to the potter. Following a method of exegesis that falls strangely on the ears of a modern interpreter, this collection of ideas is understood to have been fulfilled by events leading up to the purchase of a burial place for foreigners with blood money supplied by Judas' suicide. Stendahl holds that Matthew's use of the quotation from Zechariah hinges upon two Hebrew words that can mean both "potter" and "treasurer/treasury" (p. 796).

27:11–14 / Standing **before the governor** (in the New Testament *hēgemōn* is used of Roman legates, procurators, and proconsuls) Jesus is asked if he is the **king of the Jews**. The title reflects a gentile perspective: Jews would refer to themselves as Israel. As in 26:25 and 64, Jesus answers *sy legeis* (lit., "You said

[it]"). The ambiguity of the answer has been interpreted to mean that Jesus is in fact the king but not in any sense that Pilate would understand (Beare, p. 527). Jesus does not, however, answer the accusations made by the chief priests and elders (cf. Isa. 53:7). Pilate is disturbed by Jesus' refusal to defend himself. He would like to have dismissed him with the verdict "not guilty," but silence on the part of the accused could be taken as an acknowledgment of guilt. When Jesus will not answer a single one of their accusations, Pilate is left completely at a loss.

27:15–19 / Pilate's predicament was that, although his sense of justice called for him to release Jesus, the political pressure of the Jewish populace was frustrating his desire to resolve the issue fairly. One possible escape from the dilemma presented itself in the custom of releasing a prisoner chosen by the crowd. Being held in custody was a **notorious prisoner** (*episēmos* [bearing a mark, *sēma*] here in the bad sense of **notorious** rather than the good sense of "notable"), by the name **Barabbas**.

The GNB follows the less well attested (but probably to be preferred) reading in verses 15 and 16 that includes the name "Jesus" to supplement the patronymic "Barabbas." (The UBS text puts *Iēsoun* in square brackets indicating that it is disputed. The NIV decided to omit it.) **Barabbas** in Aramaic would mean "son of Abba," that is, "son of the father" or perhaps "son of the teacher" (*bar-rabban*). The balance of phrase in verse 17 (**Barabbas, or Jesus who is called Christ**) strongly favors inclusion. "Jesus" as the given name of Barabbas may have been dropped by an early copyist out of regard for Jesus Christ. Outside of the Gospels there is no strong evidence of releasing a prisoner during a religious festival. Josephus (*Ant.* 20.208–210), however, mentions the custom (see also m. *Pesahim*, 8.6).

Pilate, faced by the crowd, asks which "Jesus" they wished to have released. He was certain they had turned over Jesus (the Messiah) **out of envy** (v. 18), and he probably felt that their antagonism to him was not sufficiently intense to lead them to favor an insurrectionist and murderer (cf. Mark 15:7).

Matthew now includes a note to the effect that while Pilate was "still on the Bench" (v. 19, TCNT) his wife sent a message warning against any involvement with **that innocent man**. She had been deeply troubled during the night in a dream about Jesus. Tradition has given her the name Claudia Procula (or Procla), and in the Eastern church she is regarded as a saint. There is no evidence that she was a convert to Christianity, nor is there any substantial reason to accept the testimony of the apocryphal *Acts of Pilate*, which reports that just before Pilate was beheaded a voice from heaven said, "All the generations and the families of the Gentiles shall call thee blessed."

27:20–26 / Apparently this interlude provided sufficient time for the chief priests and the elders to persuade the crowd to ask for the release of Barabbas and the death of Jesus. When asked by Pilate what should be done with Jesus, the mob shouted back **Crucify him!** (v. 22). Deuteronomy 21:23 taught that "anyone who is hung on a tree is under God's curse," and Judaism had transferred the saying to those who were crucified (*TDNT*, vol. 7, p. 574). The demand for crucifixion stemmed from the desire on the part of the religious leaders of Judaism to demonstrate that Jesus' entire life and message were under the curse of God. When asked to name his crime, "their voices rose to a roar" (v. 23, Phillips), **Crucify him!** (the imperfect tense in *perissōs ekrazon* indicates that they kept crying out more loudly than ever).

When Pilate saw that he was getting nowhere but rather that a riot was under way, **he took water and washed his hands** in full view of the mob, declaring himself **innocent** of the death of Jesus. The responsibility was theirs. The practice of washing the hands as a symbol of purging oneself from guilt is based on Deuteronomy 21:6–9 (cf. Ps. 73:13). Since it was not a Roman custom and would appear to be beneath the dignity of an official such as Pilate, some have rejected this incident as an attempt on the part of the early church to minimize Roman involvement in the crucifixion. Tasker counters, "But exceptional men under exceptional circumstances act in exceptional ways" (p. 262).

The chilling response of the frenzied crowd was, **Let his blood be on us and on our children!** (v. 25). Beare says that "no such cry was ever uttered" and muses how appalling it is for a Christian to contemplate the suffering that has been inflicted upon the Jews throughout the ages, partly as a result of this "completely fictitious scene" (p. 531). Green adds that since Christians have used this passage to fix the guilt for the crucifixion of Christ on the Jewish people, "[Matthew] has much to answer for" (p. 221). Although no morally sensitive person would for a moment exonerate those who are guilty of racial abuse, the answer is not to rewrite Scripture. In the delirium of the moment, a mob determined to crucify one who apparently violated what they held to be sacred would not hesitate to accept full responsibility for what they were about to do.

Pilate then released Barabbas, and after he had Jesus scourged he **handed him over to be crucified**. The purpose of scourging was to weaken the prisoner prior to crucifixion. The victim was stripped and tied over a post, where he was lashed with a long leather whip in which bits of sharpened bone and pellets of lead had been secured. Beatings of this nature were extremely cruel, and sometimes the victim would die before ever reaching the actual crucifixion.

27:27–31 / After the scourging, Pilate's soldiers took Jesus into the Praetorium (the governor's residence while in Jerusalem as well as barracks for his official guard) where, before the entire detachment, **they stripped him and put a scarlet robe on him**. Manuscripts reading *endysantes* ("clothed," note similarity to *ekdysantes*, "stripped") assume he was taken naked from the scourging. The chlamys was a short mantle that fastened at the left shoulder. The **scarlet robe** would be the red (signifying war) cape worn by the Roman soldiers of that day. It is not important that Mark calls it a "purple robe" (Mark 15:17), the colors are not very different. The **crown** (Gk. *stephanos*) that they placed on his head was a wreath **of thorns**. It has been suggested that the long thorns may have been turned outward in a mocking imitation of the radiate crowns pictured on the coins of Tiberius Caesar (H. St. J. Hart, *JTS*, vol. 3, pp. 66–75) rather than inward so as to inflict pain. The major purpose of the soldiers was to mock Jesus: they had already beaten him cruelly. They put a staff **in his right hand** (in imitation of a royal scepter), **knelt** before him in jest, and exclaimed, **Hail, king of the Jews!** They spit on him, and taking the staff, hit him repeatedly (*etypton* is imperfect) on the head. When they had finished making sport of him, they dressed him again in his own clothes and led him away to be crucified.

27:32–34 / After the prisoner had been condemned and scourged, it was common practice to make him carry the cross beam (*patibulum*) to the place of execution. The upright post remained in place like a mediaeval gallows. As the procession

moved through the city (taking the longest route in order to serve
as a warning to as many as possible), the prisoner carried around
his neck a placard indicating his crime. When the cross beam with
its victim had been hoisted in place and joined to the upright,
the *titulus* was nailed over his head.

On the way to **Golgotha** (so called either because it re-
sembled a skull [the word means **the Place of the Skull**] or because it was a place of execution) Jesus, weakened by the ordeal,
apparently was unable to carry the cross beam without help. The
soldiers compelled (*angareuō* is a Persian loanword that means "to
force into service") **a man from Cyrene** (in North Africa), **named
Simon** to carry the cross for Jesus. Mark mentions that he was
"the father of Alexander and Rufus" (Mark 15:21), whom tradition holds to have become believers (cf. Acts 19:33 and Rom.
16:13). Arriving at the place of execution, they offered Jesus **wine
. . . mixed with gall** (v. 34), **but after tasting it, he refused to
drink**. According to the Talmud (b. *Sanh*. 43a), a person about
to be punished could have wine laced with a bit of narcotic to
dull the pain. Mark 15:23 says that the wine was mingled with
"myrrh," a delicacy that would make the wine more palatable
and also dull the pain (cf. Prov. 31:6-7). If those who gave Jesus
the wine were soldiers, then the myrrhed wine (supplied by the
women?) was made bitter (another cruel joke?) by the "gall" (v.
34, RSV) added by the executioners.

27:35-44 / Many have commented on Matthew's
"remarkable restraint" in speaking of the crucifixion. In the Greek
text the clause translated **they . . . crucified him** is simply an aorist
participle (and personal pronoun) attached to the main sentence,
which deals with the division of Jesus' clothing. Crucifixion was
a cruel and degrading form of punishment. The Romans apparently borrowed it from the Phoenicians and Carthaginians to use
only for slaves, foreigners, or criminals of the lowest class. Barclay quotes Cicero (the first-century B.C. Roman statesman and
orator) as calling it "the most cruel and the most horrible torture"
(vol. 2, p. 364).

Jesus had spoken of his coming crucifixion (cf. 20:19; 26:2).
Matthew interprets the events in the light of Psalms 22 and 69.
The wine mingled with gall reflects Psalm 69:21 ("they put gall
in my food and gave me vinegar for my thirst"), and the dividing
of his clothing by the soldiers fulfills Psalm 22:18 ("they divide

my garments among them and cast lots for my clothing"). It was common practice for the clothing of the prisoner to go to the executioners. As Jesus hung on the cross, the soldiers sat there maintaining a guard (the participle *kathēmenoi* is present, and the verb *etēroun* is imperfect) lest someone remove him before he actually died. The *titulus* that he carried along the *Via Dolorosa* (the sorrowful way) was nailed above his head with its proclamation, THIS IS JESUS, THE KING OF THE JEWS (v. 37).

On either side of Jesus were two thieves, whose names, according to popular tradition, were Zoatham and Camma. Three groups of antagonists gathered around the cross. Tasker (p. 265) calls them the "ignorant sinners" (the passersby who nodded their heads in derision, vv. 39–40), the "religious sinners" (members of the Sanhedrin who kept taunting him, partly in order to quell any possible rise of sentiment in his favor that might lead to a change of verdict, vv. 41–43), and the "condemned sinners" (the thieves who insulted him in the same way, v. 44). The derisive challenge of the crowd (**save yourself . . . if you are the son of God!** v. 40) recalls the temptations by Satan in Matthew 4:3, 6. The "mocking" of the chief priests and elders (v. 41) suggests that their actions were like those of silly children (*empaizontes* is from *en* and *paizō*, "to play as a child").

The insults of those who passed by recalls Psalm 22:7 ("All who see me mock me; they hurl insults, shaking their heads"), and the taunts of the religious leaders come from Psalm 22:8 ("He trusts in the Lord; let the Lord rescue him"). Rejected and despised, Jesus hangs alone on the cross, the object of scorn and ridicule. It is true that he was unable to come down from the cross and save himself, for then he would have been unable to save others. It was the power of love, not nails, that kept him there.

27:45–53 / Mark (15:25, 34–37) indicates that Jesus was placed on the cross about the third hour (nine a.m.) and died shortly after the ninth hour (three p.m.). His period of physical suffering was shorter than most: some hung for days before death claimed them. **From the sixth hour until the ninth hour** a supernatural **darkness** covered the entire land. It could not have been an eclipse of the sun, because Passover took place during the full moon. The prophet Amos spoke of a day in which God would "make the sun go down at noon and darken the earth in broad daylight" (Amos 8:9). The suggestion that Matthew is using apocalyptic and eschatological language that requires no historical base is persuasive only to those who wish to reinterpret the events of Jesus' death and resurrection in figurative terms.

About the ninth hour, Jesus cried out in a loud voice, *Eloi, Eloi, lama sabachthani?* (some mss. read the Hebrew *Eli, Eli* instead of the Aramaic *Eloi*; cf. Mark and the allusion to Ps. 22:1). It means, **My God, my God, why have you forsaken me?** Beare's opinion that it would be physically impossible for Jesus to cry out in a loud voice after six hours on the cross (p. 535) stems from an unwillingness to allow for anything out of the ordinary. Theologians have pondered the significance of this unusual utterance. What does it mean for God (the Father) to forsake God (the Son), when they are one in essence? Perhaps an answer is not forthcoming because the question is stated incorrectly. Could it not be that in the loneliness of that awful hour Jesus' thoughts turned naturally to the psalms, and that in the lament of David, as expressed in Psalm 22:1, Jesus found words that expressed his profound sense of alienation from having taken upon himself the sins of the world? It has been suggested that Jesus was reflecting upon Psalm 22 in its entirety and that, although the psalm begins in dejection, it ends in soaring triumph. Barclay writes that although the idea of Jesus reciting the entire Psalm to himself is attractive, "On a cross a man does not repeat poetry to himself" (vol. 2, p. 368; cf. Filson, p. 297).

Hearing Jesus' cry, some of those standing near understood him to be **calling Elijah** (*Eli* [UBS] was heard as *Elias*). One ran and got a sponge soaked in wine vinegar and hoisted it on a stick for Jesus to drink (v. 48). Others said, "Wait, let's see if Elijah will come to his rescue." The wine offered to Jesus was posca, an inexpensive sour wine popular among the soldiers and those of the lower ranks of society (*oxos*, BAGD, p. 574). Although some would have denied to Jesus this "one reported expression of human kindness in the last hours of [his] life" (Filson, p. 297), John 19:30 indicates that Jesus did at least taste the wine. Those who understood Jesus to be calling for Elijah were obviously aware of the Jewish belief that Elijah (who did not die but was taken to heaven alive; 2 Kings 2:11) would come to help the righteous in times of great distress (Str.-B., vol. 2, pp. 769-71).

The death of Jesus is reported with stark simplicity: **when Jesus had cried out again . . . he gave up** (or released, Gk. *aphēken*) **his spirit**. John 19:30 tells us that the triumphant cry was "It is finished" (a single word in Greek, *tetelestai*). Jesus did not die as a victim overcome against his will, but, as Augustine said, "He gave up his life because he willed it, when he willed, and as he willed it" (cited by Robertson, *WPNT*, vol. 1, p. 235). At that very moment **the curtain** that separated the Holy of Holies from the Holy Place was **torn in two from top to bottom**, signifying that by the death of Jesus access into the presence of God had been provided (cf. Heb. 10:19).

At the same time there was a shaking of the earth, **the rocks split**, and tombs were opened (vv. 51–52). Out of the graves came holy ones of old who, after the resurrection of Jesus, appeared openly in Jerusalem. The resurrection of the righteous was one of the great events that was to accompany the End. It was thought that the Mount of Olives would split apart and holy ones of the old covenant would rise to share in the reign of the Messiah. That they did not appear in the Holy City until after the resurrection of Jesus is usually explained as appropriate in view of Jesus' being the "firstborn from among the dead" (Col. 1:18; Rev. 1:5). The events reflect Old Testament imagery (e.g., earthquakes, Isa. 29:6; opening of tombs, Ezek. 37:12–13; rising of the dead, Dan. 12:2).

27:54–56 / When the Roman centurion (a leader of one hundred men) and the soldiers with him saw all that was happening, they were filled with awe and said, **Surely he was the Son of God!** Although the Greek has no article before "Son" (*theou hyios*), Matthew (and Mark, as well, 15:39) wants his readers to understand the confession in the same sense as intended in 4:3, 6, where "Son" also lacks the definite article. Gundry correctly notes that the "absence of the definite article before 'Son' allows but does not demand an indefinite meaning" (p. 578). Some are of the opinion that the centurion intended "a son of God" (in the secular sense of an unusually gifted individual) and that Matthew took the designation in the Christian sense of "the Son of God." In either case, the Roman guards were the first to acknowledge that Jesus was no mere man paying with his life for his religious convictions.

Many of the **women** who had **followed Jesus from Galilee** and had helped **care for his needs** were **watching from a distance** all that was happening. Among them were **Mary Magdalene** (who had been cured of evil spirits, Luke 8:2), **Mary the mother of James and Joses** (John 19:25 calls her "the wife of Clopas"), **and the mother of Zebedee's sons** (apparently "Salome" of Mark 15:40). The presence of these women at the crucifixion (especially in view of the absence of the disciple band) witnesses to the depth of their devotion and their willingness to be identified with a crucified Messiah.

27:57–61 / **As evening approached** (it was still Friday: the Sabbath began at sundown) **a rich man from Arimathea, named Joseph**, went personally to Pilate to ask for the body of Jesus. Arimathea has been identified with the modern village of Rentis some twenty miles northwest of Jerusalem. According to the apocryphal *Gospel of Nicodemus*, Joseph of Arimathea founded the church at Lydda (nine miles southwest of his home town). He himself had been a disciple of Jesus. Granted his request, **Joseph took the body** and wrapped it in a clean linen shroud. He then **placed it in his own new tomb**, which had recently been hewed out of solid rock. Rolling **a big stone in front of the entrance**, he left, but **Mary Magdalene and the other Mary** remained in front of the grave.

Roman law allowed the relatives of a criminal to claim his body for burial. Otherwise it would be left on the cross for wild dogs and vultures. Beare holds the account of Jesus' burial to be "legendary" and surmises that, like those of other criminals, his body was put in a trench and covered over by the soldiers (p. 538). No such reworking of the text is necessary. Isaiah, speaking of the Suffering Servant, says that "he was assigned a grave . . . with the rich in his death" (Isa. 53:9). Jewish custom required that the body of a man hung on a tree not remain there overnight but be buried on the same day (Deut. 21:22–23).

27:62–66 / On the following day (it was a Sabbath, although the Greek avoids mentioning the holy day and calls it **the one** *meta tēn paraskeuēn*, **after Preparation Day**), the chief priests and the Pharisees went as a group to Pilate to ask that a guard be set up at the tomb. They remembered that while he was still alive Jesus had claimed that after three days he would come back to life. Therefore it was necessary to set a guard in order to prevent the disciples from stealing the body and claiming that he had been raised from the dead. **This last deception** (a false rumor that he had risen) would be even **worse than the first** (his false claim that he was the Messiah and the Son of God).

Some have wondered why the disciples forgot the promise of resurrection while the Jewish leaders remembered it. Beare takes the entire paragraph as "one of the most extravagant of inventions," which can "only be regarded as a Christian fabrication devised to counter the current Jewish assertion that Jesus was not raised from the dead" (p. 539). However, for the disciples it was a time of overwhelming grief and despair in which the promise of resurrection seemed too unreal to grasp. For the religious leaders of Israel there was the haunting possibility that Jesus was in fact the Messiah and, if so, the totally unexpected could well take place.

Pilate answers, **Take a guard**, go and make the tomb "as safe as you think necessary" (Phillips). The Greek *echete* is probably imperative ("you have" in the sense of "take a guard/you can have a guard") rather than indicative ("you have a guard of your own [the temple guard], you'll need no help from me"). So the chief priests and Pharisees secured the tomb by sealing the stone and placing a guard on watch. The stone would be sealed by means of a cord stretched from side to side and sealed at each end (cf. Dan. 6:17).

Additional Notes   §27

27:2 / **Pilate**: For information on Pilate, see Harold Hoehner, *Herod Antipas*, pp. 172–83. Ancient texts include Philo, *Legatio ad Gaium* 38; Josephus, *Ant.* 18.2.2; 18.3.1f.; 18.6.5; *War* 2.169–177; Tacitus, *Ann.* 15.44.

27:8 / **Field of Blood**: Acts 1:19 says the field was called "Field of Blood" because of the way Judas met his death (by bursting open from a fall). There is no reason that a well-known plot could not have several ways of accounting for its name. It is also correct to say that "Judas bought a field" (Acts 1:18) since, although negotiated by the chief priests (Matt. 27:7), it was purchased with money provided by Judas. Some have suggested that the Acts reference to "Akeldama" should be "Akeldamak" ("field of sleep," hence, "cemetery").

27:16 / "Jesus": See Metzger, *TCGNT*, pp. 67–68, for the UBS' committee's decision to include *Iēsoun* ("Jesus") in square brackets.

27:32 / **Simon**: Acts 6:9 reports that there was a Synagogue of the Freedmen in Jerusalem that included Jews from Cyrene. Simon may have been a member.

27:33 / **Golgotha**: The traditional site of Golgotha is in the present Church of the Holy Sepulchre. Gordon's Calvary is a favorite alternative for many tourists. For a complete treatment of the subject, see A. Parrot, *Golgotha and the Church of the Holy Sepulchre*.

27:35 / The three types of crosses were the Saint Anthony cross (shaped like a capital T), the Saint Andrew's cross (like the letter X), and the *crux immissa* (the traditional two beams). Since the *titulus* was placed above the head of Jesus (cf. v. 37), it was the latter form of the cross that was used for Jesus. Recent excavations (in 1968 a team of archaeologists under V. Tzaferis discovered four tombs near Jerusalem) suggest that victims were nailed to the cross beam through the arms (rather than the hands), with the weight of the body borne by a plank nailed to the upright and the feet twisted back so that both heels could be fastened with a single nail. Death normally came from hunger and exhaustion.

27:51 / Josephus records a number of remarkable events that were said to have taken place before the destruction of the Jewish temple (*War* 6.288–309). One was the automatic opening of one of the doors in the sanctuary.

27:57 / **Joseph**: Several legends have gathered around the name of Joseph of Arimathea. The most widely known connects him with the town of Glastonbury in England and relates how Joseph came to England preaching the gospel and bearing the chalice that had been used in the Last Supper.

27:64 / **Until the third day**: This must be taken in the inclusive sense of "up to and including the third day," otherwise the posting of a guard would not help, since Jesus was to rise "after three days" (v. 63).

§28 The Resurrection (Matt. 28:1-20)

The resurrection stands as the cornerstone of the Christian faith. The crucial importance of this historic event is clearly set forth by Paul in the fifteenth chapter of First Corinthians. If there is no resurrection, then Christ has not been raised (v. 13), faith is useless (v. 14), the apostolic witness is false (v. 15), believers are still in their sins (v. 17) and are to be pitied (v. 19). The account of the events surrounding the resurrection is given in each of the four Gospels. John tells of Mary Magdalene finding the tomb empty and running to tell Peter and John. Jesus then appears to Mary and later that evening to the eleven disciples who had gathered behind locked doors.

The synoptic accounts run parallel, but several differences are found. It is hardly correct, however, as Beare contends, that Matthew has "radically revised the Markan story" (p. 541). The major differences are, first, that Mark (16:1) has Salome go with the two Marys to the tomb; second, that Matthew (28:1) says they "went to see the tomb," whereas Mark (16:1) says they "bought spices . . . to anoint him"; third, that Matthew (28:5) has an "angel" speak to the women whereas Mark (16:5) says it was a "young man" (Luke 24:4 has "two men"); and fourth, that Matthew (28:8) says the women departed, "afraid yet filled with joy" and "ran to tell his disciples," whereas Mark (16:8) says that "trembling and bewildered," they "said nothing to anyone." All such variations are of little significance in parallel accounts of an event as unprecedented in human history as the resurrection. Had they been carefully harmonized in every detail by the synoptic writers, we would have serious reason to doubt their veracity. Upon examination they appear to be rather easily understood and present no grave problem for the interpreter open to the possibility that the bodily resurrection of Jesus was a historical occurrence.

It is instructive to note that in the biblical account there is no actual description of the resurrection. The major point is the empty tomb. By way of comparison, the narrative as recorded in the second-century noncanonical *Gospel of Peter* tells of three men who emerge from the tomb with a cross following them. Two of the men (whose heads "reached unto heaven") were sustaining the third (whose head "overpassed the heavens"). A voice from heaven asked if he had preached to those that sleep and is answered in the affirmative by the cross (10:39–42).

28:1–10 / **At dawn on the first day of the week, Mary Magdalene** and **Mary** the mother of James (cf. Mark 16:1) went to the tomb where Jesus had been buried. The Greek text has been interpreted to mean either late on the Sabbath when the first day of the week was about to begin (hence, Saturday evening) or late in the night after the Sabbath when the new day was about to dawn (hence, Sunday morning). Probably Knox is right in his translation, "On the night after the Sabbath, at the hour when dawn broke on the first day of the week."

Matthew records a violent shaking of the earth, followed by the descent of an angel from heaven, who rolled away the stone and sat on it. There is no definite indication as to when these specific events happened, although the imperfect *ekathēto* ("was sitting") suggests that it was before the women arrived. The earthquake and heavenly descent recall passages such as Exodus 19:18 and 1 Kings 19:11–12. In verses 1–10 the demonstrative particle *idou* ("behold/lo") is used four times (vv. 2, 7 [twice], 9), marking the striking nature of the events. Matthew says that the **appearance** (perhaps "face") of the angel was **like lightning** and that his clothes were **white as snow** (cf. Dan. 7:9 and 10:5–6; also Rev. 1:14). When the guards saw the heavenly visitor, they trembled with fear and "collapsed like dead men" (Phillips).

The angel encouraged the women not to be afraid (v. 5). They were looking for the crucified Jesus, but the angel knew that Jesus had been raised from the dead. The angel invited the women to come and see for themselves **the place where he lay**. The women are then told by the angel to **go quickly and tell his disciples** that Jesus had been raised and was going to Galilee ahead of them and would see them there. Leaving the tomb at once, frightened, **yet filled with joy**, they ran to break the news to the disciples.

Since both Luke and John record the appearance of the risen Christ in Jerusalem (Luke 24:36–49; John 20:19–29), some have questioned Matthew's Galilean account. It should be noted that the entire twenty-first chapter of John takes place in Galilee as well. The angel did not say that he would not see any of them in Jerusalem, only that he was making a definite appointment to meet them in Galilee. To "go before" (*proagō*), v. 7) may mean "to go ahead (and wait)" or "to go to the head of" like a Palestinian shepherd. Green holds that the second meaning is also present in the charge (p. 228). There is no discrepancy between "afraid yet filled with joy" in Matthew (2:8) and "trembling and bewildered" in Mark (16:8). The mingled emotions of awe and ecstasy would be expected. That the women **ran to tell** the **disciples** (Matt 28:8) but "said nothing to anyone" (Mark 16:8) may indicate no more than that they did not share the remarkable news with anyone but the disciples.

As the women were on their way to tell the disciples, Jesus appeared in their path and greeted them (the AV "all hail" is a bit stilted, whereas Williams' "good morning" is too contemporary). The women fell before him according to custom and grasped his feet as a sign of submission. Jesus encouraged them not to fear but to go and tell his **brothers** (even as the risen Christ he retains the family relationship) to set out for Galilee for the appointed meeting.

28:11-15 / While the women were still on their way to tell the disciples what had happened, some of the guards went into the city to report to the chief priests. Since Pilate had placed the Roman guards at the disposal of the Jewish leaders (Matt. 27:62-66), it would not be unusual for them to report to the chief priests rather than to Pilate. In the *Gospel of Peter*, however, the guards go to Pilate and beg him to order that no one say anything about what had happened (9:45-49). Matthew reports that after meeting with the elders the chief priests agreed to give **the soldiers a large sum of money**, with the instructions that they were to say that during the night while they were asleep the disciples came and stole the body of Jesus (vv. 12-13). Schweizer questions the incident, noting that "to ask them to say they had fallen asleep while on watch and allowed what they were guarding to be stolen is asking them to sign their own death warrant" (p. 526). True, but what was the alternative? The Jewish leaders who had successfully engineered the crucifixion of Jesus promised that if news of the incident reached the governor they would intervene and persuade him (against taking any action). They would **keep** the soldiers **out of trouble** (v. 14). Matthew adds that the guards did as they were told and that this story has been making the rounds in Jewish circles ever since.

Beare holds that verses 11-14 are "completely incredible as a whole" (p. 543). Stendahl would argue that it is "reasonable to suggest that the resurrection tradition in the Gospels has its nucleus in an experience of an empty tomb," although around this basic tradition Matthew has added legendary and apologetic material (p. 798). All such decisions reflect an attitude toward the reliability of the text that arises more from basic presuppositions than from critical study itself. Otherwise, scholars would not read the same material and come up with widely differing conclusions. The position held throughout this commentary is that the text of Matthew is reliable and supplies us with a trustworthy record of what Jesus said and did during his time on earth.

28:16-20 / The **eleven disciples** (cf. death of Judas at 27:5) went to Galilee to the mountain where Jesus had arranged to meet them. When they saw him there, they **worshiped him** (*proskyneō* taken literally means "to prostrate oneself [in homage]"), although **some doubted**. Since the following verse says that **Jesus came to them**, we should understand verse 17 as taking place when the eleven first saw Jesus at some distance. From that vantage point, "some were in doubt" (Goodspeed) or were "somewhat skeptical" (Norlie) that Jesus was really there. Throughout the resurrection accounts there are a number of instances of uncertainty (the encounter on the road to Emmaus, Luke 24:13-35; Mary outside the tomb, John 20:11-18; the disciples fishing in the Sea of Tiberias, John 21:1-8). It has been suggested that those who doubted were not the eleven but some of the "more than five hundred brethren" mentioned in 1 Corinthians 15:6. That Jesus had arranged to meet them there would account for the large group.

Jesus stepped forward and delivered to his disciples what has become known as the Great Commission. It begins with the powerful proclamation that God had given to him (**has been given to me** is a reverential circumlocution) **all authority in heaven and on earth**. In Daniel's vision of the Four Beasts, "one like a son of man" receives from the Ancient of Days "authority, glory, and sovereign power" (Dan. 7:13-14; cf. Phil. 2:6-11). *Exousia* (**authority**) in this context refers to absolute power and jurisdiction. There is nothing outside the sovereign control of the risen Christ. It is on that basis that the disciples are to **go and make disciples of all nations**. The Greek verb *mathēteuō* means "to make a learner" (coming, as it does, from *manthanō*, "to learn"). A disciple is not simply one who has been taught but one who continues to learn.

The full scope of making **disciples** involves **baptizing them** (v. 19b) and **teaching them** (v. 20a). Both *baptizontes* and *didaskontes* are participles governed by the imperative *mathēteusate*. The gist of the sentence is "make disciples by baptizing and teaching." Much has been written about the trinitarian formula **in the name of the Father and of the Son and of the Holy Spirit** (v. 19). This is the only occurrence of the formula from the first century, with the possible exception of *Didache* 7.1 (a church manual normally dated second century A.D.). Elsewhere baptism is said to be "in the name of Jesus Christ" (Acts 2:38; 10:48) or "in the name of the Lord Jesus" (Acts 8:16; 19:5). Mention of Father, Son, and Spirit occurs in 1 Corinthians 12:4-6 and 2 Corinthians 13:14, but not as a specific formula. Questions regarding the divine essence and the relationships between the members of the Godhead belong to the later theological development of the church. That Jesus should gather together into summary form his own references to "the Father" (11:27; 24:36), to himself as "the Son" (11:27; 16:27), and to "the Spirit" (12:28) in his final charge to the disciples seems quite natural. Though we are not dealing with an advanced trinitarian formulation, we certainly have more than the concept of God as going beyond the intellectual to include "the instant experience of love" and "also the assurance of future love" (Schweizer, p. 534).

Making disciples includes teaching as well. Note that the teaching is here set forth as ethical rather than doctrinal. The disciples are to teach the new converts **to obey** all that Jesus has commanded them. But discipleship is not a lonely road, because the risen Lord promises that he will be with them **always, to the very end of the age**. The present age will end when Christ returns in glory and the eternal state begins. Until that final moment in human history, Jesus, who in Matthew 1:23 was given the name "Emmanuel," will be to them exactly what the name indicates, "God with us."

Additional Notes §28

28:1 / **After**: *opse* with the genitive of separation may mean "late from" in the sense of "some time later." *Epiphōskō* may mean "to draw near" (as in Luke 23:54), but here it has the normal meaning "to dawn/shine forth." See Gundry (p. 585) for the view that the women come on Saturday evening. Robertson allows for two visits and, to avoid any discrepancy, asks, "Why allow only one visit for the anxious women?" (*WPNT*, vol. 1, p. 240).

28:11–15 / Schweizer sees in this section a counterattack by the Christian community that reveals a considerable amount of arrogance. He writes, "Perhaps this shows that a faith that is too unshakable, unfamiliar with any sense of doubt, is in particular danger of giving false explanations, thus losing those who are closest to having faith" (p. 527).

28:16 / Some have taken *etaxato* ("appointed") to refer to Jesus' appointment of his disciples in chap. 10.

For Further Reading

Commentaries on Matthew

Albright, W. F., and C. S. Mann. *Matthew*. Anchor Bible. Vol. 26. New York: Doubleday, 1971.

Allen, W. C. *A Critical and Exegetical Commentary on the Gospel According to St. Matthew*. International Critical Commentary. 3rd ed. Edinburgh: T. & T. Clark, 1912.

Barclay, W. *The Gospel of Matthew*. Rev. ed. 2 vols. Philadelphia: Westminster, 1975.

Beare, F. W. *The Gospel According to Matthew*. San Francisco: Harper & Row, 1981.

Bruce, A. B. "The Gospel According to Matthew." In *The Expositor's Greek Testament*. Vol. 1, pp. 61–340. Grand Rapids: Eerdmans, 1951.

Bruner, F. D. *The Christ Book*. Waco: Word Books, 1987.

Bultmann, R. *History of the Synoptic Tradition*, rev. ed. New York: Harper & Row, 1976.

Daube, D. *The New Testament and Rabbinic Judaism*. New York: Arno Press, 1973.

Fenton, J. C. *The Gospel of St. Matthew*. Pelican New Testament Commentaries. New York: Penguin Books, 1963.

Filson, F. V. *A Commentary on the Gospel According to St. Matthew*. Harper's New Testament Commentaries. New York: Harper & Brothers, 1960.

Green, H. B. *The Gospel According to Matthew*. New Clarendon Bible. New York: Oxford, 1975.

Gundry, R. H. *Matthew. A Commentary on His Literary and Theological Art*. Grand Rapids: Eerdmans, 1982.

Hill, D. *The Gospel of Matthew*. New Century Bible. London: Marshall, Morgan & Scott, 1972.

Johnson, S. E. *The Gospel According to St. Matthew*. Interpreters' Bible. Vol. 7. Nashville: Abingdon, 1951.

McNeile, A. H. *The Gospel According to St. Matthew*. London: Macmillan, 1915.

Minear, P. S. *Matthew: The Teacher's Gospel*. New York: Pilgrim Press, 1982.

Plummer, A. *An Exegetical Commentary on the Gospel According to S. Matthew.* 5th ed. London: E. Stock, 1920.

Schweizer, E. *The Good News According to Matthew.* Translated by D. E. Green. Atlanta: John Knox Press, 1975.

Senior, D. *Invitation to Matthew.* New York: Doubleday, 1977.

Smith, R. H. *Matthew.* Augsburg Commentary on the New Testament. Minneapolis: Augsburg, 1989.

Stendahl, K. "Matthew." In *Peake's Commentary on the Bible.* Edited by M. Black and H. H. Rowley. New York: Nelson, 1962. (Pages 769–98).

Tasker, R. V. G. *The Gospel According to St. Matthew.* Tyndale Bible Commentaries. Vol. 1. Grand Rapids: Eerdmans, 1961.

Other Works Cited

Abrahams, I. *Studies in Pharisaism and the Gospels.* New York: Ktav Pub. House, 1917–24.

Barclay, W. *A New Testament Wordbook.* London: SCM Press, 1955.

Barker, G. W., W. L. Lane, and J. R. Michaels. *The New Testament Speaks.* New York: Harper & Row, 1969.

Beasley-Murray, G. R. *Baptism in the New Testament.* Grand Rapids: Eerdmans, 1973.

_____. *A Commentary on Mark Thirteen.* New York: Macmillan, 1957.

Blinzler, J. *The Trial of Jesus.* Westminster, Md.: Newman Press, 1959.

Bishop, E. F. *Jesus of Palestine.* London: Lutterworth Press, 1955.

Busch, F. O. *The Five Herods.* London: R. Hale, 1958.

Carrington, P. *The Primitive Christian Calendar.* Cambridge: Cambridge University Press, 1952.

Catchpole, D. R. *The Trial of Jesus.* Leiden: E. J. Brill, 1971.

Cullmann, O. *Baptism in the New Testament.* Chicago: W. Regnery, 1950.

_____. *Peter: Disciple, Apostle, Martyr.* Philadelphia: Westminster, 1953.

Davies, W. D. *The Setting of the Sermon on the Mount.* Cambridge: Cambridge University Press, 1964.

Dodd, C. H. *According to the Scriptures.* New York: Scribner, 1952.

_____. *The Parables of the Kingdom.* Rev. ed. New York: Scribner, 1961.

Flemington, W. F. *The New Testament Doctrine of Baptism*. New York: Macmillan, 1948.

Freyne, S. *The Twelve: Disciples and Apostles*. London: Sydney, Sheed & Ward, 1968.

Gerhardsson, B. *The Testing of God's Son*. Lund: C. W. K. Gleerup, 1966.

Grant, R. M. *Hellenistic Religions: The Age of Syncretism*. New York: Liberal Arts Press, 1953.

Gundry, R. *The Use of the Old Testament in St. Matthew's Gospel*. Grand Rapids: Eerdmans, 1975.

Hare, D. R. A. *The Theme of Jewish Persecution of Christians in the Gospel According to St. Matthew*. Cambridge: Cambridge University Press, 1967.

Hoehner, H. W. *Herod Antipas*. Cambridge: Cambridge University Press, 1972.

Hunter, A. M. *Interpreting the Parables*. Philadelphia: Westminster, 1968.

_____. *The Work and Words of Jesus*. London: SCM Press, 1950.

James, M. R. *The Apocryphal New Testament*. Oxford: Clarendon Press, 1924.

Jeremias, J. *The Eucharistic Words of Jesus*. 2nd ed. New York: Macmillan, 1966.

_____. *Jesus' Promise to the Nations*. Philadelphia: Fortress, 1958.

_____. *New Testament Theology*. New York: Scribner, 1971.

_____. *The Parables of Jesus*. 2nd ed. New York: Scribner, 1963.

_____. *The Prayers of Jesus*. Naperville, Ill.: A. R. Allenson, 1958.

_____. *The Sermon on the Mount*. Philadelphia: Fortress, 1963.

_____. *Unknown Sayings of Jesus*. New York: Macmillan, 1957.

Jülicher, A. *Die Gleichnisreden Jesu*. 2nd ed. Tübingen: 1910.

Krutch, J. W. *The Twelve Seasons*. New York: W. Sloane Associates, 1949.

Kümmel, W. G. *Promise and Fulfillment*. 2nd ed. Naperville, Ill.: A. R. Allenson, 1961.

Ladd, G. E. *The Presence of the Future*. Grand Rapids: Eerdmans, 1974.

Lane, W. *The Gospel According to Mark*. Grand Rapids: Eerdmans 1974.

Linnemann, E. *Jesus of the Parables*. New York: Harper & Row, 1966.

Lohmeyer, E. *"Our Father."* New York: Harper, 1965.

Manson, T. W. *The Sayings of Jesus.* 2nd ed. Grand Rapids: Eerdmans, 1979.

Martin, R. *New Testament Foundations.* 2 vols. Grand Rapids: Eerdmans, 1975–78.

Montefiore, C. J. G., and H. M. Loewe. *A Rabbinic Anthology.* New ed. New York: Schocken Books, 1974.

Moore, G. F. *Judaism in the First Centuries of the Christian Era.* 3 vols. Cambridge: Harvard University Press, 1927–30.

Morris, L. *The Gospel According to Luke.* Grand Rapids: Eerdmans, 1974.

Parrot, A. *Golgotha and the Church of the Holy Sepulchre.* London: SCM Press, 1957.

Perowne, S. *The Life and Times of Herod the Great.* London: Hodder & Stoughton, 1956.

Robertson, A. T. *A Grammar of the Greek New Testament in the Light of Historical Research.* New York: Hodder & Stoughton, 1934.

Schweitzer, A. *The Quest of the Historical Jesus.* 3rd ed. New York: Macmillan, 1954.

Sherwin-White, A. N. *Roman Society and Roman Law in the New Testament.* Grand Rapids: Baker Book House, 1965.

Stauffer, E. *Jesus and His Story.* New York: Knopf, 1959.

Tasker, R. V. G. *The Gospel According to St. John.* Grand Rapids: Eerdmans, 1960.

Taylor, V. *The Gospel According to St. Mark.* London: Macmillan, 1957.

Vermes, G. *Scripture and Tradition in Judaism.* 2nd rev. ed. Leiden: E. J. Brill, 1973.

Via, D. O. *The Parables: Their Literary and Existential Dimension.* Philadelphia: Fortress, 1967.

Wallace, R. S. *Many Things in Parables.* New York: Harper, 1955.

Zeitlin, S. *Who Crucified Jesus?* New York: Harper & Brothers, 1942.

Subject Index

Scripture Index

NEW TESTAMENT